TEX

The Father of Texas Swimming

ROSS LUCKSINGER

foreword by Kay Bailey Hutchison

First Edition Paperback

ISBN 978-1492214922

www.rosslucksinger.com

Printed in the United States of America

CONTENTS

BOOK 5
IT ONLY TAKES A SPARK...
THE LEGACY OF TEX ROBERTSON

Foreword

by
Kay Bailey Hutchison

Tex Robertson embodied Texan virtues. He strove for greatness through action and commitment, and will forever be remembered for the institutions he established. Tex was never intimidated by a challenge, daunted by an obstacle, or halted by uncertainty. A typical Texan, he coupled an entrepreneurial spirit with determination and his trademark "attawaytogo" attitude. He proved that nothing can stop a person driven by purpose.

A gifted swimmer and athlete, Tex loved competition. Though he enjoyed a successful swimming career of his own, this natural-born leader took more pride in coaching and shaping young men than any of his own accomplishments. Tex focused his unrelenting energy on creating new opportunities for the men on his team and, later, the campers at Camp Longhorn. As a matter of fact, before he even reached Austin, Tex was recruiting swimmers for the yet-to-be-established University of Texas swimming team. Laying claim to a non-existent head-coaching position for a team without a program or university support is just the sort of feat Tex was known for accomplishing; creating something from nothing. This entrepreneurial Texan did not just build teams however, he also erected buildings.

Like the tough and rough forefathers of his sworn state, Tex loved nature with a passion. His enthusiasm is echoed by continued traditions at his pride and joy, Camp Longhorn. Born from his own experiences at a camp in Michigan and a love for coaching, Tex held fancy the notion of starting a camp for boys in Texas. However, his methods for establishing and growing Camp Longhorn were all but traditional. With a team of swimmers ready to give their lives for the coach they adored, Tex directed his athletes through a combination of strength and conditioning, manual labor, and carpentry at the site of his new camp. After its first summer, Camp Longhorn emerged with a proud new director, a team of exhausted Longhorn swimmers, and a few cabins. Running water and electricity were luxuries that would not arrive until years later, but Tex and his favorite saying gave his team all of the encouragement they needed. "Attawaytogo!" was the most common phrase heard from Camp

Longhorn's Commander-in-Chief. Tex had the qualities of a true leader, not solely because of his insatiable commitment to achieving his objectives, but also due to an ability to inspire those around him. Not a single person ever worked for Tex out of compulsion. People gave him their hearts and souls because they wanted to. His campers desired nothing more than to please Tex. In order to inspire confidence in their actions, a reward system was established at Camp Longhorn to reward campers who were polite, hard-working, and considerate. As always, the champion-maker of UT Swimming and the hero of Camp Longhorn led by example with typical Texan courtesy and dignity. However, it was the balance of stern kindness, encouragement, and creativity that made Tex a perfect candidate to help establish the training regimen for what is now the most elite military special ops program in the world.

When war broke out across the globe, Tex Robertson answered the call of duty for his country. Much to his chagrin, the brave Texan would never see the front lines of battle. Rather, he was called to the shores of Florida to train a new special Navy unit at Ft. Pierce. There, young and unmarried men known for being athletic and brave were recruited from the Navy's SeaBees, Bomb Disposal School, and Mine Disposal School. In keeping with Tex's practice, Tex and his fellow drill sergeants went through training with the recruits to boost morale. Alongside their instructors, these future American heroes began their journey through training "Hell Week." Those who survived and did not drop out became known as the U.S. Military's toughest fighting unit of WWII; they were the Underwater Demolition Team (UDT), also known as Frogmen, and ultimately renamed the Navy SEALs.

No matter his undertaking, Tex Robertson approached monumental tasks with an unrelenting dedication and fearlessness. He built a devoted network of supporters and followers, and utilized their assistance to make his dreams come true. An exemplary Texan, Tex took pride in accomplishments that allowed others to achieve their goals. Coach Robertson trained champions rather than furnish his own trophy case because his joy was found in helping others achieve victory, whether on the battlefield or in the swimming pools. Still to this day, his legacy, Camp Longhorn, shapes the lives of thousands of boys and girls, including mine, every year. In his eyes, that is the greatest legacy he could ever leave, and he will forever be remembered for it.

TEX

The Father of Texas Swimming

Prologue

At the International Swimming Hall of Fame, with flags of all represented countries hanging behind him, Tex Robertson stood at the podium ready to deliver his speech. The Gold Medallion Award from the ISHOF, a life-time achievement recognition, is one of the highest honors a swimmer can receive and in 2003 it was being given to Tex at the age of ninety-three.

It was well-deserved. This was a man who trained the original Navy SEALs. He revolutionized his sport by inventing many of the swimming techniques still used today, including the now-ubiquitous flip turn. After winning a pair of national championships as a swimmer at the University of Michigan, he named himself the head coach at the University of Texas, accepted an offer of no pay, and took the program to national prominence.

As he spoke of his love for the sport, he wore a crisp tan suit. A large black bow tie flowered forth from his collar. He also wore, to the simultaneous confusion and amusement of the crowd, swimming goggles and nose clips.

Grinning beneath the headgear, he strung together a series of puns, mostly at the expense of his oldest pupil, Olympic gold medalist Adolph Kiefer. Tex had borrowed the clips and goggles from Kiefer, who had opened a swimming supply company after his athletic career. Tex concluded the ribbing by holding aloft a copy of *Kiefer Magazine* that had been tucked in his jacket.

"You'll notice on this catalog, the first thing it says is 'Everything but the water,'" Tex said. "Well now he's got that too." He poured his water bottle onto a random page and then tossed the half-filled plastic projectile into the crowd. With his formal wear soaked in said water, he smiled and held forward the Gold Medallion sash that the ISHOF gave him at the beginning of the ceremony, as if to say, *That's right, you gave your highest honor to this guy*. Flashbulbs popped. Tex basked in it, appreciating the intentionally ridiculous image of himself he'd created.

It seemed a contradiction. Tex Robertson had lived a life that required a great deal of toughness. He was born on the West Texas frontier. After his mother's death when he was fifteen, he rode box cars out to California where he became one of the great athletes of his era. He developed into, and still was at ninety-three, a tenacious, unstoppable, certified American paragon. And there he stood, resplendent in his golden award sash, with goggles on his head, clips on his nose, and an ear-to-ear grin as he sprayed water on the front row of dignitaries to uproarious laughter.

But this wasn't a contradiction to him. Most speeches, conversations, and interactions with Tex were collections of non sequitur jokes, but there was a message hidden in his revelry. His achievements were many, yet his real obsession was the joy, improvement, and greatness of those around him. Even when told to focus on his own accomplishments, his mentality was that of a coach.

In 1936, when he was acclaimed as "one of the nation's outstanding hopes" for gold in the Berlin Olympics, he was much more concerned with coaching Kiefer, who Tex believed to be the world's next great swimmer. (Tex was vindicated in Berlin, with Kiefer winning the 100-meter backstroke in Olympic record time – a record Kiefer would set in the prelims and break twice more on his way to gold.)

At the conclusion of Tex's national championship career, Michigan coach Matt Mann predicted that in a few years Tex Robertson would rank as the best swimmer in the world. But at the height of his swimming ability he gave it up. He instead became the first head swimming coach at Texas rather than pursue a path as a professional swimmer – a profession that would likely have earned him more money than his starting salary at UT of zero dollars. It was through coaching that he found himself standing on that stage at the ISHOF in 2003 receiving an award given to a former competitive swimmer "whose life has served as an inspiration."

He was also a man with an uncanny ability to get people to do things...things under normal circumstances they wouldn't imagine themselves doing.

"Tex, I can't treat an alligator," said veterinarian George Lillard, who would make regular trips out to Camp Longhorn to look after Tex's unique wildlife collection at the camp's zoo.

"Sure you can," replied Tex, without hesitation.

Sure you can. It was always his response to consternation or complaint about a request. It's a response he would continue to give, no matter how many times someone said "no." In a way he was "a man who wouldn't take no for an answer." But this doesn't accurately capture his attitude. To say that someone "wouldn't take no" does express persistence, but it also implies aggression. Tex wasn't aggressive, but he certainly wasn't going away until he had his way. Most of it was simply likability.

"People liked Tex," recalled his eldest son, John, with a smile.

Tex would travel to the state capitol building in Austin with a breast-pocket full of candy sticks and stop by the office of each relevant representative – or any unrelated representative or staffer, for that matter. And he got what he wanted, whether it was specific camp safety regulations, water and land rights, or stopping year-round school. And those representatives would remember him, thanks to his charming demeanor, the joke he led with (or perhaps the pun that took you about four minutes to get), or the candy stick with a Camp Longhorn merit attached. Mostly they remembered him because they knew if Tex didn't get what he wanted, he'd be back again. And again. And again. And again. And the letters wouldn't stop. Nor the phone calls. Each time he was his smiling self, never angry, but he wasn't giving up.

"It's not that Tex didn't take 'no' for an answer," John said, "it's that to him the answer was already 'yes.' You just didn't know it."

He saw the world as he wished for it to be and, as a result, the world around him changed to fit his vision. All of the organizations and places he created were already there in his mind. He knew they existed, even if others did not. When he told his coach at Michigan that he was going to return to Texas to create a summer camp just like Mann's Camp Chikopi, in essence it was already reality. It was going to happen. When he declared to UT athletic director Jack Chevigny, "I am your swimming coach," he was the head swimming coach for the Texas Longhorns. The way Tex saw it was the way it was going to happen.

But this story is not just an examination of what Tex Robertson did. It's also an exploration of who Tex Robertson was, how those events shaped him as a person, and how people continue to be shaped by his work – a story of all that a single person can create by sheer force of will.

BOOK 1

FROM MUDHOLE TO MICHIGAN
THE STORY OF TEX THE SWIMMER

Chapter

"I learned to swim in a West Texas mudhole."

It was Tex's answer any time he was asked how he got his start as a swimmer. It's not far from the truth. Putting aside the humor of the statement and the wry smile with which he would deliver it, a look at the other top swimmers of his era reveals that Tex's place of birth was a bit of an oddity. The American Olympic medalists of the 1930s had birthplaces encompassed entirely by three regions: the Pacific, the Atlantic, and the Great Lakes. From the west came greats such as Buster Crabbe and Jack Medica. From the east came Al Vande Weghe, Ralph Flanagan, Alice Bridges, and Helen Johns. From the lakes came Helene Madison, Paul Wolf, and Josephine McKim.

It stands to reason. If you want to find a swimmer, go to water.

Sweetwater, Texas, despite its aquatic name, is not where we should find an American record-holder in the 440-yard freestyle, a Big Ten and national champion, and a man who revolutionized the sport. It's a dusty town on the West Texas plains located about forty-two miles west of Abilene and is known much more for wind power than water sports. That, and the annual Rattlesnake Round-Up – the largest round-up in the world, I might add. Understandably, Sweetwater has its share of liquid, with a set of four man-made lakes serving as a welcome relief to the arid climate of the western expanse that sits just below the high plains of the Llano Estacado. But around the turn of the twentieth century there was little more than a creek, which only flowed when the fast-moving storms willed it.

Yet this supposedly inauspicious location is where the story begins.

Julian William Robertson – Tex's birth name, which he was never overly fond of – was born in Sweetwater around the time Sweetwater was born. His date of birth, April 23, 1909, came just seven years after the town was fully incorporated. Before then it was simply a way station for buffalo hunters who arrived as the first Anglo settlers to the area around 1870.

The site proved attractive because the water in the creek lacked the bitter taste found in most of the wells in the immediate area. The bitterness was a result of a high concentration of gypsum in the ground water, which is nonpoisonous but still rather off-putting to the pallet. This particular creek carried little of the crystallized mineral, earning it the name "Sweet Water" – coincidentally the same given to the area long before by the Kiowa natives, who called the site "Mobeetie," their word for the same concept.

This outpost known as "Sweet Water" was named seat of the newly partitioned Nolan County in 1881, despite consisting of only a few tent stores and zero permanent buildings. Billie Knight would welcome hunters into his temporary depot, the only place to get dry goods in the sparsely populated region, for supplies and rest. Yet if we move forward to 1910, just a year after Julian's birth, the population of Sweetwater and the surrounding country had swelled to 11,999 residents.

The area went from a couple of tents to a community of 12,000 people in such a short time because of the railroad, as it was for so many settlements in the newly opened American West. Following Reconstruction, the unrelenting march of the "Iron Horse" became the symbol of ingenuity and technological power in the reformed United States. Railroad mileage tripled between 1860 and 1880 (it would triple again by 1920). From 1880 to 1900, the U.S. overtook Great Britain as the world's leader in industry, increasing its share from 14.7 to 23.6 percent of the entire planet's manufacturing output. This was the era of titans such as Andrew Carnegie, John D. Rockefeller, Jay Gould, and Charles Crocker, monopolistic financial barons of each of their respective industries. This was the era of the first billion-dollar corporation in J.P. Morgan's U.S. Steel.

Simultaneous to this second industrial revolution came access for these eastern industries to a host of untapped resources in the west. The American West was "newly opened" because the last significant battles with the native population of America had been fought. In Texas, this came with the surrender of Comanche chief Quanah Parker and his Quahadi warriors, the last free band of Plains Natives, in 1875. The Texas-Indian Wars ended, much of the native population of the state forcibly relocated to the Indian Territories of Oklahoma.

Railroads began to crisscross the American West and fully

developed communities began popping up seemingly overnight in what were once remote locations. Texas received much of this expansion through rapid growth of the Atchison, Topeka, and Santa Fe Railway Company (or just Santa Fe, for short). Thanks to generous land grants from Congress, the railroads carried for essentially no cost travelers willing to buy said land from the railroad companies, facilitating a rapid population expansion into West Texas.

Which is how Tex's parents, Francis Garland Robertson and Nancy Emerson Robertson, came to Sweetwater.

Frank – as he was more commonly known – was a railroad engineer for the Santa Fe. Until finally stopping in Sweetwater and switching careers by opening a wholesale grain business, Frank traveled up and down the rails, covering much of the state of Texas and never staying in one place for long.

But this is not unusual for a Robertson.

Following direct paternal lineage back from Tex, even going all the way back to the American Revolution, it turns out that not a single one of those relations stayed in the same place for more than a generation. Tex's father, Frank, Jr., came to Sweetwater from Huntsville, Texas. Tex's grandfather, Francis Garland Robertson, Sr., came to Huntsville from Greene County, Alabama. He married Ida Jimmie Hightower there in Huntsville but died soon after, leaving his young wife still shy of her seventeenth birthday and his six-month-old son. Two years later Ida would marry Eugene Luther Angier and together they raised Frank, Jr.

Frank, Sr., was born in Greene County, Alabama, after his father, Henry C. Robertson, moved there from Virginia. Henry was born in Virginia in 1806, just eighteen years after Virginia became the tenth state to ratify the U.S. Constitution, making him first in the line to be born in the new nation and the one who started the Robertsons' four-generation jaunt across these United States.

Tex's father, ever the sturdy railroad engineer, was known for his even keel and temperament. He kept a tightly trimmed mustache and even in the West Texas heat he would wear a three-piece suit and black bowler hat. It fit his personality. Outside of the family he kept few close and was often described by those who knew him as a "serious" man. This was especially the case for those who met him through Tex. Due to Tex's boisterous, over-the-top personality, they often expected Frank to welcome them as warmly as Tex did and share a similar sense of humor.

He did not. Those close to Tex would try their best to get to know his father. For the most part it was in vain.

"I was never was close to him at all," said Pat, Tex's wife for sixty-seven years. "I tried, but it wasn't too effective."

Tex's children had similar experiences with their gruff grandfather. However, Frank's personal writings reveal a man who, inside this shell he built around himself, privately held a great sensitivity. He showed love especially of nature, a theme he consistently returned to in his letters to his step-siblings. Though he spent most of his life in the twentieth century as a Los Angeles businessman, he repeatedly stated how much happier he was living a country life in Texas.

He wrote in a 1938 letter to his stepbrother Gene:

...Los Angeles is a beautiful, interesting City for young people; with all its noise, and gay night life; traffic jams; murders; robberies night, and day. And while it is life to many, it is also death to some. I am fed up on it all; and long for a quiet, peaceful life...Yes, Bud, I am like you about having no love for City life; I love the country; I love to work in the soil; to stroll in the woods; to fish in the streams. I am a natural lover of Nature. The City is too artificial to please me.

His short, stream-of-consciousness statements highlighted his poetic use of language. It's a style he'd slip into often, possibly because of his interest in poetry itself, as he would occasionally clip and send his favorite poems to his stepsister Ida.

But Frank's intelligence was most often defined by his proclivity for success at whatever he set his mind to – no matter how varied the task. Over the course of his life he was a railroad engineer, founded a grain business in Sweetwater, and later founded Robertson Brokerage Company in Los Angeles, which handled imports, exports, and high finance (a company that even expanded later into popcorn manufacturing, a surprisingly profitable industry in the Depression-wracked 1930s). He can be attributed as a source of his son's work ethic. Most of what Tex created throughout his life was by sheer force of will and his father shared that rare drive.

And if Tex's work ethic came from his father, Nancy Emerson Robertson was the source of his heart. While few were close to Frank, his mother was described by those who knew her as "universally loved." Reverend G.S. Hardy of First Methodist Church in Sweetwater stated in no uncertain terms that "she always saw the good in everyone" and that she "made lives happier and more worthy by her sunny disposition, cheery smile, and kind words." A writer from the *Sweetwater Reporter* described her as someone "whose every effort while on earth was to make her community a better and finer place to live in."

Frank, a headstrong, emotionally stiff railroad engineer, and Nancy, an exceptionally loving, exceptionally loved homemaker wife, carved out a life in the hinterland of turn-of-the-century Texas. This image is incomplete, though, without a brood of rough and tumble children.

Filling out those ranks were Frank and Nancy's four boys: Francis Garland Robertson III (born in 1900 in their original home in Huntsville), LaClaire Elkins Robertson (1903, further up the rails in Seymour, Texas), Eugene Emerson Robertson (1906, the first to be born in their new home of Sweetwater), and finally Julian William Robertson (1909). Compared with modern conventions their names appear a bit extravagant, but they were every bit the wilderness whippersnappers you'd expect – and later in life they'd pick up the more appropriate monikers of Frank, Pas, Jack, and Tex.

They were muddy, ornery boys who got into as much trouble as possible on the ranches and farms that were beginning to dot the area. They played in the streams and hunted for various plains critters. Their base of operations: a shack they collectively built about four miles from home out of stolen road signs, boards, and other debris. The rickety shanty was located on the edge of the railroad company's water reservoir, in which they'd row their homemade raft.

Hunting wasn't a hobby taken on for pure entertainment – though Julian and his brothers did derive a great deal of entertainment from it. Pelts represented spending money. Each morning the adolescent Julian would get up, run his trap-lines, skin whatever jackrabbit, squirrel, badger, or raccoon he'd find and sell it in town. The family wasn't starving, but they were by no means wealthy, so skins became his allowance. And if the particular animal was good for stewing, all the better.

It was also the beginning of a passion for the wilds of Texas that Julian would hold throughout his life. He and his father may have differed dramatically in personality, but their love of nature was the same. This is reflected, as were so many elements of Tex's personality, in Camp Longhorn. Swimming was the original inspiration for the camp, but exploration of the natural world is always a significant part of the program. He took great pleasure in doling out snippets of zoology to campers and would tell stories about trapping in the woods outside Sweetwater with those helping him set traps to catch animals for the camp zoo.

Not that it was ever a consistent narrative. If Tex told a story, it was to make a point. For as much as he was a talker, he didn't talk directly about himself a great deal. When interviewed for a newspaper story or some such, he'd typically respond to a question about himself with a purpose-driven story. He was a huge promoter, but not a true self-promoter, and if he was promoting himself it was always in the context of some project he was attempting to put forward, according to his oldest son, John.

"When I started working at camp we did the whole father-son facing desk thing and even if you'd ask him about these sorts of things, he'd always move on to another subject," John said. "He didn't tell the stories to tell the stories, he told them to make a point."

He'd talk about working in the grain mill with his father only when extolling the value of hard work. That rickety shack constructed by he and his brothers would come up while building a new cabin for Camp Longhorn.

But, since promotion of swimming was the ever-present goal in Tex's life, the one place he would most frequently return to in his stories was a wilderness area about a half mile from his family's home in Sweetwater.

WHEN TEX WOULD TELL THE STORY, he was specifically referring to Cottonwood Creek, which would often flood just enough for a boy to submerge himself (mostly). However, his first experience swimming, as his father would tell it, quite literally involved a West Texas mudhole.

According to Frank – in a story he told the *Sweetwater Reporter* when the paper asked him how the then-champion Tex Robertson got his start – the first attempt came when little Julian was not but three years old.

While at home, his mother suddenly realized that Julian had gone missing. She searched all over the house but the toddler was nowhere to be found. Frantic, she ran from house to house organizing a party of anyone who was willing to search for her baby boy. Just when this hastily arranged posse was about to depart, Julian came waddling up to the house, covered head to toe in mud, and triumphantly announced he had been 'fimming'.

He'd managed to open the front door and wander to the nearby Lewis Ranch, where the toddler encountered a fresh mudhole filled with about a half-inch of water. He was gone for so long because, well, it was a hole full of mud and he was a three-year-old. That's about all that's needed for entertainment, much to the distress of his mother Nancy, who Tex – in the rare moments that he would talk about her – described as "loving and very protective."

Mudhole 'fimming' aside, for the first twelve years of his life Julian was a non-swimmer. As a child he was frightened of standing in water higher than his knees, though he did enjoy watching his brothers – who all started swimming at a much younger age – play in Santa Fe Lake.

At the time of Julian's birth there was no standing body of water to swim in, but three years later in 1912 the Gulf, Colorado, and Santa Fe Railways constructed a lake by damming up Kildoogan Creek just northeast of town, primarily for irrigation purposes. Santa Fe Lake quickly picked up the nickname "Country Club Lake" and before long it was used as much for recreation as it was for agriculture. It's where the Robertson boys would do their swimming, minus Julian, who stood at a safe distance away due to their repeated threats to "throw him in."

Nancy prolonged the dry spell by saying, as Tex put it, "My boy's not going in that water until he learns to swim." Julian, a few years and a thousand miles away from being known as "Tex," was embarrassed by his inability. His desire to swim started to grow. But he just wanted to learn so he could have fun in the water with his older brothers. His true fascination began at age nine, when he left Sweetwater and had his first encounter with competitive swimming.

In the summer of 1918 the family moved to the state capital, Austin. Frank originally left the rails to start his wholesale grain company to sell to the growing number of farmers and ranchers in the area. But growth of the business still required a steady influx of people coming up those railroads and in the 1910s it slowed significantly. The rail companies in the state had shifted their focus back east thanks to the Texas Oil Boom. Spindletop in East Texas became the most productive oil field on the planet, moving the United States to number one in production and encouraging rapid infrastructure development in Texas. Historians have referred to the Texas Oil Boom as the beginning of humanity's so called "Oil Age."

With the new oil infrastructure forming in East Texas, the trains, and thus the jobs, started going back the way they came. With that, the family packed up and left their home in Sweetwater for a temporary stay in Austin. Nancy's justification to her four boys for the sudden move away from their friends was a chance to experience a larger community. Of course with a population at the time of 34,876, Austin wasn't terribly bigger than Sweetwater. But there were jobs to be had, so the adventure in the "big city" began.

And it was an adventure. With the new family home located one block from the University of Texas campus, nine-year-old Julian had a new wilderness to explore, a wilderness populated with something he'd never seen before: buildings taller than a couple stories.

While his father and oldest brother worked (Frank III was eighteen at the time), Julian would spend his days wandering the UT campus. Though he wasn't yet a swimmer, he very quickly became a climber. Showing no fear of heights whatsoever, Julian's favorite activity was sliding down the fire escapes on the side of university buildings. If run off by an employee due to his horseplay, Julian would scamper his way over to another structure on the 40 Acres and resume his climbing and sliding. He quickly became familiar with the ins and outs of the campus. It was a familiarity he would occasionally make use of later in life (when John got to UT, one of the first things his father showed him was how to break into Gregory Gym in case he wanted to do some late-night swimming).

But it wasn't just buildings to scale that drew him to the university. The inner workings of this mysterious place captivated him. He was a nine-year-old from a railroad community in West Texas suddenly amongst university students and professors. It was the beginning of his love for the University of Texas, one of the places where he would make his mark on the world of swimming later in life. His family was in Austin for only a few months, but the experience stuck with him all the way through his swimming days at the University of Michigan.

Austin was also where he discovered competitive swimming. There was no official swim team at the University of Texas at the time, but there was a YMCA. In the basement there was a swimming pool. On one of his random wanderings, Julian went below the Y and saw something that helped set the course of his life.

This wasn't a muddy creek or an irrigation reservoir. Here he saw a beautiful pool with lane ropes and filled with competitive swimmers moving gracefully through the water. Julian took several trips to the YMCA that summer, mostly just to sit and watch the swimmers. He didn't know how to swim yet, but he knew he had to learn.

He didn't get many opportunities, though, as the family was on the move again, bringing his Y-watching and campus-climbing days to a halt. That fall the Robertsons moved south to San Marcos looking for new job opportunities before moving west for a brief stay in El Paso. In January of 1919 the family picked up once again. This time, though, it was to head back home.

Frank had decided to give the wholesale grain business in Sweetwater another shot. He'd picked up some experience working in finance during his time in Austin, San Marcos, and El Paso and he was confident in the business' success. Julian's thoughts, however, were on the University of Texas and on swimming.

IT WAS SLOW GOING at the start of Julian's swimming career. It took him another few years to gain the confidence to finally get his head underwater, something to that point he was deathly afraid of.

During the late spring and early summer of 1922, the thirteen-year-old would take daily trips to Cottonwood Creek. With his home located on the edge of town it was only a half mile to the wilderness area where he'd take clandestine self-taught swimming lessons. He preferred the solitude, anyway.

"I had few friends my age, I was afraid of girls, and I hated school," Tex wrote in a brief summary of his adolescence.

With only his dog as witness, Julian waded into the creek for the first time. After getting comfortable with the idea of being partially submerged, his next step was the crawl. And not the American Crawl or the Trudgen stroke. Literally crawling in a foot of muddy rainwater in a ditch on the West Texas plains.

Humble men have humble beginnings. It's debatable whether the great promoter Tex Robertson was a "humble man," but humble certainly describes the beginning of his swimming career.

After several days worth of crawling, he was comfortable enough being horizontal in the muck to duck his head underwater and start to experiment with floatation. He had no training in swimming strokes, but from what he saw in his brief time at the 'Y' and in news reels, he pieced together a crawling, dog-paddling stroke that managed to propel him forward. He was soon pushing off and swimming across the drying up creek in late June with the enthusiasm of a five-year-old at age thirteen.

By mid-July his swimming hole had dried up into the standing hole it was for most of the year. But it wasn't time to jump into the lake and join his brothers just yet. Julian felt he still needed some practice before taking the plunge into water that really could drown him. But with the creek dried up, Santa Fe Lake was the only place to swim. He found his solution on the nearby Chapman Ranch.

Dr. Chapman had on his ranch a two-foot-deep concrete horse trough. When nobody and no horse was around, Julian would sneak onto the property and jump in. He never got sick, and the ten trips he took to the Chapman Ranch were enough for Julian to perfect his version of the dog paddle. In fact, later in life that horse trough became the design model for a large bathtub Tex built in his house at Camp Longhorn, which he used to teach his children how to swim before they graduated to larger tanks.

Julian was finally ready to swim in Santa Fe Lake. Armed with his self-taught stroke, the next time the family was at the reservoir, much to the surprise of his brothers – and horror of his mother – he flung himself off the pier and into the water. But he did not drown. He happily swam in the lake, as he would every single day for the rest of the summer of 1922.

His first competition came one year later. By the summer of '23 Julian had picked up a reputation as the "fastest swimmer in Sweetwater." His siblings quickly noticed that their little brother, though he'd never practiced before the age of thirteen, could swim faster than any of them. His title as the fastest in town became official on July Fourth. Sweetwater Country Club decided to hold a pair of swimming races with various items from local merchants as prizes. There were two events: a short swim of about twenty-five yards around Santa Fe Lake Bath House Pier and a long swim of roughly 175 yards across the lake.

Julian won them both. Since he still had no formal training, his technique wasn't exactly pristine. It was basically a breast-stroke kick awkwardly combined with a crawl arm stroke. But he moved a lot more naturally through the water than any of his competition. His most-prized trophy was a red inner tube from City Garage. In addition he was awarded some odds and ends from Glass Grocery.

The win got people talking. The event was well attended because the rodeo was in town, so plenty of people saw that lanky Robertson kid swim faster than anyone around. Now, there's always a great deal of bragging and speculating that surrounds any rodeo. A discussion between a few riders led to a lively debate about whether a horse could beat a man at running and swimming. Well, it just so happened that the main attraction at the Sweetwater Rodeo that year was an old cowboy who wasn't opposed to taking on a challenge.

His name was Samuel Thomas Privett, Jr., but he was known by all as simply Booger Red (a nickname he picked up after he mangled his face in a fireworks accident at a young age). Red was a man with no shortage of Texas lore surrounding him. He was one of the most accomplished bronc riders of the early twentieth century. It was said there wasn't a horse he couldn't break, and he even had a standing offer to pay $100 to anyone who could bring him a horse he couldn't ride (an offer he never had to pay). It was said that he never fell off a horse during a show and that once a horse fell on him and broke his leg, but he refused to get off and held on until the horse righted itself. He won twenty-three first prizes at various rodeo competitions and his appearances included a performance at the 1904 World's Fair in St. Louis.

When he came through Sweetwater in 1923, Red was on tour

with a wild west show and circus and at the age of fifty-eight was near the end of his riding days (he would retire one year later). Ever the showman, he readily accepted the challenge to have he and his horse pitted against the fastest swimmer Sweetwater had to offer.

Rules were hastily thrown together. It was to be a hundred-yard run and a seventy-five-yard swim across the shorter end of Santa Fe Lake. Red would have to stay on his horse all the way through the run and the swim while Julian would be on foot. And Glass Grocery threw in a prize for the winner.

About ninety people, including a writer from the *Sweetwater Reporter* and one from the *Abilene Reporter-News*, followed Booger Red and Julian over from the rodeo to the lake. There Julian stood next to a Texas legend, who was grinning down at him from a hulking chestnut bronco. Tex said in an interview once that while he kept a smile on his face for the crowd, all he felt leading up to the race was fear. A pistol commandeered from the wild west show was raised into the air, fired once, and off went Tex and Booger Red.

That first hundred yards was a rout. Booger and his horse arrived at the water's edge well before Julian. However, since there was no practice for the event beforehand, the horse was not prepared to throw itself into the lake. No matter how much Booger Red spurred his horse the bronco refused to move beyond the shallow end. As Red was fighting with his horse, Julian came running by and into the water.

That next seventy-five yards was a rout. The horse wouldn't swim and Julian zipped through the water for an easy victory. The race over, Red hopped off into knee deep water and stomped away in disgust. Julian swam back across the lake, grabbed the horse's reigns, and led it out to the cheering crowd.

He was awarded his Gold Medal...a sack of Gold Medal Flour from Glass Grocery. With that, the legend of Julian Robertson in Sweetwater had begun. His risk-taking swimming exploits didn't bother his mother. After his race with Booger Red, she just shook her head, smiled, and said to him: "You're too mean to drown."

Those were halcyon days for newly crowned town hero Julian Robertson. It was one of the happiest times of his life. But those blissful days would end abruptly.

2

Chapter

It was called the "longest funeral procession in the history of Sweetwater" by the local paper, and indeed it seemed the whole of the city had shown up to First Methodist. It came as no surprise to any in attendance to see the church packed.

Nancy Emerson Robertson had died.

Julian was fifteen when he lost his mother. In the summer of 1924 an infection had left her and his oldest brother bed-ridden. After a lengthy illness Frank III pulled through, but during Nancy's recovery she suffered a stroke and died instantly.

It was a shock to the town that the beloved community leader was gone at the age of forty-nine. News of her death was on the front page of the *Sweetwater Reporter*, as was the story of the funeral, which captured the scope of the service:

> (Reverend G.S.) Hardy spoke from behind a long tier of flowers and wreaths, floral offering sent by scores and scores of the many friends of Mrs. Robertson. The flowers were heaped high across the front of the rostrum making a solid bank of beauty over 20 feet long. The Methodist Choir occupied the platform, but a chair on the front row was vacant except for a covering of wreaths and flowers, placed there by the choir in memory of her who was their leader for many years...The crowd which completely filled the church was allowed to pass by the beautiful casket and see for the last time the remains of the one so universally loved during life. Relatives and members of the family, all stricken with grief, also glimpsed for the last time on earth, the face of the wife and mother.

She was the heart of the family. That heart had been suddenly torn out. Julian, his father, and three brothers were crushed. His father was distinctly inconsolable. The already emotionally withdrawn Frank became a despondent wreck.

There's an old Robertson family photo album that Frank and Nancy maintained together. There are notations in the margins from each, with names of relations and locations and some cheerful comments here and there, mostly from Nancy, about a particular time or place.

After July 24, 1924, there are no more entries, save for a single sentence written by Frank:

"Here my life ends."

For the rest of his life that outlook never wavered. In one of the last available letters written by Francis Garland Robertson II – this one to his stepbrother's wife, also by the name of Nancy, in 1951 – he would still fondly look back to the days before his wife died as his happiest: "I just had a letter from Will Allen telling me that he and I are the only ones of the old [railroad] crew left that we used to work with. Those were happy days, and they continued for me until I lost my precious darling about 25 years ago."

Frank lived to the age of ninety-three and never remarried.

As for the four boys, they would speak little of the difficult experience the rest of their lives. All that could be done to manage the pain was to focus on their individual passions. For Julian, that was swimming.

Through the connections he'd built with the rodeo folks, he learned about a unique race, the San Antonio Steeplechase. It would take place at a rodeo down in the Alamo City and it required its participants to run a half mile, ride a horse a half mile, and swim a quarter mile. Julian didn't have a great deal of experience riding horses, but he accurately guessed he could make up time on the back end with the swim.

By that point his technique had improved quite a bit. Not from any formal training, but rather because he saw newsreels of swimmers preparing for the 1924 Olympic Games in Paris. At the time he didn't understand how to execute a proper flutter kick – he assumed the swimmers were creating a splashing effect by shaking their feet – so he kept his bizarre scissor style, but watching Olympic freestylers in action did cause him to change his rolling one-arm over the top sidestroke into a proper Trudgen crawl. (He didn't know the technique had a name; he just knew he went faster with his head down in the water.) Getting rides from whomever could take him, Julian worked his way down to San Antonio and entered himself in the steeplechase.

As expected, he was one of the last competitors to dismount from his steed and enter the water. But a quarter of a mile is a long way to swim and he was the first to exit the water, giving him his first victory outside of his home town.

Brimming with confidence (perhaps a bit too much confidence), he decided to go straight from random rodeo contests to the most prominent swimming competition in the state of Texas: the mile swim at the Galveston Splash Day and Bathing Beauty Review. From San Antonio, Julian hitchhiked his way down to the Texas coast, where he received a cultural experience.

In 1924, there wasn't a hotter place to be than the Free State of Galveston.

During the 1920s, Galveston Island became a famous resort town and celebrity getaway thanks to the city's very, very popular decision to stop enforcing U.S. law when it came to gambling and liquor. (Hence the "Free State.") Prohibition was in full force in the rest of the country, but businesses in Galveston made little attempt to hide their prolific rum-running. If a state or national agency attempted an investigation, the local sheriff, Frank Biaggne, would tell them to move along because everything was just fine the way it was on the island. And the Maceo Mafia family would see that the sheriff was rewarded.

There were casinos aplenty, the crown jewels being the Hollywood (which was just outside of the city limits with the view from the street sheltered by thick vegetation) and the Balinese Room (located at the end of the pier, which allowed only single file-entry and had plenty of back doors, lest some fed did decide to raid the place). The Maceos had slot machines in three hundred establishments, including restaurants, barbershops, and groceries. Even junior high schoolers would bet on football games while in class, thanks to betting cards distributed by students whose fathers worked for the Maceos.

As Paul Burka of *Texas Monthly* put it: "When Texas ranchers were still driving their cattle to market over the Chisholm Trail and

Houston was a quagmire hardly fit for habitation, Galvestonians were [living in] $250,000 houses, sipping French wines, and hearing their city called the New York of the Gulf."

This was Julian's introduction to the Roaring Twenties.

One of the premiere events in "The Republic" – another nickname of the era given to the island – was the Galveston Splash Day and Bathing Beauty Review. The event was overseen by the public face of the Maceo family, Salvetore Maceo, or just "Sam" to Galvestonians. Sam also was nicknamed the "Velvet Glove" because of his reputation as a smooth talker (and to contrast him with his brother, crime boss Rosario Maceo, who was the "Iron Glove"). The event itself was a weekend-long beach party, the main feature of which was an internationally famous beauty contest said to be the model for the modern Miss America Pageant. With the population of the island tripling during the event, beachfront hotels would fill up immediately, leaving no room for the thousands more who would show up with no lodging. Many of those would make their way to "tourist courts," lines of small bungalows along the water. Or they just passed out on the beach.

While the "bathing beauties" were the main attraction (and might have been the genesis of a very popular method of raising money for UT swimming Tex concocted later in life), there were events all over the island, from acclaimed music acts at the casinos to the mile swim, all in a carnival-like atmosphere.

Julian took in the sights, but his main reason for making his way to Galveston was the race. He wasn't entering the mile swim just to test himself in a distance race. He wanted to test himself against his first true hero from the world of swimming.

One of the local celebrities was lifeguard LeRoy Columbo. At the age of seven, an attack of spinal meningitis caused Columbo to go deaf in both ears. Undeterred, Columbo would go on to be a champion ocean swimmer and lifeguard, winning races at distances as long as forty miles and saving the lives of swimmers on the beaches of Galveston. He once saved nineteen swimmers at a single Splash Day and was famous across the state as "the man who saved 1,000 lives." (*Guinness World Records* officially has him at 907 rescues over forty years.) Julian read of the deaf lifeguard's exploits and wanted to see how he stacked up against a real champion.

Turns out, he didn't stack terribly high. Columbo won the mile swim at Splash Day for the ninth year in row while Julian finished officially in seventy-eighth place. (Though Tex insisted he actually finished seventy-seventh.) It was the first swimming competition Julian lost, though it's not surprising since before Galveston the quarter mile at the San Antonio Steeplechase was the farthest he'd ever swum for a race. Considering the hundreds entered in the event, ranking in the seventies wasn't bad for a fifteen-year-old with no formal training (and who was swimming with pretty much all arm because he had yet to learn the flutter kick).

Still, it was a valuable experience that exposed the teenager to a very big world outside of Sweetwater. It also gave him a chance to jump right into the middle of a unique time and place in American history, because "The Republic" didn't last long. By the 1940s, with the Maceos moving on to Las Vegas and law enforcement finally catching up with Galveston, the Free State was no more. As the crowds waned so did Splash Day and the spectacle eventually faded out of existence – though it has been revived several times over, most recently as an annual gay pride event.

The hoopla of Galveston was another turning point in Julian's life. He knew he wanted to swim and he knew he needed to leave Sweetwater to do it.

He graduated high school that next spring, though just barely. (Even his father being president of the school board didn't help the frequently absent, consistently distracted student.) As soon as his final semester ended, Julian left Sweetwater for a city with a bit of a different pace: Los Angeles, California.

Julian Robertson the swimmer was finally headed for water.

By 1925, all four of the Robertson boys had departed Sweetwater. Julian chose Los Angeles because two of his older brothers, Frank and LaClaire, had matriculated their way to the West Coast as well. Through their letters back to Julian, they painted a picture of beautiful weather, LA beaches filled with ten times the bathing beauties he saw in Galveston, and jobs aplenty.

As for the remaining brother, Jack, he was even more of a loner than Julian and took a much different path. Filled with an insatiable wanderlust, Jack made off to the north and wouldn't be seen by his brothers for nineteen years.

Julian headed west in whatever fashion he could. With twelve dollars tucked in his sock, he hitchhiked most of the way, picking up rides from passing motorists – a much more common practice in the 1920s. When there was not enough traffic to get him to the next town, Julian would hop the trains with the hobos to whichever stops would get him closer to his destination.

After avoiding getting tossed from any of the box cars he hid in, he arrived in LA. Luckily for Julian, his brother Frank had a job waiting for him. Frank worked for the Studebaker Automobile Company as a car salesman. Studebaker was one of the oldest car companies in the United States, switching in 1902 from the wagon business to cars. It quickly grew into one of the world's largest automobile companies, building the world's biggest car plant in 1923 and selling 145,000 cars that year. By 1925 the Studebaker company owned 5,000 dealerships across the country and it was at one of those in Los Angeles where Frank Robertson III worked.

Though Julian was only fifteen, Frank was able to get his youngest brother a job in the parts department. Julian proved surprisingly adept as a salesman. His immediate usefulness to the company is probably what saved him from losing that job after the "incident" that occurred not long after he started work.

As a manager, Frank was able to take Studebakers around the test track at the San Bernardino plant. Julian was eager to get behind the wheel of one of the vehicles, so after one of his rides with Frank the two switched seats. Julian managed to flip the brand new Studebaker when he took a turn at too high of velocity. Fortunately no bones were broken in the crash, but both Julian and Frank were covered in gasoline when the tank ruptured, which caused them both to blister up. As they healed from their injuries, the brothers did have a friendly competition to see who could remove the biggest single piece of skin from their blisters.

Dermatological oddities aside, with a job in hand Julian was able to pursue the passion that drew him to the Pacific. From what his memories of Austin told him, if you wanted to be a swimmer you went to the YMCA. So that's where he went.

Walking into the Central Los Angeles YMCA brought back the same feeling he had as a nine-year-old watching competitive swimmers for the first time. Just like in Austin, there in the basement of the LA Y was a sixty-foot, four-lane beauty of a swimming pool. It was also a swimming pool filled with swimmers a lot better trained than Julian. As in, trained at all.

He was back to being a beginner, as evidenced by his unsuccessful try-out attempt for the YMCA relay team. Hampering his speed was a refusal to give up his scissor kick, which by that point felt to him like the most natural way to get through the water. The race teams wouldn't have him, but there did happen to be one water-based team at the Y that didn't care about his unusual kicking stroke: water polo.

The lanky Texan could tread water for hours, was willing to scrap with the best of them, and could get the ball in the goal. Due to this, Julian was placed in the key position of center-forward, giving him plenty of goal-scoring opportunities. But more than that, his fellow water polo players at the Y liked him. This was new for Julian. Sure, plenty of people had known him before and he'd been a town celebrity back in Sweetwater, but the fact of the matter was he didn't have many friends. He was the odd kid who spent a lot of time out in the woods and, when he was around, was only interested in swimming. It made him simultaneously well known and a bit of an outcast. There were a select few friends from Sweetwater who, even until late in life, he did keep up with, but the YMCA in Los Angeles was the first time he had a group of friends who shared similar interests. It was the first real community he felt himself a part of. He could laugh with them and learn, at an astoundingly quick rate, the intricacies of the game.

Within weeks he was voted team captain. Within a month he was captain and co-head coach, teaching the details of techniques he himself had only just learned. He always coached with a smile, encouraging his teammates in his affable West Texas drawl. The accent in particular amused them, since most of the players at the Y grew up in California. (Water polo in the United States has always been a California-dominated sport; every single men and women's NCAA water polo championship has been won by a team from California.) So they started calling their captain "Tex."

It stuck. Julian Robertson was no more. Tex loved his new name and began using it at all times, formal or informal. At no point in his life would he go by Julian again.

In a very real sense the identity of Julian was gone. Many of the qualities that defined Julian Robertson didn't apply to Tex Robertson. Julian was a loner and Tex was a leader. Julian didn't know anyone and Tex never met a person he didn't like. The first team he ever coached didn't just give him a cute pseudonym, it was the beginning of his insatiable urge to coach.

TEX ACCLIMATED TO LIFE IN SOUTHERN CALIFORNIA. Of course, he was still a country boy at heart and would take sabbaticals to the woods in the form of twenty-eight camping trips to Mt. Wilson. (The fact that he remembered that oddly specific number of twenty-eight is a good indication of the importance of camping to him.)

By this point Tex had been promoted to parts director at the Studebaker plant and was enrolled in nearby San Bernardino Junior College. He'd joined the racing teams at Central YMCA now that he learned the right way to kick through the water, though his main focus at the Y remained playing and coaching water polo. Los Angeles was a big city, but like he did as a child on the University of Texas campus he found plenty of hidden places to amuse himself. For example, there was that nice patch of grass at the top of the hill overlooking the Rose Bowl where he'd watch each game while in California.

His camping led him to Catalina Island and his first job as a camp counselor. The rocky island twenty-two miles off the coast was (and still is) a popular tourist spot with a number of youth summer camps operating on its shores. Learning about the camps and deciding that the island might not be a bad place to spend a summer, Tex applied for and received a job at Camp Treasure Island. He'd worked with people his age, but this was his first time working directly with kids on the fundamentals of swimming.

He loved it. Couldn't get enough. He reveled in the kids' enthusiasm and energy. The simple joy of a child after splashing through the water for the first time on their own made Tex happier than anything else in the world. Perhaps it was because he was always a kid himself.

"Most kids by the age of 13 have ambitions of becoming successful adults," Tex wrote, "but all I ever wanted was to camp and swim."

The campers on Catalina always crowded around the tall, smiling Texan. His favorite activity at the camp was breaking the kids up into teams that would compete against each other, but in such a chaotic, constantly changing fashion that nobody could really tell who ranked where and who was better than anyone else.

He didn't stay on Catalina for the whole summer because there was work to do back on the mainland. His water polo team had developed a reputation, beating each of the other YMCA teams from around the city in exhibition matches. This led to an important turning point for Tex's swimming career, the 1929 California YMCA Water Polo Championships. It was where he was discovered by Fred Cady.

The greatest athletes in LA did their training at the Los Angeles Athletic Club. A total of ninety-seven Olympic medals (forty-seven gold) have been won by LAAC athletes. The biggest stars of Hollywood, such as Charlie Chaplin and Douglas Fairbanks, did their training at the Y. The club itself stood twelve stories tall and it was the first building in Southern California with a swimming pool on an upper floor, and even that pool's lifeguard was three-time gold medalist Duke Kahanamoku, the father of modern surfing.

Fred Cady was the club's swimming coach. He attended the YMCA championships to scout prospective talent for the LAAC and it was there he saw center-forward Tex Robertson lead his team to victory. After the championship – in which Coach Tex was the team's leading scorer – Cady approached Tex and offered him a spot on the LAAC's Water Polo team.

This was no small honor. Back then, the U.S. Olympic water polo team *was* the Los Angeles Athletic Club's team. Rather than selecting water polo players from around the country, the U.S. Olympic Committee would instead host a tournament between the top club teams, the winner of which would comprise the Olympic team. In the '20s and '30s, that was typically the LAAC.

Tex accepted immediately. With an opportunity to train at the LAAC every day, Tex had no desire to remain in San Bernardino. The offer to join Coach Cady caused him to bring to a sudden halt everything else that was going on in his life. He quit his job at the Studebaker plant, transferred from San Bernardino to Los Angeles Junior College (primarily because they had a swimming team), bought a new Ford Roadster with the money he'd saved up, got work at a service station in Hollywood, and moved into an apartment in West LA.

He began his work at the LAAC initially as a water polo player but his career as a race swimmer took a giant leap forward when he was taken under wing by the best in the world: Johann Peter Weißmüller.

As far as the U.S. Passport Office is concerned, there was no Johann Peter Weißmüller. There's just Johnny.

With five gold medals, fifty-two U.S. national championships, and sixty-seven world records, there wasn't a better swimmer around than Johnny Weissmuller. But America's greatest swimmer wasn't American.

According to his passport, Peter John Weissmuller was born in Windber, Pennsylvania, on June 2, 1904. Weissmuller indeed was born on that date, but it wasn't in Windber. Johann Peter Weißmüller was actually born in the small town of Freidorf in the Banat region of Romania, which was part of Hungary before boundary changes in 1918. His parents immigrated to the United States via Ellis Island when he was just seven months old.

Since he grew up in the United States, he wanted to represent the U.S. in the 1924 Olympics in Paris, so he gave his birthplace as Windber (his younger brother's place of birth) when obtaining a passport thanks to a false affidavit written by his father. He not only kept his foreign birth a secret through his three gold medals in Paris and two golds in Amsterdam in the '28 Olympics, amazingly he kept it secret from his all five of his wives, his closest friends, and his only son, Johnny, Jr. It wasn't until after his death in 1984 that his true place of birth came to light.

The elaborate ruse wasn't necessary for him to compete in the Olympics. It would have been easier to just swim under the Hungarian or Romanian flag, but he loved the U.S. He didn't just want to win Olympic gold, he wanted to do it for the country he grew up in. As far as Johnny Weissmuller was concerned, he was nothing but American.

Weissmuller did his training at the Los Angeles Athletic Club, where in 1929 he met a young water polo player named Tex Robertson. The world champion could see that Tex was full of talent but very short on training. The plucky Texan had been succeeding on pretty much just grit. Recognizing his ability, Weissmuller agreed to train Tex for free during his off hours.

It's saying something when the best swimmer on the planet decides to coach someone for no charge, especially someone who had previously received no formal training. Each Saturday afternoon, Tex would meet Johnny at the Ambassador Hotel's swimming pool and work with him on stroke techniques, fundamentals, and every little trick he knew to shave those precious seconds.

Tex swam for both the LAAC and the YMCA, posting faster times every week. At the 1930 YMCA National Championships, Tex won the 200 freestyle and came in second in the 100. In a year Tex had gone from unable to make any YMCA racing team to national champion. In the spring of '31 he won his first collegiate championship, taking first in the 220 and the 440 at the Junior College National Championships.

Tex also got a lot friendlier with the Pacific Ocean. Most of his long distance work took the form of ocean swims. Much like Galveston, swimming competitions were a popular part of various beach events in Los Angeles. Tex made a regular habit of entering ocean swims and won every time. Well, every time except when Buster Crabbe entered.

Clarence Linden "Buster" Crabbe was an All-American swimmer for the University of Southern California and teammate of Tex's at the Los Angeles Athletic Club. They were about the same age (Crabbe was born in 1908) and the two formed a close friendship and an amicable rivalry in the pool at the LAAC and in the ocean. Whereas Weissmuller was the coach who taught Tex his techniques, Crabbe provided the second piece of the puzzle that leads to a jump in ability: an ever-so-slightly better rival. Ocean distance swimming came naturally for Buster, who grew up in Hawai'i and won a bronze medal at the 1928 Olympics in the 1500-meter freestyle. Tex earned plenty of first place trophies along the beaches of LA, but he'd always get second when Buster swam.

Tex also spent plenty of time at the beach because, on top of his work at the service station, he'd picked up a job as a lifeguard in Santa Monica. It was at that job he discovered a surreptitious source of income that he would tap intermittently throughout his life when he felt it necessary.

Abalone.

Sea snails, basically. *Big-as-all-get-out* sea snails. The shells of red abalone can grow to about a foot in diameter. They're also considered quite a delicacy, for which restaurants would pay handsomely. Because of this, abalone fishing is highly regulated. Sale of sport-obtained abalone is illegal and it's illegal for even a licensed fisherman to be in possession of more than three at a time.

Occasionally when he would get off work at the beach in Santa Monica, Tex would swim out to spots in the ocean he had previously scouted and dive for abalone. With a snorkel, a mask, and a tow sack in hand (swim fins weren't popularized until the '40s), he would dive to the bottom, put abalone in the sack and tie it to a rock just off shore. That night he would return, retrieve his stash, and sell his catch to high class restaurants looking to serve the delicious – and expensive – mollusc.

The Hollywood service station, lifeguarding gig, and cloak-and-dagger abalone hunts gave Tex enough money to put himself through college while still training at the LAAC, the YMCA, and at the Ambassador with Weissmuller. Those finances got a big help in 1931, when Fred Cady offered him a scholarship to USC.

Along with coaching at the LAAC, Cady was also the head swim coach for Southern Cal. Tex jumped at the opportunity and joined his pal Buster Crabbe on the USC swim team. Since it was his first year as a scholarship athlete, USC listed him as a freshman, even though he'd already won a pair of JUCO national championships at Los Angeles Junior College. (This would come back to haunt him three years later at Michigan.)

But while Cady was officially the head coach, with the 1932 Los Angeles Olympics fast approaching his attention was on the Los Angeles Athletic Club and scouting talent. With Cady spending most of his day over at the LAAC, much of the work by the USC swimmers that year was done without him.

Officially Tex's first collegiate head coaching job was at the University of Texas, but in the fall of 1931, he was basically the unofficial head coach of the USC Trojans. One of the reasons for stepping into the role of coach (aside from the fact that it's what he would do in all situations) was his interest in helping his friend Buster.

Crabbe already had a bronze medal in the 1500, an NCAA championship in the 440, and a number of ocean swim titles to his name, but what struck Tex was how much of it he was doing on just sheer talent. Because of his work with Johnny Weissmuller (and the way in which he absorbed these sorts of things), Tex had extensive knowledge of the intricate little techniques that could make a big difference as those split times add up.

Not that he didn't have Olympic dreams of his own. In the spring of 1932 he left USC to focus on the games. Tex got his old job back at the Studebaker plant in San Bernardino, which helped him make the money he'd need to travel to Cincinnati for the U.S. Olympic Team Trials. Even though he was no longer attending/swimming/coaching at USC, Tex would work the early shift at the plant so he could privately coach Buster in the afternoon as each prepared for the trials.

In the summer of 1932, Tex, Buster, and all the other top swimmers from around the country traveled to Cincinnati to vie for the few spots on the U.S. Olympic swim team. The prelims in the 200-meter and 400-meter freestyle went very well for Tex, swimming a great opening heat and securing himself a spot in the finals of each event. But the finals were as far as he made it. He secured alternate status, but his times put him one spot off the U.S. Olympic team.

Tex was happy for his friend Buster, who made the team by winning the 400, but coming so close was a tough pill to swallow. However, there was another route onto the team. Coach Cady called his star center-forward back to LA to prep for the Olympic trial in a different sport.

FRED CADY had been busy. While Tex was filling in for him over at USC, Cady was putting together a world-class water polo team.

This was expected. The best water polo players in the U.S. lived in California and the best water polo players in California worked out at the LAAC. As the Olympics approached, Cady and newly added water polo coach Frank Rivas put their all-stars in place: Austin Clapp, Philip Daubenspeck, Charles Finn, Dutch McCallister, Wally O'Connor, Cal Strong, and goalkeeper Herbert Wildman. And Tex. Cady picked up Clapp, McCallister, O'Connor, and Strong in one go from the dominant Stanford water polo team, which gave the squad a tremendous boost in talent.

In their qualifying matches, the LAAC beat their LA rivals, the Hollywood Athletic Club and the Olympic Club, before traveling and beating the top teams from around the country, most notably the Chicago Athletic Association, the Illinois Athletic Club, and the New York Athletic Club. By beating all of its competitors, Tex's team was chosen to represent the United States in the 1932 Olympics.

With all the swimming and coaching and water polo, Tex had missed a lot of work at the Studebaker plant. Even with the last couple of matches before the Olympics approaching, the patience of the higher ups at Studebaker ran out. If Tex missed work again to go play water polo, he wouldn't have a job to come back to.

Tex knew he didn't need to be there for his team to make the Olympics. He'd played in four qualifying games already and by that point it had become apparent he and his LAAC teammates would roll the competition. Plus, this was 1932. It was the height of the Great Depression. Tex was lucky to even *have* a job, especially steady work as the manager of the parts department. He could miss the last two games, keep his job, and be ready for the '32 LA Games.

What he did not know was that the qualifying tournament rules stated that the official Olympic roster had to be the winning team's roster in its final game. If you're not on that roster, you're not on the Olympic roster.

But the winning team was able to select a group of players to serve as alternates. Unsurprisingly, Cady immediately selected Tex. So Tex would head to the games as a representative of the U.S., but just as an alternate in both the races and now in water polo as well. All he could do was keep himself ready in case there was an injury. That, and coach Buster.

When the Opening Ceremony arrived on July 30, 1932, Tex marched into Los Angeles Memorial Coliseum with the rest of the U.S. team in front of 95,000 fans. During the games, he'd spend his days at the Los Angeles Swimming Stadium, the 10,000-seat aquatics center built next to the Coliseum, and his nights at the Olympic Village with the other athletes.

The LA games were the first to feature a fully constructed Olympic village for the athletes. (Well, at least for the male athletes;

female athletes were housed at the Chapman Park Hotel on Wilshire Boulevard.) In the Baldwin Hills, Olympic organizers constructed a 500-building village that included its own post and telegraph offices, amphitheater, hospital, fire department, and bank. Athletes from across the world mixed and mingled. Even though each country had its own dining area, many athletes would choose to eat in a different country's dining hall each day.

Each day started early, in fact earlier than Tex and his teammates had planned. The U.S. eight-man rowing team (which took gold at the games) had to be awake early for training over at Laguna Beach. They decided it would be particularly amusing to wake the water polo team by banging their oars on the sides of the little houses where the swimmers slept. The startling prank turned into a welcomed wake-up call. The U.S. would always be the first water polo team to the Swimming Stadium each day thanks to the early morning wall rattling from American oarsmen.

As for the competition itself, with Tex out the team had to rely on Wally O'Connor even more than ever. But that was one heck of a player to rely on. O'Connor is considered, with very few objections, the greatest U.S. water polo player of all time. In his long career, O'Connor was selected to five Olympic teams (1924, 1928, 1932, 1936, and the canceled 1940 games). He was the flag bearer for the '36 U.S. Olympic team. Tex may have been the captain of the water polo team at the Y but on the LAAC squad Wally ran the show.

With the talented team the U.S. put in the pool, the goal was for a silver medal. Normally the goal is gold but nobody was going to beat Hungary in 1932. In the five games the Hungarians played on their way to the gold medal, a grand total of two goals were scored against them. They scored thirty against their opponents.

The United States' top competition for the silver was Germany. The two countries played a tough, scrapping, back-and-forth game, but at the end of regulation the Americans made a tactical error. Apparently Tex wasn't the only player to suffer due to some rules confusion. U.S. player Cal Strong explained in a 1988 interview with the Amateur Athletic Association of Los Angeles:

> Well, of course, the Hungarians were outstanding. Not being sour grapes, but they should have been good because they

worked for the government and could practice anytime as much as they wanted. The Germans were good – and that was one of the big disappointments in all my years of playing; the fact that we were stupid and didn't know that they didn't play off ties. And at the end of the German game we were tied (4-4) with them and were all fired up to play an overtime period, and were told that under the Olympic rules you didn't play off ties, which I think is the only sport I know of anywhere that you don't play off a tie. The same thing happened in the 1984 Olympics. There was a tie that gave the United States team a silver medal instead of a gold.

In 1932 it gave the U.S. bronze. Both the U.S. and Germany finished with the exact same record, so the silver was determined by total goals scored. The Germans had two more. Silver for Germany; Bronze for the United States of America.

But that bronze medal never hung on Tex's wall. He was a part of the team, certainly. He'd been selected and played in qualifying games. But he was an alternate and alternates didn't get medals. He instead had to watch his teammates play while sitting with the other five alternates: Duke Kahanamoku, Frank Graham, William O'Connor, and Raymond Rudy from the LAAC and Fred Laur from the Illinois Athletic Club.

It was the same story at the races. Tex swam an exhibition relay before the actual event, but was an alternate for the 4x200 rely team, which got the silver, finishing second to a Japanese team that crushed the world record by more than thirty-five seconds.

At least Buster managed to make it to the top of the podium.

Buster Crabbe's gold in the 400 freestyle prevented a complete Japanese sweep of the men's races. Using underwater cameras to watch swimmers during training, the Japanese team put an impressive amount of work into refining the most efficient swimming stroke possible. It paid dividends in Los Angeles, with Japan winning gold *and* silver in the 100 free, 1500 free, 100 back, and 200 breast, and winning gold in the 4x200 free relay. That's every swimming race at the games save the 400.

In a photo finish, Crabbe beat France's Jean Taris in the finals by a tenth of a second with an Olympic record time of 4:48.4.

Tex was thrilled. That night Tex celebrated with the swimmer he'd helped win gold, Buster Crabbe, and the gold medalist who helped him, Johnny Weissmuller. They were each a significant part of Tex's development in Los Angeles. And they were good friends. But Tex never saw Buster or Johnny after he left LA at the conclusion of the '32 games.

Weissmuller left coaching and would go on to become the iconic "Tarzan." Many actors have played Edger Rice Burrough's famous feral man on the silver screen, but Weissmuller was the definitive Tarzan, appearing in twelve films. The iconic, ululating Tarzan yell – created by combining the sound of a soprano, an alto, and a hog caller (frankly, hog caller is an under-utilized register of classical chorus) – first appeared when he played the character.

Though he and Tex never crossed paths again, a notable coincidence is that after Weissmuller became famous as Tarzan, he was invited to Splash Day in Galveston by Salvetore Maceo, where he won the mile swim Tex had participated in way back in 1924.

Crabbe was also bound for Hollywood, where the speedy swimmer would make a name for himself playing, appropriately, Flash Gordon. Crabbe even stepped in for Weissmuller and played Tarzan once, making him the only actor to play Tarzan, Flash Gordon, and Buck Rogers.

As for Tex, he wasn't done swimming yet. Though he didn't swim in any of the official events, those who scouted the sport knew the impressive times he'd put up in Cincinnati. There were coaches from the top swim programs from around the country attending the 1932 Olympics and Tex, in classic Tex style, made sure he met every one.

The disappointment of being an alternate turned into excitement at the opportunities laid before him. He was offered by Cady to return to the scholarship he gave up at USC. Yale coach Bob Kiphuth, who would become the winningest dual meet coach in history (528-12), asked him to come to the East Coast and swim for the Bulldogs. According to Tex, he was also invited to swim for a university in Japan. He did not recall which school but, looking at the potential destinations of the time, the most likely possibility is Keio University in Tokyo, considering that it not only had a strong swimming program but also a distinct openness to foreigners (Albert Einstein gave his first lecture after winning the Nobel Prize in Physics at Keio). Plus, 1932 silver medalist Koike Reizo would set a new world record in the breaststroke a couple years later while swimming for Keio.

Nevertheless, he did not choose to swim for Keio, USC, or even Yale. At the 1932 Olympics Tex met the person he'd model the rest of his life after: Michigan's Matt Mann.

Tex had met several of Mann's swimmers at the Olympic trials and at the games and was consistently impressed by how much they loved their school and loved their head coach. They were always upbeat and yet always focused.

When Tex got out of the pool following his exhibition swim at the Olympics with the 4x200 team, he found Mann waiting for him.

"Kid, why don't you come over and swim with us?" Mann asked in his distinct Northern English accent.

It was settled. Tex decided right there that he was a Michigan man.

Chapter

"Coach Mann! This is Tex. I'm here!"

Tex stood at the University Union on the Michigan campus, where he'd borrowed a phone to let Matt Mann know he was ready to enroll for the fall semester of 1932. It was August 28, just two weeks after the closing ceremonies of the Olympics. That was all the time it took for Tex to settle his affairs in Los Angeles and make his way to Ann Arbor.

He quit his job at the Studebaker plant, gave his car to his brother Frank, and left town the same way he came in: hitchhiking and hopping rails with the hobos. All he brought with him was a single cloth bag containing a change of summer clothes, a toothbrush, and an Olympic sweat suit. The whole of his fortune, eighty-five dollars, was pinned to his underwear.

After hopping off the train he went straight to the University Union and called Mann, eager to start swimming for the legendary coach he'd already absorbed a great deal of information about. Born in England in 1884, Mann became the country's boy swimming champion by age nine. Playing an integral role in the development of college swimming, Mann is the only person to coach at both Harvard and Yale. From there he went on to the Detroit Athletic Club and became Michigan's first full-time swim coach.

"That's great, kid," Mann said. "See you at workout tomorrow."

"Wait, wait a minute," Tex said. "Where do I stay? When does my scholarship start?"

"Scholarship? Son, the Big Ten doesn't have scholarships."

With workouts starting the next day, the swimming part at Michigan was taken care of, but for the time being he needed to find a place to bed down. That night it would be at Mann's house, where he and a freshman diver – perhaps facing the same issue as Tex – slept.

The next morning he managed to obtain financial aid from the university (the eighty-five dollars pinned to his underwear wouldn't cover tuition). He got a loan to cover the rest of his tuition and simply used the library for his studies, since he wasn't able to afford any textbooks. The first workouts with the Michigan swim team were that afternoon for the freshman swimmer.

Michigan put him down as a freshman for the third time (fourth if you include San Bernardino, though he didn't swim there). This would come up later in his career, but as far as the Big Ten Conference was concerned, he was a freshman.

After Tex stayed at his house for a week, Mann worked out a deal with the Delta Kappa Epsilon fraternity. Tex could live in the basement if he washed dishes. Thankfully he wasn't alone in the task. Stuck in the basement with him was a sophomore named Jerry, whom Tex developed a close friendship with. As a member of the fraternity, Jerry had his own room but he was on clean up duty, which meant spending plenty of time in the basement drying the dishes Tex washed. Jerry was also a fellow athlete. As a football player, he played linebacker and center on back-to-back national champion teams for the Wolverines.

It was Jerry who introduced Tex to life at Michigan, as well as many of the other athletes at the university. Athletics was obviously a common topic of conversation for the two dishwashers at the ΔKE house. Along with talking plenty of football (Tex was a big fan of the sport thanks to his complimentary viewing of games at the Rose Bowl), they talked just as much swimming. Tex, ever the enthusiast for his craft, sold Jerry on the athletic benefits of the sport.

According to Tex, that friendship and those conversations are why, forty-three years later, when Jerry became President of the United States, he decided to build a swimming pool at the White House.

Tex would remain a supporter of his old college buddy Ford and send him money when he could for campaigns as Jerry navigated his way up the ranks. They stayed in contact through post over the years, even after Ford took the Oath of Office following Richard Nixon's resignation. He would not be the last U.S. President to have a friendship with Tex Robertson. Tex received a lot of letters with the White House stamp on it.

He had a basement to bed down in and an introduction to the social life of his new university; he just had to keep himself from going hungry. With no money left to his name, he survived for a couple weeks by stealing apples and pears from the trees on the university's golf course. He was able to buy some proper meals once he strung together a series of jobs. He waited tables, cleaned the football stadium, raked leaves, shoveled snow, and did all manner of other jobs to keep himself eating and in school. As Tex described it: "The first school year was fun, cold, and tough with a few hungry days."

After the parade of professions he got more steady work by operating a linoleum floor cleaning business. He even hired some of his fellow swimmers.

It was a tough life, but he loved it. As a twenty-three-year-old third-time college freshman, he was operating his own business, living with good friends, and swimming with and learning from the best. And for the first time he was a pretty good student. His first semester at Michigan he passed Astronomy 101, a course he'd taken at three different schools.

He majored in physical education and it was in the phys-ed program he met professor Harold D. Copp. Discovering his young student's financial and nutritional issue, Copp invited Tex to move out of the boiler room and into his house, where Tex served as a babysitter for Copp's grade school-age sons.

Tex spent the spring semester of '33 living at Professor Copp's house. Copp also owned a cabin and about ten acres along the Huron River, which would later serve as the beginning of Tex's camp-building experience.

But the future wasn't on Tex's mind yet. He just was happy to be a Michigan Wolverine swimmer. As freshmen could not compete on the varsity back then, Tex couldn't swim at the Big Ten or NCAA meet, but he could compete in Amateur Athletic Union events as a member of an athletic club outside the university. Given his previous membership in the prestigious Los Angeles Athletic Club, he was immediately admitted to the Detroit Athletic Club. In New York, Tex represented the DAC at AAU nationals, where he placed sixth in the 220 freestyle and got third in the 300-yard medley – there were only three portions of the medley, as the butterfly wouldn't be established internationally until 1956 – finishing behind two of the Spence brothers. (New York Athletic Club swimmers Walter, Wallace, and Leonard Spence were inducted together into the International Swimming Hall of Fame in 1967.)

As for Michigan meets, Tex had to sit and watch during that first season, a relatively disappointing one for the Wolverines. Michigan won yet another Big Ten Championship, but the back-to-back defending national champions were upset at the NCAA meet by Northwestern, a team Michigan had beaten in both a dual meet and at the conference championships. At the previous year's NCAA championship, the Wolverines won titles in four races. Yet in 1933, Richard Degener's victory in three-meter diving was the only title the Wolverines had to show from their trip to the national meet at Yale.

The significance of Northwestern's upset would be put into perspective as time went on, given that Michigan won team national titles in each of Tex's two remaining years at Michigan, 1934 and 1935, as well as the next six national championships after that.

Tex traveled with the team that first season and began his tutelage under Mann. There was no person Tex respected more than Mann. He already had the coaching itch, as evidenced by his willingness to volunteer himself as coach in all situations possible, but it was Mann who taught him the way to win championships and inspire a group of swimmers, athletes participating in a decidedly individual sport, to sacrifice personal gain for team titles, such as willingness to swim a stroke they were not as skilled at to pick up extra points.

Tex asked questions whenever possible about overall season strategy, meet-to-meet strategy, practice structure, teaching style, and technique refinement. Tex claimed that by the end of his Michigan career he would always be Mann's "first or second option" when it came to composing meet strategy and that he greatly appreciated his teammates' acceptance of his coaching while he "interfered with Matt on the deck."

"During my competitive years, I was more a coach than a swimmer," Tex said in a 1981 speech to the College Swim Coaches of America. "Most workouts I spent so much time as unofficial coach I missed the workouts, so I swam alone at night or odd times." Tex also joked that he was the real reason for Michigan's national championships but Mann got all the credit. In addition, Tex worked as the swim coach at University High School in Ann Arbor during his remaining two years at Michigan.

He knew he wanted to be head coach at an NCAA program. A very specific NCAA program. While working with Mann, Tex decided someday he would return to his home state and become the head coach of the Texas Longhorns.

This was not a statement of preference. It was a statement of fact. He had no familiarity with the athletic department at the University of Texas. He knew no one at the University of Texas. But he knew he was going to be the Longhorns' head coach because he decided he was going to be the Longhorns' head coach.

That was how Tex operated. And he usually got his way because of it.

But that was just part one of Mann's influence on the direction of Tex's life. Mann was also the founder of the world's first sport-specific camp. On Ahmic Lake, in the forests about 185 miles north of Toronto, he created Camp Chikopi. From 1920 until his death in 1962, Mann spent every summer at Chikopi training young swimmers, eighteen of whom went on to be hall of famers (including Buck Dawson, the founder of the International Swimming Hall of Fame). Fully aware of Tex's love of camping, Mann invited his freshman freestyler to join him for a few weeks as a counselor up at Chikopi.

Tex was in his own personal heaven. He was working with the person he admired most and doing what he loved most (teaching swimming) in the wilderness of Canada.

During the second week of camp, there was a quiet moment where Tex and Mann sat on a porch overlooking the lake, sipping ice tea, and spitting the saw dust that came from the method the camp's 300-pound blocks of ice that were pulled from the lake the winter before were stored. It was in a quiet moment on a lazy afternoon in the shade that Tex made the singular and conclusive declaration that would define the rest of his life.

"I'm going to have a camp like this and call it Camp Longhorn. And, like you, I'm going to coach swimming at the University of Texas."

"Good work, son."

Tex remembered those words, specifically, as Matt Mann's response. It meant a lot that his mentor approved of him adopting the same lifestyle. It's odd, though, that Mann would respond in an implied past tense, as if something had already been accomplished, even though Tex was simply giving a statement of purpose.

But perhaps Mann was as confident as Tex that it was going to happen because he knew it could be done. After all, he had done it. Maybe Tex's mudhole reminded him of practicing his swim strokes in the sluice-ways draining from the woolen mills in Leeds, England. Maybe Tex's rail-hopping and surviving on his wits (and some stolen golf course fruit) reminded him of showing up to Toronto in a sealed railroad car with two dollars in his pocket after getting sent away from Ellis Island for insufficient funds.

Or maybe that was just his manner of speech.

Regardless, Tex's life plan was in place. Now he just had to get to coaching and camping. His next opportunity came immediately after his return from Chikopi.

Through Ford he'd become friends with a group of Michigan track athletes who were heading across the lake to Chicago for the 1933 World's Fair. Tex joined them and, like Galveston in '24, it was something to see.

Over twenty-two million paid admissions were sold that summer to the World's Fair and the "Century of Progress," celebrating the city's centennial. The theme of the fair was technological innovation, though, ironically, Tex's first job there was pulling a rickshaw. But he did get to take in his share of the science fact and science fiction on display at the fair. There were concept cars, the arrival of the German airship Graf Zeppelin, and the "Homes of Tomorrow." He also saw the premiere of the ten-minute short, *Buck Rogers in the 25th Century: An Interplanetary Battle with the Tiger Men of Mars*. Six years later it would be turned into the famous twelve-part serial film *Buck Rogers*, the role of Buck played by his old friend Buster Crabbe.

Rickshaw pulling made for great training for Michigan's track stars, but after two days and two sore knees Tex stopped his cart at the Baby Ruth Swimming Pool. He was made the pool manager and life guard and was given a part in the aquatic show billed as "Michigan's Olympic Champion." The big draws to the show were exhibitions from Pete Desjardins, a diver who won two gold medals at the 1928 Olympics, and Helene Madison, who won a gold medal in all three freestyle events at the Los Angeles Olympic Games.

Tex's favorite part of the job was between shows, when he would coach a group of five Chicago Westside boys who got a free swim and a pass to the fair. Their free passes were a result of their willingness to be a part of the entertainment. Suspended over the Baby Ruth Pool was a long pole covered in grease. Attached to the end of the pole was a one dollar bill. Before the show, as the crowd was getting settled, the boys would one by one attempt to walk across the pole. If they could make it to the end, they got the dollar. This mostly resulted in entertaining spills into the water, much to the delight of the crowd.

There was one boy in the group who was particularly skilled at the contest. He would build momentum and go sliding right off the end, taking the dollar with him into the pool. He would emerge, dollar in hand, to cheers. Or at least that's how the kid told the story. Tex had a different version.

"He never did get close to it. His long ol' feet would kind of curl over the thing and he'd slide off," Tex said. "Between shows I had a swimming team – I had a team everywhere I'd go. So I found out that nut after a few little workouts could kick faster than he could swim, those big ol' feet and so forth – just a natural."

They each had their own version of the meeting. According to Tex, he discovered the fifteen-year-old junior lifeguard at the Baby Ruth pool and immediately saw his potential to become the world's greatest backstroker. According to the fifteen-year-old junior lifeguard, it was he who went to Tex and pestered him until Tex finally agreed to become his coach.

"He was a national collegiate champion and here's poor little me," said Adolph Kiefer, a ninety-two-year-old man when I met with him at his business near Chicago. "But I didn't give up following him around because I wanted to be coached by the great swimmer Tex Robertson."

"MY FATHER DIED IN 1931. He had a brain tumor, and I was one of eight children. One died very young, who I never met, another one died in 1918, the year I was born. The rest, four brothers and a sister, they're all dead. I'm the last of the Mohicans of anybody in that family.

"My mother and father migrated here from Germany, like everybody else. He came as an inventor of candy. He had a process of making soft-centered hard candies, like raspberry and maple and all that. He invented flavors and he invented the machinery. So he was pretty inventive and he was hired by a candy company in Chicago.

"We had cousins and neighbors all with German names and we

would go to Lake Michigan on these little picnics. I seemed to be one of the first ones who'd swim in the lake and play in the water. My father was Catholic and my mother was Lutheran. We went to Lutheran school and Sunday my father would pick us up, all the little kids, and take us to Lake Michigan, big Lake Michigan right over here. We didn't know how to swim, but we'd always play in the water. We always got an ice cream, a black walnut ice cream cone.

"The first time I really swam was when my cousin came to the house. Our house was alongside a little stream that ran into a drainage canal, a great, big, wide, deep drainage canal. And there's a great big falls and cement abutment. I ran along that abutment showing off and I fell in. I never swam before and I was in my clothes. So I rolled over on my back and paddled on my hands and feet. That was the beginning of the backstroke for me. I thought I'd invented the backstroke.

"So I go into swimming and there was this city meet. I didn't know much about how to do it right but tried it anyway and I got second. My father, he was proud. He gave me a dollar and he said, 'Son, you're going to be the best swimmer in the world.' So I said, 'By gosh, I'm going to do that.' That was right before he died.

"When he died it was during the Depression, and I mean the real Depression. He had an apartment, but he lost that before he died. Everyone lost everything.

"No smoke from the factories. No life. Everything was dead. People on the streets everywhere doing nothing. As a result, as a little kid I started to sell magazines and newspapers and popcorn. Anything just to work and make money, because we didn't have any money. We're talking about total poverty. Holes in my shoes. But it didn't make any difference. You don't think of those things.

"Then in the summer I'd go work on a farm with my aunt and uncle. I lived with a lot of different people. Our family was so big it was broken up when my father died. Two of my older brothers had to go to work in the brewery in Pittsburgh where another uncle was the brew master, another German. My sister had to leave college and she had to get a job, working for fifteen dollars a week or something like that. My mother was really suffering from depression, so we really didn't know our mother that well.

"That's why Tex, when I found him, became more than a coach.

He was a senior mentor to me and in some respects, yes, a father.

"Before I met him I hadn't been coached, but I had been swimming. I'd gotten a job as an elevator operator at the Lake Shore Athletic Club. I ate at their cafeteria so I had some food and I'd swim for two or three hours at a time and take the street car home. Then a swimming coach from the junior high school got me the job as a junior life guard at the Baby Ruth Swimming Pool.

"Here we go. This is where Tex comes in. The pool was right there on Lake Michigan and there were so many people there, all with their wool bathing suits on. Yes, we wore wool. Jantzen Swimwear, that was the big name then. Everybody wore Jantzen.

"The job paid four dollars a week, I think that was it. Street cars at that time were three cents for children, so I thought that was great. We had world champions Pete the Shark and Helene Madison. She was the big shot. She won three freestyle gold medals. Lots of the lifeguards were great swimmers as well. And one of the lifeguards was Tex Robertson.

"Tex was a good looking guy and a damn good swimmer. I had to push the girls away because he had a lot of girlfriends. I said, 'Get away get away get away.'

"Well, finally, he said, 'Ok, let me see what I can do for you.' So he took a liking to me and I would follow him around. Everybody would see me walking behind him, even with his girlfriends. So we found a bond of sincerity, with me following him around there like a watchdog. But I wanted to be coached by Tex Robertson because he was a great swimmer.

"He then started telling me about swimming and strokes. When the World's Fair was over he said, 'Kid, here's what I want you to do. I want you to go to Lakeshore Athletic Club and see Stan Brauniger and work out there, because he can help you. And I'm going to write to you with instructions on how to work out. Also, when you have weekends or holidays, you come over here and I'll get you in the pool and we'll have you swimming at the University of Michigan swimming pool.'

"So, I would hitchhike – at that time people would hitchhike – to Ann Arbor, Michigan. There I would find Tex Robertson. Tex at that time was working in the student union behind the counter, so I could eat, no charge. Then he put me up in one of the dormitories, where I could have a place to sleep a couple of nights on the weekend. He'd take me over to the pool when he was free and have me swim in the pool. And then during the week he would come to Chicago and coach me."

"ADOLPH DIDN'T KNOW IT, but I also had a hot girlfriend in Chicago," Tex once confided.

But I imagine Kiefer had an inkling. He brought up, multiple times, how Tex was always surrounded by girls when he was at the pool. Adolph would not be the first nor the last of those I interviewed to describe Tex as "good looking."

"I'd characterize him as a character, and a good looking man," said Texas athletic director DeLoss Dodds.

"Marvelous looking, just marvelous," said Pat, Tex's wife. "Have you seen that old picture in the bedroom? Marvelous looking."

Combine his appealing personality with those looks and his athleticism and we have a truly charismatic figure. Pat actually announced that she was going to marry him the moment she saw him.

Tex's relationship with Kiefer was the first time he became a true father-figure to someone. He'd been a coach and a counselor for kids at camps, but this was different. He wanted Kiefer to be successful not just because he was one of his swimmers but because this kid looked up to him in a way no one had before.

Tex spent several weeks at a time in Chicago. During the day Tex worked at Sears and Adolph sold hot dogs and popcorn at Cubs games. In the evenings Tex trained Kiefer at the Lake Shore Athletic Club and the Lawson YMCA.

Because of their close relationship and the tremendous talent Kiefer showed, Tex decided to have the kid work on techniques he was experimenting with in his personal research on more efficient swimming strokes. One of these was a straight-arm recovery Tex had been using in freestyle. With Tex's experimental arm recovery applied to the backstroke and his improved starts, Kiefer began shaving seconds off his time. But his leap in performance wasn't truly apparent until...

"Who's that kid in the pool?!"

Tex looked up in surprise to see Coach Mann stomping his way across the deck.

Tex smiled, spread his arms wide and said, "Well that's Sonny Boy

Kiefer."

He used nicknames to give people an air of credibility. After all, that's not some kid named Adolph. That's the famous 'Sonny Boy' Kiefer. How could you not know who 'Sonny Boy' Kiefer is? It's a skill Tex would make frequent use of later in life.

"Sonny Boy Kiefer's one of the best swimmers around," Tex said.

Mann considered for a moment.

"Well, let's see what he can do."

So Mann took out his stopwatch and said, "Swim the 100."

Down and back went Kiefer. As he got closer to the finish, Mann's eyes grew. When Kiefer touched the wall, Mann clicked his watch and exclaimed, "I can't believe this! Kid, do that again."

He did it again. All Mann could do was stare at his watch. Finally he looked up at Tex.

"That kid's gonna be a world's champion," Mann said.

59.4.

No one had ever swum the 100-yard backstroke in under a minute and a high schooler had done it off the cuff. His world record was made official when he swam at the Illinois High School State Championships, lowering the mark to 58.5 seconds.

Kiefer was on his way to Olympic glory and Tex his first breakthroughs in stroke development. Tex had been bugging Michigan teammate Taylor Drysdale about his backstroke recovery, but up until this point Drysdale had been unimpressed with what the sophomore freestyler had to say. Following Kiefer's time trial, Drysale begrudgingly admitted there might be something to it and adopted the technique, much to the delight of Tex.

Tex always seemed prouder of his innovation of little techniques like the straight-arm recovery rather than the invention of the flip turn, though he was obviously much more famous for the latter. Then again, Drysdale would go on to build the atom bomb as a part of the Manhattan Project after obtaining his master's degrees in nuclear physics and mathematics. Perhaps it's all relative.

Before the flip turn came about, swimmers would simply touch the wall with their hand, shove off, and start swimming the opposite direction. With the flip turn, the swimmer dives underwater, flips over, and pushes off with the feet, giving a boost to speed.

That's a simplified explanation of the technique and it gets even more complex when it's applied to the backstroke. But Tex didn't have Kiefer just swimming the backstroke. He was a believer in getting swimmers outside of their comfort zone and having them swim all strokes and swim them a lot. No weight training or running. Just swimming. Lots and lots and lots of swimming. (Even after his career, Tex would continue to swim at least a mile every day.)

Since Kiefer was already Tex's guinea pig for his new stroke techniques, he went ahead and had him start flipping over when he hit the end of the pool while he was swimming freestyle. The flip turn still needed a lot of refining, but the potential was obvious from the slight drop in Kiefer's freestyle times.

It was Kiefer who suggested applying it to the backstroke. There was just one problem. The rules at the time required a backstroker to touch the wall while still laying on their back. That made fitting in a flip turn a rather difficult proposition. But Adolph and Tex still managed to work it out.

Kiefer explained: "You throw your opposite hand to the opposite shoulder, put your head back, put your arms out some, bring your knees up to your chest, and pivot with the free hand, spin around, get both feet against the wall firmly, shove off, power stroke underwater, come up. At that time you were only allowed one stroke underwater. You didn't get fifteen feet out. All the rules have changed."

Even with the added complexity of getting into the flip, the boost off the wall more than makes up for the time lost flipping. But despite the time he spent with Tex working on it, Kiefer didn't use the flip turn in the 1936 Olympics when he won gold in the 100-meter backstroke. Tex never used the technique in his own swimming while he was at Michigan and its use didn't spread until he became the coach at Texas, when other schools saw his freestyle swimmers using it at nationals. And even with some NCAA schools using it, the flip turn didn't make an appearance in the Olympics until 1956.

There are a number of factors that kept the flip turn on Tex's drawing board and out of the swimming pool for a long time. The first was risk. The flip turn is now ubiquitous in swimming, but in the '30s and '40s it wasn't something swimmers had trained on their whole lives. It was just an idea bouncing around in Tex's head. An improperly executed flip turn could ruin a race for a swimmer.

"If you missed it, you lose and you lose by a lot," Kiefer said.

In addition, wall touching rules were so specific at the time that judges would raise an eyebrow if a swimmer flipped. There was just as much risk of disqualification. The rules have changed greatly since then (Tex played a role in that, writing many letters and attending many meetings with NCAA and IOC officials), but there was a debate at the time as to whether or not the flip turn itself should be allowed.

Then there was World War II. Kiefer should have many more Olympic medals than the gold he won at the age of sixteen, but the 1940 and 1944 Olympics never happened. A swimmer winning with the flip turn at any Olympics would have caused rapid spread of the technique. But without an Olympics, a honed version of the flip turn spread slowly, primarily at the collegiate level. Even at the 1948 and 1952 Olympics the flip turn wasn't used.

It wasn't until the 1956 Olympics, when the rules were changed to clearly allow the flip, that it gained widespread usage. (It wasn't the only rule change; the '56 games also saw the introduction of the butterfly as an Olympic stroke.)

It certainly helped one country. Australian Olympic coach Forbes Carlile, who obtained his masters degree in physiology from the University of Sydney and was an innovator in swimming himself, was aware of Tex's work and already had his swimmers training on the flip turn before most other Olympic teams.

The Australian men's and women's teams won eight of thirteen gold medals – more swimming golds than Australia had won in all previous Olympics combined – and swept gold, silver, and bronze in both the men's and women's 100-meter freestyle. More than half of the golds won by Australia on their home soil in 1956 didn't take place on soil but rather in the water.

As for Kiefer, within a couple years of meeting Tex he'd set the official world record in both the 100-yard and 100-meter backstroke (58.5 and 1:04.8, respectively) and broken records in six different countries on a European tour. He easily found himself on the U.S. Olympic team and off to his parents' country of birth for the Berlin games.

While training in the pool at the Olympic village, Kiefer was told to get out because the Führer himself was on his way. Turns out he was coming specifically for Kiefer. Adolph Hitler had heard of the American swimming star of German descent who shared his given name. Flanked by a cadre of bodyguards and Hermann Göring at his side, there was Hitler.

"He was a little guy, just like his pictures. He was very straight and erect, with a little mustache," Kiefer said. "But very piercing eyes."

Hitler shook Kiefer's hand and through an interpreter said, "This young man is the perfect example of the true Aryan."

Kiefer was confused by the remark. He only thought of himself as American and had never heard the term "Aryan." So he simply smiled, nodded, and shook the hand of the man who would start World War II.

"At the time, I was honored to meet this important head of state," Kiefer said. "If I had any idea of what he was about to do, I'd have drowned him in the pool."

In the 100-meter backstroke, Kiefer set a new Olympic record in the preliminaries, the semi-finals, and the finals on his way to gold. Kiefer's Olympic record would stand sixteen years until it was broken by American swimmer Yoshinobu Oyakawa, wearing the nylon swim suit Kiefer invented. The silver in '36 was taken by Al Vande Weghe. The gold medalist from the 1932 Olympics, Kiyokawa Masaji, got the bronze, barely beating Drysdale. Tex's Michigan teammate had beaten Kiyokawa in the semifinal race, but the three-time national champion slipped when pushing off the starting block in the finals and got fourth.

While Tex was preparing Kiefer for those Olympics, he was building on his own swimming career as well. "Michigan's champion swimmer" as he was inaccurately billed at the 1933 World's Fair quickly became, in reality, Michigan's champion swimmer. He went from watching in '33 to winning in '34. As a sophomore he was named an All-American, winning the Big Ten Championship in the 440-yard freestyle and the national championship on Michigan's 400-yard free relay team, along with Ogden Dalrymple, Henry Kamenski, and Robert Renner.

Tex managed to build some stardom of his own in Ann Arbor. "Matt Mann's best" he was called by the papers. The attention grew as his freestyle times got closer and closer to the American records held by his old mentor, Johnny Weissmuller. Heading into the 1935 Big Ten Championships, there was speculation he might break Weissmuller's record in the 220. Tex won the 220 but fell short of the record by 3.5

seconds. Instead, it was in the 440 where he blasted his old coach's time out of the water, beating it by more than two seconds (4:49.6).

No Big Ten swimmer had ever swum the 440 faster than five minutes. Tex did it in under 4:50.

Stricken with the flu right after his record-setting performance, he didn't swim the 220 or the 440 at nationals, but he still managed to compete again in the 400 free relay, again winning a national championship, this time with Drysdale leading off and Renner and Dalrymple coming back for another go around.

After each win, he'd send newspaper clippings and heat sheets back to Los Angeles. By that point, his father had joined his brothers in LA and founded Robertson Brokerage Company. Before the Big Ten Championship, where Tex set a new American record, the telegraph office informed him he'd received a one-sentence wire from his father.

The message: "You're too mean to drown, so get along doggie."

HE WAS AGAIN on top of his world. After the NCAAs, Tex was named All-American once more and his Michigan teammates voted him team captain for the following season. By proving himself one of the fastest swimmers in America (and the fastest at one distance), his senior season would be one for the ages, except that the Big Ten finally figured out that he should have already been a senior. If he swam in 1936 it would be his seventh year in college and sixth year on a collegiate swim team, if you count the fall of '31 when he practiced with Southern Cal.

"Taking into consideration the improvement the curly-haired southerner has shown this year," read an article in the local paper, "the Conference ruling...is robbing Michigan's swimming team of the greatest middle-distance star ever developed here."

Even with the sudden end to his collegiate swimming career, there were plenty of options laid before him. Matt Mann predicted that in a few years Tex would "probably rank as the best swimmer in the world." He'd bested Weissmuller's mark in the 440 and crushed the Big Ten record by more than ten seconds.

He could prep for the 1936 Olympics. He could swim for the Detroit Athletic Club and stay at Michigan as a student, since he'd (still) not finished his degree in physical education. He could join the professional ranks and start earning some cash; something he was certainly in need of. Most professional swimmers of the day participated in surprisingly profitable swim shows and exhibitions. Tex had plenty of 'carnival barker' in him and could have joined Billy Rose's show at the Great Lakes Exhibition. And swimmers were all the rage in Hollywood. Tex was a natural performer and could have joined his old pals Johnny and Buster in Tinseltown.

He didn't want it. He said no to the Olympics, no to the money, no to Hollywood, and ended his swimming career. He didn't want any of it. He just wanted to coach.

Tex Robertson's life was an example of what can be created with a razor focus. He didn't fall into coaching. He had a lot of obvious choices and rejected them all, instead starting his coaching career by force of will. And he knew exactly where he wanted to start it.

Tex was headed back to Texas.

Afterword
by
Bill Robertson

Dad loved humor almost as much as he had a passion for water. He would drink eight *full* glasses of water every day, just as Dr. Joe prescribed. He would joke during cocktail hour while others drank *fool* glasses he would finish his full glass. There always seemed to be a lesson with the humor.

When Dad was about sixty-five years old he started competing in Masters swimming meets. He noticed that as he got older he would get slower despite the effort he would put out during workouts. He would write his times on the concrete steps by the edge of the pool for various lengths. I once was baited into asking him about this trend and he said "adding time is what I am trying to achieve." He always bragged about how swimming kept him alive so long. When people asked him if he still swims a mile a day, he would reply, "Yes and that's how long it takes me."

Dad had many loves in his life. He cared deeply for Mom, his children, nature, politics, community, and camping, but his passion for swimming was at the heart of his life and it would be what became an integral part of mine.

For as long as I can remember I was in the water almost every day practicing. I think I was two years old when I first competed in a meet. I never really cared for or appreciated the workouts. We had summer lake swims during quiet time, workouts on every vacation, and after Rob and Nan left for college I worked out every night when dad came back from the office at 8:30 p.m.

Although Dad was always working, he had time for swimming. This was quality time with Dad even though my face was in the water for an hour and I was usually not very happy about the training. He was focused on me and our goals.

Every night before we went to bed we would visit and he would pull out his spiral notebook (one for each kid) where he kept track of our pay. We were paid for jobs, merit questions, but most of all for workouts and reaching goal times. We all knew it was a bribe to keep us swimming. As I reflect, I am so thankful for the bribes as I was able to experience swimming through college. There I met the love of my life, Carol, also a swimmer. We have raised all four of our children to be strong swimmers as well.

I am honored to continue Dad's legacy through the organizations he founded and the inspiration he gave me to promote aquatics. Considered by most to be the pioneer of Texas Swimming, Dad was alive to see the rebirth of the Texas Swimming and Diving Hall of Fame to honor him and all those that have brought notoriety to aquatic sports in Texas. The museum is located on the UT Campus and in the facility Dad worked so hard to see built, the Jamail Swim Center.

The WETS (Working Exes for Texas Swimming) is also alive and well and I know Dad would be proud of all those involved helping this organization that has the goal of honoring the past accomplishments of UT swimmers and divers. Promoting the present and future success of Longhorn Swimming, and to provide a common forum for all former Texas swimmers, divers, coaches, and fans to gather and stay connected. After almost fifty years since Tex created WETS, the Longhorns have won fifty-five conference and nineteen national championships.

Dad was a remarkable man and accomplished so very much in his lifetime. He had a unique ability to get things done and inspire others to carry out his missions. I am grateful that he touched my life and the lessons I learned are still with me today. Swimcere thanks!

BOOK 2

LONGHORNS AND FROGMEN
THE STORY OF TEX THE COACH

Chapter

Jack Chevigny is the epitome of Notre Dame football.

After Knute Rockne's "Win one for the Gipper" halftime speech, it was Chevigny who scored the tying touchdown against Army, calling out "That's one for the Gipper!" as he crossed the goal line. He was an assistant coach under Rockne following his playing career. He went on to be the head coach of the NFL's Chicago Cardinals, then St. Edward's University in Austin – a sister school of Notre Dame – before becoming head coach of the Texas Longhorns, where he famously took the Longhorns into South Bend and upset his alma mater. Sometime after the victory, Fighting Irish head coach Elmer Layden gave him a fountain pen with the inscription "To Jack Chevigny, a Notre Dame boy who beat Notre Dame."

Marine Lieutenant Chevigny died at the Battle of Iwo Jima in World War II. As Notre Dame legend has it (though this has never been confirmed), the pen was discovered on V-J Day, September 2, 1945, in the hands of one of the Japanese envoys on the U.S.S. *Missouri*. After the pen was sent home, the inscription was changed to read "To Jack Chevigny, a Notre Dame boy who gave his life for his country in the spirit of old Notre Dame."

Steeped in legend, there are few more important figures in Notre Dame lore than Jack Chevigny. But on a warm afternoon in the summer of 1935, this legend wanted to know one thing.

Who the hell is Tex Robertson and why is all of his mail showing up in my office?

Letters from a number of swimmers had arrived to the Longhorn athletic director and football coach's office declaring their commitment to swim for the University of Texas and the institution's new coach, Tex Robertson. Jack Chevigny had never heard of Tex Robertson, at least not until Tex arrived to pick up his mail.

Bursting into the athletic director's office came the showman himself, arms full of medals, newspaper clippings, and various other credentials. He expounded on the great swim program he was already in the process of creating, as he'd been busy recruiting swimmers to Texas long before Texas knew he was recruiting swimmers to Texas.

How Chevigny's brow must have furrowed. This swimmer from, of all places, Michigan – the Irish-Wolverine rivalry got so heated that Michigan was in year twenty-six of its "boycott" of Notre Dame football – was the one responsible for all these letters showing up to his office. Chevigny explained to Tex that he had no intention of paying for a varsity swim coach.

"Good, I'll accept the job under those terms," Tex replied.

Tex left the bewildered Chevigny sitting in his office and began work as Texas' volunteer head coach, the university's first swim coach. Or, that's how Tex liked to frame it. In many ways he was the first coach at UT. Tex was the first person to be recognized as the hired swim coach, the first to take the team out of state for competition, and the first to coach scholarship swimmers.

But let's give Shorty Alderson his credit because credit is due. Starting in 1926, swimming was a minor sport with teams organized into campus clubs that would swim against each other. In 1931 it was given varsity status at UT and in 1932 the Southwest Conference organized its first conference championship, with Texas, Texas A&M, Southern Methodist, and Rice participating. In its first four years the varsity team was run by C.J. "Shorty" Alderson during his four years as a swimmer at Texas. In 1935 he handed the team off to fellow swimmer Bob Nall. Under Alderson and Nall, the Longhorns won each of the first four Southwest Conference championships.

Tex was determined to have a recognized, hired coach for the University of Texas swim team and immediately set to coaching the Longhorns, though he had received no such designation yet.

After a couple of months of meeting with swimmers and organizing tryouts for the 1935-36 team, the athletic council agreed to pay him $300 a year to lifeguard the pool during open swim. In his time at the swim center Tex made many allies, including a physical education professor named Ed Barlow, who finally convinced Chevigny to recognize Tex as his head swimming coach. Barlow spoke to his friend Chevigny of Tex's sincerity and desire to help build UT in to a national power in swimming, though his most compelling argument was simply, "Jack, he's already down there coaching anyway."

On November 12, 1935, the University of Texas officially hired Tex as coach for the 1936 season. His coaching salary was still zero dollars. But thanks to Barlow he was in. Ed would prove to be a valuable ally throughout Tex's tenure at Texas. Along with being an advocate in the administration, Tex asked Barlow to help him add a "toughness" to his squad of swimmers.

Barlow, the Texas PE director in charge of swimming, was an old military man with a belief that all athletes could benefit from getting knocked around a bit, even if they were participants in non-contact sports. On Saturdays, Tex would have the varsity swimmers meet with Barlow for a game of "Barlow Polo." It was basically water polo, except Barlow Polo has just one rule: put the ball in the goal. That's it.

"You could cheat any way you wanted, kick, fight, shove people underwater. It was all legal," said Bill Johnson, one of Tex's early swimmers. "Ed was a tough cookie. But he knew what he was doing. The war was coming. He was trying to make people tough, because Ed knew what war was like. He was an old-timer and a good man."

The old-timer and the energetic, twenty-four-year-old Tex made an unorthodox and highly effective team. Barlow respected Tex and had no problem checking him, if he felt it necessary.

"Ed was the only one who could see straight through any of Tex's manipulations and would say something if he didn't like what Tex was doing," Johnson said, "but he appreciated Tex and what he was doing for swimming and why he was doing it. He obviously was not coaching to make money or make a name for himself. He was pushing swimming."

The future of swimming in Texas mattered to Tex. In 1935 it mattered more to him than anything in the world. He'd given up the '36 Olympics. He'd given up a considerably promising professional swimming career. He was a coach. It's why as a teenager he took over the Central Los Angeles YMCA water polo team. It's why he taught Buster Crabbe. It's why he created swimming teams on Catalina Island, in the 1933 World's Fair, and at Camp Chikopi. It's why he studied everything Matt Mann did at Michigan.

He'd done it, just as he told Mann he would. He was the head coach of the Texas Longhorns. Now, with no budget, no scholarships, and no salary, he was going to take his Horns to national prominence.

WHEN TEX ROBERTSON'S IN CHARGE, the first step to prominence is always promotion.

But his form of promotion was never straight forward. He lacked the funds for advertising, but advertising was rarely the method he chose to promote swimming or anything else. Instead, he'd create a situation where others did the promotion work for him on their own initiative. Favors for Tex didn't occur because of a tit-for-tat agreement. He put people in positions where they'd *want* to do things for him. When selecting the first student manager for his team, he didn't pick a physical education student or someone with any background in swimming. He gave the job, and the varsity letter in swimming that came with it, to Stanley Gunn, who happened to be the editor of *The Daily Texan*, UT's student newspaper. Prominently featured articles about swimming showed up immediately in the *Texan*. The trend would continue throughout Tex's time at UT, as Gunn was just the first of these student managers.

"At the end of one season I looked at the list of all who had lettered in swimming and there was a fella named Gabe Warner. I didn't remember swimming with any Gabe Warner," Johnson said. "Well, he was a *Daily Texan* reporter that went with us to Mexico and sent wires back to the newspaper. Tex honored the people that were promoting swimming... The newspapers were all interested in baseball, basketball, and football, but Tex had the art of publicity."

While Tex was the coach at UT, swimming was covered as a major sport thanks to the amount of time he'd spend at the offices of the *Texan* and the honors and awards he'd make up for the writers. It was a common tactic for Tex. He'd invite an administration official or other potentate to a swim meet as an honorary guest with some elaborate title or create some sort of award for them to receive at the meet. Instead of asking them to support swimming, he'd give people a feeling of obligation to the program.

The first of those articles showed up in December, with an announcement for swimming team try-outs that brought eighty-eight hopefuls to the pool. That number dwindled considerably when they were informed that they were expected to practice five nights a week from 8:00 p.m. to 10:00 p.m. But with those that did stick around and the returning swimmers from the year before, Tex was able to put together a team for the 1936 season, a team that had little clue what it was in for.

In January, a series of articles detailed a "Pre-Olympic Swimming Carnival" to be held at Gregory Gym. The day of the event, January 9, the *Texan* reported that a world record was expected to be broken by the Horns' new head coach.

"Robertson," read the article, "who is a former all-American tank star of Michigan, will attempt to break the World and American Record in the 100-yard medley swim..."

That next day, the *Texan* reported the results of Tex's attempt: "One World's record and two conference records were unofficially broken before 1,500 spectators who crowded into every inch of sitting and standing room at Gregory Gym pool last night to witness the first annual 'Pre-Olympic Swimming Carnival.'"

The world record in the 100-yard medley was "unofficially" broken because there was no world record in the 100-yard medley. It didn't exist as an event. Thus, record. It would be the first of many "records" broken at Tex's carnivals. The 75-yard freestyle, the 150-yard breaststroke, the backstroke relay, all of these not actual records would be set. But fake record attempts was only part of the act. Tex was given a crowd to entertain and a group of young swimmers willing to take part in the show. The result was pure, entertaining chaos.

There were floating obstacle races, tight rope walks over the pool (often by swimmers who were not told beforehand they would be tight rope walking), trapezes, and clown diving. A swimmer once ate from a can marked "SPINACH," stuffed paper into his shirt to give the appearance of Popeye's arms, and was then yanked into and through the pool by a wire tied to a car out in the parking lot. The show featured a fire dive, where a swimmer wearing a fire suit dove off the high board while, well, on fire.

The Aqua Carnival was born. The one-night show turned into a three-night event the next year. Eventually it became a five-night extravaganza, each a sell out. It became the primary source of funding for trips across the country for dual meets. It's important to remember that wide distribution of commercial television did not occur until the early 1950s. Live shows were more frequently attended and for a week in January, the Aqua Carnival was the hottest ticket in town. But according to those who participated in Tex's grand swimming exhibition, the swimmers weren't what brought the crowds. The main event was a beauty contest voted on by the swimmers.

"One thing we used in recruiting was you got to be on the board that picked the bathing beauties," Johnson said. "We had twenty some-odd or thirty come out and we'd have to pick ten for the finals. So everybody had a girlfriend in there."

Initially the Aqua-belles, as they were called, were dressed in sport clothes rather than swim suits because the administration "frowned upon" the whole affair – it was not until 1940 that the girls dressed more "appropriately," as Tex put it.

The contest ensured a sell out every night.

"They wouldn't come to see us swimmers. They'd come to see the girls," said Eddie Gilbert, a swimmer of Tex's and a member of the United States' gold medal 4x200 relay team at the '48 London Olympics.

"My first wife was one of them," added his friend Johnny Crawford, an All-American breaststroke and butterfly swimmer. "Plus Kathryn Grant was one of the queens of the Aqua Carnival. She married Bing Crosby. Real pretty girls there each time."

Lest one think female spectators were left out, the participants in the pageant also judged a "Handsomest Man on Campus" contest. Initially it was just members of the swim team participating, but athletes from other sports were soon roped in. Hall of Fame Dallas Cowboys coach Tom Landry, then a UT football player, took the Handsomest Man crown at the 1947 show.

The Aqua Carnival would continue to be a popular attraction on the Texas campus long after Tex's retirement. Wally Pryor, a freestyler and the leading scorer for UT's 1949 water polo team, carried on organizing the show after Tex left. He was the obvious choice. Wally had been heavily involved in planning the show since his arrival to UT.

"I probably could have been a better swimmer, but I had a lot more fun working with the ten Aqua Queens," Pryor said.

Pryor is most famous for being the "voice of Memorial Stadium" at University of Texas football games for forty-eight years and that announcing career began with the Aqua Carnival.

With no budget for the show, Tex pulled in favors from friends he'd developed in the maintenance department for paint, lumber, and other supplies. Equipment came from his allies in other sports. With football receiving the majority of the athletic funds, Tex encouraged the other sports to work together, building connections and friendships with the same rapidity he showed at Michigan.

"He was a very forceful person, but very ethical in all his activities," recalled Denton Cooley, a Texas basketball player at the time, who would later perform the first successful heart transplant in the United States and the first clinical implantation of a total artificial heart. Tex built these supply lines because there was no money for swimming. This did not change with the arrival of Texas' new athletic director, a man Tex would butt heads with repeatedly.

Dana Xenophon Bible was a longtime Texas A&M coach, whose Aggies had three undefeated seasons, including a 1919 team that was not only undefeated and untied (10-0), but not a single point was scored against them (275-0). In 1929, he was hired by Nebraska and won six Big Six Conference titles in eight years. In 1937, he was hired away from the Cornhuskers to become Texas' new football coach and athletic director for $15,000 a year (inflation adjusted to 2013, that's $245,000), a very high salary at the time for a coach. This was controversial for a couple reasons; it was the Depression and because University of Texas president H.Y. Benedict made $8,000. Nowadays it's common for a football coach to make more than the university president. That was not the case in 1937. In response, the state legislature more than doubled Benedict's pay, which only added to the "where's all this money coming from?" controversy.

As such, swimming received little support. Much of the equipment had to be purchased on Tex's own dime and there were no scholarships available; scholarships he'd promised to some of those star swimmers from across the country; swimmers he asked to commit to the program he wasn't yet coaching. His solution was to pay for as much of his swimmers' scholarships as he could with his own money. Admirable, but clearly not allowed under NCAA rules.

"Tex never did anything wrong, he was only interested in helping people, but he crossed some rules on the way," said Eddie Reese, the current Texas swimming coach. "Morally fine. Ethically fine. NCAA-ly, he was a dead man."

He didn't have much money to give, but he put all of it into Texas swimming. During his first few years on campus, he and many of his swimmers lived together in Little Campus Dormitory, a Civil War barracks with no heat or running water. He strung together as many jobs as he could manage. His most profitable, by far, was with Coca-Cola. At the 1933 World's Fair he'd seen some of the first Coke vending machines. Tex contacted Coca-Cola and started his own franchise. He installed the first machines on the University of Texas campus and spent much of his day refilling and servicing the machines when he wasn't lifeguarding, gardening, or at another of his myriad of jobs. Swim practice was from eight to ten at night because he spent all day putting together the money needed to run the program.

Soon he would be married. Soon after that a father. And he still swam a mile a day with his team. Many of those close to Tex would comment about how it seemed there were more hours in the day for him than the rest of us. Tex simply said he was "accustomed to working."

The work resulted in the program's first out-of-state meets in 1936, with Texas beating Washington University in St. Louis, Kansas, and Kansas State and losing to Nebraska. On March 28 the Longhorns won the Southwest Conference Championship and Texas had its first swimmers on the All-America team, Rollin Baker and Thurman Talley.

Tex managed to secure his first conference championship with just swimmers already available at UT. That would change in 1937, when his promised recruits from across the country began showing up.

When Tex was a swimmer at Michigan, he talked with high school swimmers at invitational meets he was taking part in, telling them about how he was going to be the head coach at Texas. The result was the arrival of a diverse cast of characters who would lead the program to a run of success that wouldn't be equaled for another fifty years.

Texas Out to End Michigan Swimming Supremacy
by Jerry Brondfield
The Austin American
December 7, 1937

Tex Robertson, former Michigan swimming star and now tank coach at the University of Texas, might be accused of treason, of biting the hand that fed him, or most anything along that line.

He's going to bring a bit of aquatic honor to the hot, dry plains of Texas, of all places – or drown in the attempt...

Four potential stars on the Longhorn freshman team are from Detroit. They are Billy Brink, who placed fourth in national diving a year ago; Bill Pioch, ace free-styler; Billy Buckinham, another corking good sprinter from the Detroit A.C., and Ira Breneman, a dash man from Massenutten academy, breeding grounds of many a good swimmer.

Included on the freshman roster is Juliard Carr of Ann Arbor, who, because he is the son of Lowell J. Carr, a Michigan instructor, just about establishes a new high in treason. He holds two state free-style records.

Then there is Al Jacobson, a Chicago lad who holds the national interscholastic breast-stroke title. He also hails from Massenutten.

Buffalo sent Walter Blake and Bill Cronisky, free-stylers, and Merrill Hickey, diver.

They even have Flanagan.

To top off a great yearling squad is Ralph Flanagan, the sensational Miami, Fla. Olympic star and holder of 15 American and three world free-style records.

Until this great crop of first year men become eligible for varsity competition, Robertson has a whale of a good nucleus, Adolph Kiefer, Chicago's Olympic back stroke titlist. Kiefer is the best in the business at his specialty.

Aiding Kiefer is Mike Sojka of Buffalo and Walter Hoffrichter of Detroit, two good breast strokers, the latter by way of Massenutten.

University officials say no money is being spent to draw this tank talent to their campus. Only a few athletic jobs are available for distribution and most of these go to football players. All the swimmers, however, have jobs, but the work they do has no connection with the university.

WALLY HOFFRICHTER was the first to arrive.

A teammate of Tex's and Kiefer's at the Detroit Athletic Club, he was an interscholastic breaststroke champion in 1936. During his successful high school career, Tex had convinced him to join him down south in Texas. When Hoffrichter showed up in Austin in the fall of 1937, he was directed to Little Campus Dormitory, where a place had been reserved for him. The city boy, complete with zoot suit, knocked on the door of his assigned room at the old barracks.

No answer. He slowly opened the door. Laying on top of one of the bunks was a man of about his age with a dusty cowboy hat drawn down over his eyes. He was nonchalantly picking at a guitar laid across his stomach. A pair of boots sat at the foot of the bunk. A piece of beef jerky dangled from a string thumb-tacked to the ceiling. Hoffrichter's eyes followed from the jerky to the ground, where a white line had been chalked down the center of the small room.

The cowboy lifted his hat. "Howdy," he said. "This is my side." He pointed to a sign that read "God's Country." "That's your side." There was a sign that read "Yankee-Land." He then retrieved the jerky from the ceiling with his bare toes and stretched his leg out in Hoffrichter's direction, offering a bite. Hoffrichter politely declined.

The Yankee had just met his roommate, a man who would become one of the most famous symbols of Texas: Hondo Crouch.

John Russell "Hondo" Crouch was a rancher, philosopher, Texas folklorist, poet, and one of the most influential figures in country music. In 1970, answering an ad in the paper offering "town – pop. 3 – for sale," he bought the old ghost town of Luckenbach, Texas, and turned it into a dance hall and haven for "outlaw" artists outside the corporate scene. Flags flew at half-mast on Nashville's music row the day he died and he was memorialized by Willie Nelson and Waylon Jennings with the song "Luckenbach, Texas (Back to the Basics of Love)."

At UT they called him the "Swimming Cowboy." He learned to swim in a cattle water tank near a windmill in Hondo, Texas, and on a team full of international stars would become one of best swimmers in Longhorn history.

He was one of a bizarre mix of supremely talented characters who came together at Texas.

"God's Country" was eventually invaded, since Chicagoan Adolph Kiefer took the bunk below Hondo. Olympic silver medalist Ralph "Alligator Boy" Flanagan showed up in 1937 as well. He wasn't called "Alligator Boy" because of his prowess in the water but rather because he brought with him from Miami a pet alligator named "Apalachicola." He kept the one-and-a-half-foot gator in a large bowl in his room, feeding it fish and raw meat once a week. He'd often bring this unofficial team mascot with him to Gregory Gym Pool on a leash to go for swims. They had to keep the alligator out of Hondo's room, though, for fear it would eat the baby skunks Crouch kept as pets. One of Hondo's favorite jokes was to keep a baby skunk in his coat and then hand it to the cashier while looking for his wallet. They were an unusual collection of northerners and southerners that joked about each other's origins and learned a great deal.

"Hondo taught me how to swear in Mexican," Kiefer said. "He said, 'Adolph, when you walk down to campus, so that people will know you and say hello, just say,' and he told me this word which really means son of a bitch. I was doing that, not knowing I was swearing. But he did teach me the ways of life."

They became a very close group. They became a wild one, too. Jeff Davis of the *San Antonio Light* related in a March 11, 1938, article a story told to him by Texas swimmer Burr Noonan:

> They were riding in a big Lincoln, and they came to Platte City, Missouri. A Swimmer named 'Hondo' Crouch, who is all Texas, thinks he'll give his teammates a laugh, so he puts on his eleven-gallon hat, and cowboy boots and all, gets out of the car and lurches drunkenly into a cafe.
>
> The boys follow him, and they order meals from a trembling waitress. When the meal is finished, one of the boys says to Crouch in a loud voice: "Git me my shootin' arns, Hondo, I'm gonna shoot up this joint."
>
> One of the waitresses slips to the telephone, and the coach, Tex Robertson, overhears her call the sheriff and say: "There's some tough Texas cowboys down here shooting up the whole place!"
>
> Robertson rounds up his boys and rushes them out to the

car. In ten minutes they are across the county line and going strong. On the way back they drove 85 miles out of the way to avoid Platte City.

The "big Lincoln" was a car Tex and six of the swimmers bought together. With seven owners, each person could use the car one night of the week and deals were struck to trade days. The team painted a big orange "T" on the side of the white car and attached a set of longhorns to the front grill.

It became the team car they used to drive all over the country for swim meets, while making some money to fund those trips by taking the Aqua Carnival on the road. Crouch, who loved to play up his "Swimming Cowboy" image, was a mainstay in the carnival. Each swimmer brought something new to the table. Invited officials were once tricked into believing a world record really had been broken at an Aqua Carnival when a swimmer appeared to shatter the 800 freestyle record by ten seconds. In fact, fresh swimmers had been hiding underwater in the wooden bulkheads, shooting out right when one swimmer started his "turn."

They were something to behold. There were wild animals living in the dorm with them. They drove across the country, to New York and California. They were a fire-diving, guitar-playing, hoopin', hollerin' bunch of college boys. And they won. Oh, did they win.

Along with continuing the unbroken streak of conference championships, a team that a few years before was a loose student organization finished in the top ten nationally in 1938, '39, and '40 (No. 8, No. 5, and No. 8, respectively). Crouch, Sojka, Kiefer, Brink, and Bob Tarlton were all named All-Americans in that span.

The Longhorns won the Southwest Conference in all thirteen seasons that Tex was coach, but no run compares to 1938-1940 and no team compares to that group of talented and insane swimmers. By 1940 that initial group of star recruits had each gone their separate ways. Some left earlier than others. Flanagan left school after the '38 season to pursue his professional swimming career. Kiefer then left because of a contract offer to be in movies for Paramount Pictures. But the core stayed together and accomplished Tex's mission of putting UT swimming on the map.

"Tex had as colorful of a career as any coach I can think of, whether it was an Olympic coach, college coach, or any coach," Kiefer said. "He did more to create and build swimming than any coach in America. I'd put him on the level with Bob Kiphuth of Yale University, who was our Olympic coach. He did a lot to promote swimming for Texas. It's obvious it worked. (Texas has) ten national championships in the last thirty years. Who could do a better job? You could list that as the outstanding swimming program, from scratch, in the United States."

But that career was abruptly interrupted, as were the careers, plans, and lives of everyone else, by World War II. The Navy needed swimming instructors and it set Tex on a path that would cause him to play a role in the origin of the Navy SEALs.

Chapter

Mr. Vice President, and Mr. Speaker, and Members of the
Senate, of the House of Representatives: Yesterday, December
7th, 1941, a date which will live in infamy, the United States
of America was suddenly and deliberately attacked by naval
and air forces of the Empire of Japan. The United States
was at peace with that Nation and, at the solicitation of
Japan, was still in conversation with its Government and its
Emperor looking toward the maintenance of peace in the
Pacific...As Commander-in-Chief of the Army and Navy
I have directed that all measures be taken for our defense.
Always will we remember the character of the onslaught
against us. No matter how long it may take us to overcome
this premeditated invasion, the American people in their
righteous might will win through to absolute victory.

-Franklin D. Roosevelt

The bombing of Pearl Harbor ended the debate over U.S.
involvement in World War II and the nation mobilized for a two-front
war.

At the onset of the war Tex continued to coach, leading the
Longhorns to another conference title in the spring of 1942. But soon
after he would join the Navy and it was his old protege who brought him
into the war.

With Congress' declaration of war, Adolph Kiefer left Hollywood
and enlisted in the Navy, turning down a standing offer to play Tarzan
(yes, another of Tex's swimmers could have played Tarzan). Because of
his athletic background, the Navy made him an instructor in the "Tunney
Fish," a physical training program named after their commander, former
world heavyweight boxing champ Gene Tunney. Kiefer enjoyed teaching
with his fellow athletes at the base in Norfolk, Virginia, but he discovered
something odd about officers in the Navy.

"I asked the Chief Petty Officer with all these hash-marks on him, 'How long have you been in the Navy?' Blah, blah, all this, all that. I said, 'Can you swim?' He said, 'No. But I'm a special this and a special that. We don't have to swim.' I asked the other Chief over there, 'Can you swim?' He said, 'No.' They're in the *Navy* and they can't *swim*."

It sounds strange, but Navy-men not being able to swim was not a new problem. Ancient Greek historian Herodotus of Halicarnassus (484-430 BCE), who is the primary historical source on the Greco-Persian Wars, noted that in the naval battle of Salamis, many, many more Persians died primarily because most Persian soldiers did not know how to swim while the Spartans and Athenians were swimmers.

The concept that most men in the U.S. Navy did not know how to swim bothered Kiefer. He began researching on his own time and determined that the Navy was losing more men to drowning than to enemy bullets.

"I couldn't sleep at night. Ask my wife. I couldn't sleep," Kiefer said.

He drove to Washington, D.C., to show a captain he knew his findings. The captain then brought him before an admiral.

"So the Navy said, 'Ok, you go back, you write a program. Go up and see the commandant of the base and we'll give you anything you want to help," Kiefer said. "So they assigned me a yeoman for the typing and writing and I talked to people who were smarter than me, like the Red Cross and people I knew and other books that I read, and I put it all together and we wrote a program."

The Navy built a new training center in Bainbridge, Maryland, where Kiefer trained 1600 instructors over the course of the war. Since it was Adolph Kiefer, he started every swimmer out with the stroke that as a boy he thought he'd invented when he fell into a drainage canal in Chicago.

"We taught everybody to swim – you're going to get a kick out of this – on their back and we had two million recruits in the world in six places learning the 'Victory Backstroke,'" Kiefer said. "So we taught them to swim on your back because your head's out of the water. And today the Red Cross has adopted teaching swimming on their back as a prelude to rolling over on your stomach."

Since the Navy needed swimming instructors, Kiefer would call upon his old coach. Tex was still coaching in Austin and building his new summer camp in the Texas Hill Country when he received a phone call from First Lieutenant Adolph Gustav Kiefer asking him to join the swimming program. Tex shut down Camp Longhorn, handed the team off to his swimmers, and signed up for the Navy.

He was not the first of his family to enlist. After nineteen years away from his brothers and father, Eugene Emerson "Jack" Robertson arrived in Los Angeles for Christmas of 1937. During the visit Jack decided to stay and LaClaire helped him find work. But Jack wasn't able to hold the job his brother procured for him and his life took another sudden shift when he decided to go into the Army as a career.

This is where the story gets hazy. On an old set of family birth and death records, where Jack's date of death should be listed it says "See Note" with an asterisk next to it. The connected note reads: "...he went into the Army as a career and 'disappeared' during World War II; whether a personal or a military disappearance not known; no further word received; no known issue." This has led to a family rumor that Jack went native during the war and lived out his days on a tropical island. But according to Tex, Captain Jack Robertson was killed in action in World War II and he said nothing more on the matter.

Once Tex signed up, Kiefer sent him to San Diego to teach new Naval recruits how to swim. His wife, Pat, came with him and they spent most of 1943 on the west coast...until Pat discovered she was pregnant. She took a train back to Texas to stay with her parents and in February she gave birth to John Hudson Robertson.

When John was six weeks old, Pat took the tike with her out to San Diego. But when she got there she found Tex troubled. He was happy to have his wife and child, but he also wanted to fight for them. He felt guilty training and sending men to fight while he stayed in the States. Tex contacted his superiors and officially asked to be sent overseas and join the front lines.

Naval command refused his request because it had a different mission for him. His training style and techniques, especially his work training soldiers to swim long distances underwater, had caught the eye of the higher-ups.

The Navy was creating an elite special forces unit and command wanted Tex to train them.

In November of 1943, over 1,000 U.S. Marines were killed taking the island of Tarawa. Most died in the utter disaster that was the initial landing. The landing boats became stuck on a reef 500 yards off shore. When the naval bombardment stopped to allow the Marines to land, the Japanese emerged from their shelters and opened fire from gun emplacements. The landing boats were soon set ablaze by Japanese artillery and mortar fire. Troops jumped out of the boats and were forced to wade 500 yards to shore under machine gun fire and the few men in the first wave who made it to the beach were pinned down. After several more assaults the U.S. was able to take the beach, but at a heavy cost.

Many of those lives could have been saved by a unit of specialists trained to scout ahead of beach landings and not only be able to report on conditions but demolish obstacles with underwater explosives. In response, Admiral Earnest King selected Lieutenant Draper Kauffman, who had organized the Naval Bomb Disposal School, to lead the training. After scouting other amphibious training bases at Solomon Islands, Maryland, and Little Creek, Virginia, Kauffman chose Fort Pierce, Florida. He chose the beaches of Ft. Pierce because it provided both sandy and rocky landing areas to train on, water temperatures that would allow for year-round training, and it was already the home of the Navy's Amphibious Scout and Raider School. Lieutenant Commander Phil H. Bucklew – the "Father of Naval Special Warfare" – started the Scouts and Raiders in 1942 to specialize in beach raids and there would obviously be a great deal of crossover in the training of these new underwater explosives specialists. Ft. Pierce was also selected because of the enthusiasm of Captain Clarence Gulbranson, the base commander, for the new organization.

Kauffman, Bucklew, and Gulbranson selected twenty-one training officers from across the Navy for the new Underwater Demolition Teams. The group was comprised of officers from the Scouts and Raiders, bomb disposal school trainers, explosives experts, and veterans of the allied invasion of Sicily. And Tex. He was promoted to Chief Petty Officer and shipped to Ft. Pierce.

It was quite a shift for Tex to go from teaching fresh recruits the "Victory Backstroke" to forging elite special forces units. But he wasn't alone. Not only did Pat and their infant son join him in Florida, but, coincidentally, an old friend and fellow Michigan swimmer was also selected as one of the training officers.

In his early days as the head coach at UT, Tex made frequent trips back to Michigan to discuss coaching with his old mentor, work at a few summer camps, and check in on the Wolverines. He also got to know the man who picked up where he left off. While he was a swimmer, Tex was Michigan's top freestyler and after his departure Tom Haynie stepped into his place. Tex won the Big Ten championship in the 220-yard freestyle, the 440-yard freestyle, and on the 400-yard free relay team. Two years later, Haynie won each of those events as a sophomore. Just as Tex had in '34 and '35, Haynie's free relay team would win the NCAA championship in '37, '38, and '39. Along with his relay victories, in his time at Michigan Haynie won five individual Big Ten titles and four NCAA titles.

At Ft. Pierce, Tex lived with Pat and John in an apartment building near the base and Haynie lived in an adjacent room, though Tex and Tom weren't the only colorful neighbors in the building.

"It was a funny little town, with an apartment with a lady who was a whore," Pat said. "Well she *was*. She had men coming in. She owned the apartment building but she had men coming in visiting all the time. I knew what she was. Tom was a real good friend of Tex's who joined the Navy at the same time and we all stayed at this apartment where the bad lady was with her gentlemen. Neither one of us knew anything about anything. We learned about the world and the Navy and everything else in that apartment."

The men Tex and his fellow officers were to train didn't have their wives with them, but not many of them had wives anyway. Due to the exceptional risks that would be undertaken by front-line underwater demolition squads, for the first batch of specialists the Navy specifically targeted unmarried men. Preferences such as this led to the unofficial assumption between officers and recruits that the UDTs would be a "seventy-five percent casualty outfit." Other requirements for these volunteers – which haven't changed very much since – were youth (age twenty to thirty-five), swimming prowess, general strength endurance, and, perhaps most importantly, no fear of explosives.

Men for the units came from three main sources: the SeaBees (Navy Construction Battalions), the Bomb Disposal School, and the Mine Disposal School. The experts in disarming these weapons were now put to the task of planting them underwater. The rest were drawn from other areas of the Navy. Kiefer also sent some recruits he considered particularly athletic and who were brave enough to volunteer for UDT.

"I would send them people going through our course. If they were unmarried, young, and a good athlete, we'd ask them if they wanted to volunteer for UDT," Kiefer said.

Training began with what was officially called "Indoctrination Week," but it has never been known as anything but "Hell Week." The brutal first week of training was created by compressing the eight-week physical training program for the Scouts and Raiders into a single week's schedule.

Every day started at five a.m. with a run on the rock jetty and thirty minutes of hard calisthenics, which was followed by a three-mile double-time march. Then came the obstacle course. Then paddling fully loaded rubber boats in six-man teams against ocean winds and tides. Then carrying the boats over rocks and dunes. For twelve to sixteen hours a day the work would continue, all in full combat gear, with physical tests getting more and more difficult. To help maintain morale, Tex, Tom Haynie, Draper Kauffman, and all the other officers went through "Hell Week" with the trainees, establishing a precedent in UDT that requires officers to demonstrate the same capabilities and endure the same hardships as their men. Those hardships were very effective at weeding out the recruits who couldn't handle the physical demands. Those who could take the punishment but had an inherent fear of explosives were taken care of with the final day of the week, referred to as "So Solly Day."

Before dawn the recruits hit the beach in landing craft. Just as the ramps dropped, heavy demolition charges on the beach were set off – not close enough to injure, but close enough for them to feel the force and get pelted with sand, dirt, and rocks. For the rest of the day they had to fight through thick swamps and non-lethal (but painful) booby traps, with explosions sending columns of mud and water into the air around them the entire time. If a recruit panicked and wouldn't press forward, an instructor would toss improvised half-pound TNT hand grenades from behind (the rules stated no closer than "ten feet" but that line got pushed now and then) to get the shaken man moving. Once they reached the target area, they had to hold their ground in foxholes while charge after charge was detonated around them. For an hour straight.

Those that couldn't take the constant concussive blasts were weeded out. Those that could became essentially immune to the shock. All in all, "Hell Week" washed out between thirty and forty percent of the volunteers. But the first group of true "Frogmen," as the UDTs were nicknamed, had survived.

After "Hell Week," the regular physical training was combined with tactical training, which occurred in all hours of the day and night to prepare the men for any potential raid. In one example of a "night problem," a five-man team would paddle along the shore in the darkness, then arrive at a selected spot and bury the boat. The team then had to infiltrate an abandoned plantation house where four sentries patrolled the perimeter, retrieve a candy bar or some other specific item, and return to the boat. Any Frogmen who were caught had to sit in the old house and let the mosquitoes have at them until the exercise ended. If all five men returned, they would dig up their boat and paddle back to camp, arriving at about three a.m. That left about two hours sleep until the start of the next day of training.

The work was meant to prepare Underwater Demolition Teams for any extreme. This resulted in limits being pushed every day. At least once it turned deadly. It was an incident that would affect Tex for the remainder of his years, physically and mentally.

Frogmen were expected to complete their mission, no matter the weather. That meant training in the elements. But with a heavy tropical storm approaching Ft. Pierce, Tex recommended ending the day's maneuvers to Captain Gulbranson. Gulbranson disagreed and sent Tex, Tom, and several teams out into the ocean.

The storm hit during the training operation. Sheets of rain fell from darkened skies, lightning flashed all around, and waves towered above the small rubber rafts.

"The boats were impossible to upright. All they'd do is flip over in the storm," Pat said. "He was trying to save them after they'd been knocked out of boats and pull them in. He was trying to hold onto two guys at the same time when he got caught in a big wave."

With the wind roaring and waves hurling the sailors in all directions, Tex held onto those two men stuck in the undertow, one in each arm, kicked with all his might, and made for shore.

He made it. The two men he pulled with him made it. Tom made it. Several recruits did not.

"Some of those guys didn't make it. They drowned," Pat said. "Tex blamed Captain Gulbranson."

His battle with the waves also damaged ligaments in both his legs, causing him knee problems for the rest of his life. This was after he'd already suffered a back injury when accidentally run over by a landing craft in shallow water. But he never complained about the aches, the stiff back, the shaky knees. Perhaps it was because he was lucky enough to make it out alive when there were others who did not.

He was furious with Gulbranson, but made no official complaint. Tex and his base commander both stayed on at Ft. Pierce through the end of World War II. Such decisions are made in war, but they never reconciled their differences over the incident and there was no chance to after the war. After overseeing 110,000 sailors at Ft. Pierce during World War II, Gulbranson died of cancer in 1947.

As for the Frogmen, those who made it through "Hell Week," "So Solly Day," the "night problems," the explosions, the pain, the heat, and the storm emerged as some of the toughest commandos in World War II. It was the Frogmen who were called upon to go in ahead of the pivotal landing of the Eastern Theater. In May of 1944, all available UDT men were sent, Bucklew with them, from Ft. Pierce to England in preparation for the invasion of Normandy.

The German defenses along the French coastline were intricate. Jutting out of the water were steel posts topped with explosives. In the surf zone there were three-ton barricades called Belgian Gates. Reinforced machine gun nests and mortar emplacements lined the beach. On the English coasts, Frogmen practiced extensively on replicas of these defenses, picking up key information, such as determining that it was possible to detonate a Belgian Gate, but it was more effective to blow out the joints on the gate rather than leave a mess of tangled debris. On D-Day, their mission would be to open sixteen 50-foot wide corridors for the landing on Omaha Beach and Utah Beach.

The initial bombardment of the beaches on the morning of June 6 was largely ineffective, meaning it was up to the UDTs to clear the way. The Frogmen were supposed to move in with the first wave, but tidal conditions and misunderstood communications caused many demolition teams to land prematurely. Despite the heavy German fire they faced, the Frogmen were still able to plant their charges and clear the way for American landing craft. Of the 175 UDT members who went ashore on Omaha Beach, thirty-one were killed and sixty were wounded. Facing less resistance, fewer men were lost in the attack on Utah Beach, with four killed and eleven wounded when an artillery shell hit a team working to clear the beach.

With Allied forces on the ground in Europe, the focus for the Frogmen switched entirely to the Pacific. New UDT bases were built on Oahu, Maui, and on the beaches of Tex's old stomping ground in California, Catalina Island, though Tex stayed in Florida until the conclusion of the war.

After World War II, the Frogmen continued to serve a key role in U.S. military operations, a role which expanded during the Korean War to include land-based missions as well. With counter-insurgency, guerrilla, and parachute training included in the reorganized UDTs, President John F. Kennedy renamed the Frogmen and in January of 1962 commissioned the creation of SEAL Team One.

Tex would leave the Navy after the war and return to Texas. His friend Tom Haynie took a similar path. It wasn't just Michigan where Haynie followed Tex's footsteps. After leaving Ft. Pierce, he went on to become the second swim coach at Stanford. In thirteen years at Stanford he won eleven conference championships. Today, Stanford and Texas are two of the most prominent swimming programs in the nation. Every Division I NCAA swimming championship from 1985 to 1994 was won by either Texas or Stanford. More than half of the NCAA championships in the last thirty years have been won by either Texas or Stanford.

Those two programs were established on the national scene by a pair of friends who swam at Michigan and together taught the first Navy SEALs.

6

Chapter

"Couldn't you have lost part of your foot instead of your hand? You always did pull better than you kicked."

"Sorry, Coach. The enemy didn't ask which I wanted."

"Well, you'll just have to swim harder."

"I don't think I'm going out for swimming."

"You've already been voted team captain. How about swimming sprints this time instead of distance?"

Eventually Bill Johnson relented, because Tex was relentless. Johnson was a champion swimmer for UT before the war, but as a member of the 5th Marine Division he was at the center of the Battle of Iwo Jima. With the 5th at the spear-tip of the invasion, no division suffered more casualties, with 1,098 killed and 2,974 wounded. Johnson was fortunate enough to not be among the former, but he was among the latter when an enemy bullet blew off part of his hand.

He met with Tex at Gregory Gym fully prepared to tell his coach that he was giving up swimming. He left with a bathing suit with a white 'T' on it and the position of team captain. Johnson was important to leadership on the team and Tex needed every able-bodied swimmer he could find, missing fingers or no.

While Tex was gone, the Longhorns' dominance in the Southwest Conference came to an end. No coach had taken over for him and the war-depleted squad just ran itself. In 1944 the Longhorns tied with Texas A&M in points at the conference meet, giving the Aggies their first share of a conference crown and in 1945 the Ags won it outright.

When Tex got back the Longhorns returned to their winning ways. With one good hand, Bill would win the 1946 conference championship in the 50-yard freestyle and at only a tenth of a second slower than the time he put up in '43 before he left for the war. UT would win the Southwest Conference that season and in each of Tex's four remaining seasons in Austin.

That was how Tex coached. He didn't give up until he got what he wanted and he won because of it. His convincing Johnson to swim in '46 wasn't much different from the first time he had Johnson jump into the pool at Gregory Gym. As a part of a fraternity that only allowed members to stay if they lettered in a varsity sport, in 1940 Johnson answered one of Tex's various calls in *The Daily Texan* for swimmers. The first day he went out for swimming, Tex said "Welcome!" and then told him to jump in and swim a mile.

"That was the type of negligent coaching that did all of us good," Johnson said. "I asked him later about that, why he didn't teach me and he said, 'Your body teaches you. If you've got to swim a mile or a half a mile, your body will find the easiest way to move. You won't grab at the water. You'll learn by trial and error and then after you know what's easiest on your body, then someone can give you some moves on how to make it better.'"

Tex's introductory methodology to teaching was "throw 'em in and let 'em figure it out." He refined them from there, often times by getting in the water with them. Fresh out of a national championship career at Michigan, when he first got to UT, Tex could swim faster than most of the swimmers he was coaching.

"You wouldn't know why you were doing some things until you'd done it," Johnson said. "If you came to the end of the pool and did an old fashion turn and he did the flip turn and he was way ahead of you, you'd see that and then you'd realize what you've got to do."

He'd swim about a mile every day with his team and would often teach by just doing. He believed in distance swimming, even for the non-distance swimmers. No weight training, just building muscle through hours in the water. Every summer he'd take his swimmers up to Inks Lake in the Texas Hill Country, where he was building his summer camp. When they weren't building cabins, up and down the lake they'd go. Before breakfast it was a two-mile swim to the Inks Dam and back to camp, then after breakfast it was a mile (or more) up to the Inks Bridge and back.

"He didn't spend a lot of time on the finer points of swimming as much as the older swimmers helped the younger swimmers," Johnson said. "What he did was to have us swim a lot of miles, and he didn't believe in weight-lifting and muscle-building. That wasn't done in those days. He saw me throwing shot-put in an intramural track meet and yelled, 'Don't do that! That'll ruin your swimming!'"

Tex was one of the most influential innovators of stroke technique in the sport, yet he did very little one-on-one work with his swimmers in terms of technique. It resulted in a style of coaching that most of his swimmers described as contradictory.

"Tex, he probably wasn't the best swimming coach in the world, but he was," said Johnny Crawford, the first scholarship swimmer at UT. "To put that another way, he wasn't the best coach, but he was always the *better* coach."

Another coach may be a better teacher, but give Tex swimmers at least half as good as his opponent and he'd win the dual meet every time. Tactically, he was brilliant. And this is in a sport where coaches didn't used to think as tactically as they do now. Recruit the best swimmers, have them swim the event they're best at, and get them to swim their best. But Tex would position swimmers tactically, squeezing every last point possible out of every meet.

The greatest example of this is Kiefer. The best backstroker on the planet never swam backstroke at Texas. Not once. Kiefer could have easily won titles in the backstroke, but those points were already covered because Tex had Bob Tarlton, who would win the Southwest Conference title in the 100-yard back three years running. Kiefer winning the same event by any greater margin wouldn't result in more points, but with his natural talent he could grab some extra points by swimming freestyle. Swimmers were willing to give up on greater glory because Tex could always find a way of convincing them to do what he wanted.

"What Tex did is he said, 'Adolph, you're not going to swim the backstroke. You hold all the world's records. So you're going to be our freestyler. You're going to swim on all the relays and you can be the best freestyler in the world too,'" Kiefer said. "So Bob Tarlton swam the backstroke and I swam the freestyle."

Tex was also the better coach head to head because he'd do anything to win. One season he sacrificed two dual meets leading up to Texas A&M by having his swimmers participate in random events, giving his opponent no idea which way to match up against Texas. And he wasn't above manipulating the rules to gain an edge. Crawford remembers a Southwest Conference Championship where an "accidental" equipment failure gave him the little bit extra he needed to win.

"I was a butterflier, but Tex said, 'Craw, if you get in there in the 440 freestyle and get fourth, we can win the meet, we can beat A&M.' So I did. Then, 100 fly was the next event. I wasn't in shape for the 440 free, but I did it and I got the place he told me to and got the points. He was exactly right. He said that would be what would win the meet; I'd get three or four points. He had it all figured out. So there I was – pant, pant – after the 440 that I wasn't in shape for."

But as Crawford stepped onto the starting block for the 100 butterfly, far too tired to win, he saw one of his lane ropes wiggling its way over toward another lane. Turns out Tex had sent one of his swimmers under the bulkhead to detach the lane rope and then told the swimmers who typically helped out with equipment, such as Wally Pryor, "Don't anybody fix it. Johnny's still got to rest."

"Finally some maintenance man came and had to fish it out," Crawford said. "By then I'd gotten my breath back. It was a ten, twelve-minute delay. That's what I needed. Then I got in there, I won it, and I broke the conference record. Swam a 1:04 100 fly."

It wasn't the first time Tex had used a delaying technique to fit his best swimmers into more events. Joe Demmer, who along with Johnson was one of the few to swim for UT both before and after World War II, was one of Tex's top swimmers, winning six individual conference championships in his time at Texas. Late in the 1946 meet, when Tex was limited in the pieces he had to work with and was looking to take back the trophy from A&M, he determined that the only way the Longhorns could win was to have Joe swim two events back-to-back.

"In those days you could jump the gun twice and the third time they threw you out," Johnson said. "Well, when you jump the gun in order to delay the start of the event, you'd just keep on swimming and pretend like you didn't hear it, until somebody stopped you. Then you'd have to swim back breaststroke real slowly and dry off. And we all did that, one after the other. Joe, in the meantime would stand up, get ready to dive in, and somebody would jump the gun and he'd sit back down and rest up and he won the meet by getting the rest that we gave him by following the rules. Not real ethical in a certain sense, so they changed the rule."

Tex played by his own rules. But he knew how to win and his swimmers loved him for it. They'd do anything for him, and once that included breaking federal law.

In 1950, two of Tex's All-Americans, Crawford and Eddie Gilbert, both missed their flight to the NCAA championship. This wasn't as much of a problem for Gilbert, given that he was in ROTC and right after World War II military personnel could hop on most flights with no problem. But Crawford was not. Their solution was to borrow a uniform and ID from a fraternity brother.

"He could have been in federal prison for impersonating an officer," Gilbert said with a laugh, pointing a thumb in Crawford's direction.

Hitchhiking on planes and then in cars from the airport, the pair arrived at the pool just in time for Eddie to squeeze into the last heat of the 220-yard freestyle, in which he swam two seconds faster than his previous best.

"The driving deal for all of us was Tex," Johnny said. "We'd go to those extraordinary lengths for him. And you made your grades on account of Tex."

"He was like a father to me," Eddie said.

"He was always trim and had a big smile on his face and eyes were just sparkly," Johnny added.

His swimmers were always loyal and that loyalty that was central to how Tex coached. He didn't win because he was a great teacher, he won because he could see the big picture and had swimmers who were willing to switch events and detach lane ropes and jump the gun and impersonate military personnel and anything else for him.

ALONG WITH THE LEGACY he created in Austin, Tex also impacted swimming on the national level in his time at UT. Aside from his alterations of stroke techniques and invention of the flip turn, he changed many aspects of collegiate swimming. He spent most of his career constantly hounding the NCAA Rules Committee with calls and letters. Apparently it had an effect, since in 1948 the NCAA went ahead and made him a member of said committee.

Within a year of being named to the committee, he had changed a significant portion of the rulebook. The biggest change was officially recognizing the flip turn as a legal technique, but other changes included twelve places counting for points at the national championship, increasing the total number of spots on the All-American teams, and raising the required water temperature at meets to eighty degrees Fahrenheit. Plus he managed to make Austin the site of the 1951 NCAA championship.

He was named NCAA coach of the year in 1948. It was also the year he finally got the University of Texas to offer scholarships for swimming. Officially it was just a single scholarship, but it got turned into two thanks to Crawford.

Crawford was originally from Texas but at the '48 Olympic swimming trials in Detroit he became friends with a diver named David "Skippy" Browning.

"Skippy talked me into going to Wayne University with him, right there in downtown Detroit," Crawford said. "We dated the country club girls and rode in Cadillacs and went out on the golf course. Anyway, come September, all those girls, the country club girls we'd been dating, they went off to girls school in the east. Then it started getting dark at 3:30, still dark at ten in the morning. It was snowing, cold. We were having a miserable time. I said, 'I'm going back to Texas.' So I wrote Tex a letter. I said, 'Detroit is not for me.' He wrote me back. He said, 'Is it possible you could get Skippy to come with you?'"

Clarence Pinkston, the Aquatics Director at the Detroit Athletic Club and an old friend of Tex's, had told Tex about a young diver he was working with whom he believed would become the best in the world. Tex offered the talented Crawford the school's first official swimming scholarship and tried to convince Bible to give him one more so he could get Skippy Browning as well. After going back and forth with the administration, the athletic council agreed to grant him an additional half of a scholarship.

"I wrote Tex back and said, 'Skippy wants to come, but his daddy won't let him come on half a scholarship' – his family just threw paper routes – 'so I want you to give him half mine.' Tex didn't tell me to do that. I wanted to do it because Tex wanted Skippy," Crawford said.

It paid off. Skippy Browning would become the Longhorns' first individual national champion, winning the one-meter and three-meter dive events in both 1951 and 1952. He then went on to win the gold medal in springboard diving at the 1952 Summer Olympics in Helsinki. Browning is also famous for being arrested at the '52 games when he shimmied up the flag pole at the stadium to steal the Olympic flag. After the Olympics he became a Navy pilot and was expected to become the first man to win two springboard diving golds, but in March of 1956, just before he was scheduled to head to Los Angeles to prepare for the Melbourne games, Lt. David Browning was killed when his jet crashed in a field in Kansas.

Seemingly every year at the Texas swimming reunion, Tex would tell the story of Skippy Browning and of how Johnny Crawford got him to UT. He would tell it both to remember Skippy and to praise Crawford. There were few actions taken by a Texas swimmer that made Tex prouder than Johnny's willingness to give up half his scholarship. But Tex seemed to bring that out of people.

"He really could. I was so proud to do it," Crawford said. "And I was so proud at the time. It put a ding in my folds and I had to sell bottles to get by on, but I made it, because I had that shining light of Tex Robertson."

He could also get people to help him even when they weren't planning to. Bill Johnson, again expecting a different outcome when he began the conversation, once called Tex to tell him that he wasn't going to ride with the team up to Fort Worth for a Southwest AAU meet.

"I was a little bit rebellious," Johnson said. "We were due at the meet Saturday morning and there was a big party, beautiful party the night before and I had a date. I said, 'I'll be there, but I can't go with you. I'm going to the dance. It'll be over by one o'clock and I'll drive to Fort Worth and I'll be there by eight o'clock in the morning.' Tex said, 'You have to go up with the team if you want to swim.' I said, 'Ok, I'm going to come anyway and watch.' He said, 'Well, if you're going to come anyway, would you bring Jane Dillard?' 'Who's Jane Dillard?'"

Jane Dillard was the woman Tex had been sneaking into the men-only Gregory Gymnasium Pool. There were no women's collegiate swimming programs anywhere in the country and most athletic facilities were off-limits – there would not be a women's NCAA swimming championship until 1982. Long after his coaching career was over, Tex finally managed to convince UT's president to allow women access to the swim center, but when Dillard showed up to Austin in 1938 to learn from him, he had to keep her workouts a secret.

Following her clandestine workouts at Texas, Dillard set the

American and world records in the 100 breaststroke and was named to the 1940 U.S. Olympic team for the canceled Tokyo games. With her likely Olympic gold taken away by World War II, as it was for so many, she met up with another of Tex's great prodigies, Buster Crabbe, and swam alongside him in traveling aquatics shows. Eventually she returned to the Lone Star State to help in the founding of legitimate women's swimming programs, which is why she is considered the "queen of Texas swimming."

"I'm sure I wouldn't have done it without Tex," Jane Dillard Hanger said. "We were never able to pay him anything, because my parents didn't have any money. That's one reason now my husband (Bob Hanger) has established a scholarship for female swimmers at the University in mine and Tex's name."

Tex, meanwhile, was not only building up swimming at UT, he was also helping other swim programs in the Southwest Conference get access to as many resources as possible. It was an odd duality of Tex. When he faced off against another program in the pool, he was brutally competitive, willing to do just about anything to win. But out of the pool he was willing to do just about anything to help build up his opponents. He cared about promoting swimming, even if it wasn't Texas Longhorn swimming.

His work with Art Adamson at Texas A&M and Red Barr at SMU helped give Texas some serious competition following Tex's departure from UT. For most of the 1950s, Texas, Texas A&M, and SMU took turns at the top, at least until 1958, when the Mustangs took the conference title...the first of twenty-three straight Southwest Conference championships.

Promoting swimming is why Tex also coached the Austin High swim team, winning a state championship in 1947. He also ran the Texas Aquatic Club in AAU competition and started the Texas Frogman Club, to add to the various other projects he was simultaneously balancing.

He carried on for years like this. It became too much when one dream began getting in the way of another.

IN 1946, eleven years after he walked in to Chevigny's office and took the job at no salary, Tex finally got paid, though it was only $900 a year. That number was raised to $2,000 in 1948 after his threat to resign made the front page of *The Daily Texan*, thanks to his always high publicity. That $2,000 was officially broken up as $1,200 for coaching and $800 for putting on the Aqua Carnival, which is just as well since the athletic department had already starting taking the ticket proceeds for itself. (The swim team made money by selling concessions and programs.) But that money still fell short of what he was starting to make from the other project he promised Matt Mann he would create: Camp Longhorn.

By this point his summer camp had grown to about 150 boys, around the amount he'd told Mann he was hoping to have – though still a long way from the 4,000 that came through Camp Longhorn in 2013.

On May 16, 1950, he announced his resignation from UT and was quoted in *The Austin American* as saying: "The swimming program at the University of Texas has developed into a big thing and the camp is taking an increasing amount of my time. Both projects are of a full-time nature and I feel I should devote all of my efforts to the camp because of the opportunities involved."

The split was presented as amiable, with D.X. Bible providing a supportive send-off: "Tex certainly will be missed. He goes with our best wishes and we expect to call on him from time to time to help carry on some of the projects he instituted."

But Tex's ever-stalwart ally, *The Daily Texan*, reported it differently. A May 17 article from the *Texan* – and the scathing column next to it that tore into the athletic department for not offering Tex more money – reported on a back and forth between Tex and Bible at the press conference.

Said Bible: "Where Tex and I differ is that Tex believes swimming here justifies a full-time coach with commensurate pay...I feel that a part-time coach is all that is necessary, and I believe Tex should combine his coaching with class instruction. Then I would feel justified in increasing his salary beyond the $2,000 figure."

Tex responded by saying that he worked fourteen hours a day, all of that at UT when preparing for the Aqua Carnival, and didn't consider his job to be "part-time." In the ensuing conversation, Bible pointed out that the University's golf and tennis coaches are employed at similar salaries, and that "keen interest" rather than high salaries have helped build the minor sports here.

The column, "Tex Robertson's Resignation Brings Student Objections," expanded on the matter:

> The Athletic Director declined to discuss prospects for next year, and when a newspaperman remarked that he couldn't understand "how a University that can spend $1,400,000 on stadium improvements can refuse to pay one of the top swimming coaches in the country $2,000," Mr. Bible brusquely retorted "Well, all right. Any other questions?"
>
> Meanwhile, the swimming team squelched any rumors that it would refuse to perform in the Aqua-Carnival, but individuals commented heatedly on the effect Mr. Robertson's departure may have on swimming in the future at the University. "We're not mad at anybody," diving champ Jack Tolar commented. "We just want our coach back."
>
> Jim McCann, captain of the team, declared that "the terms Tex wants certainly aren't unfair." He prophesied that the University would not be able to find another nationally-recognized swimming coach "for the inducement they're offering."
>
> The team will not suffer intensively this year, according to Dick White, a breast-stroke specialist, "because the bulk of the coaching for the conference meet March 19-20 was done in the fall." But Bob Tarleton [sic], All-American backstroker a few years back, opined: "Yeah, this year. Tex has brought the conference championship to UT every year he has coached here; but without him..."
>
> At the meeting Tuesday night, Tarleton said that Yale University has four or five swimming coaches, with a minimum salary of $4,000.
>
> C.T. Johnson, sponsor of the crippled children benefit broadcast of the Aggie-Texas freshman football game and well-known Austin sportsman, was greatly surprised when he learned that amount of Mr. Robertson's salary.
>
> "I have traveled all over this country," the businessman said, "and Tex Robertson is a name I hear in every important

swimming circle. Tex is to swimming what Billy Disch is to baseball. He's clean-cut, well-liked, and his record is incomparable. And $1,000 is – well, ridiculous. The word is ridiculous."

Both Mr. Bible and Mr. Robertson assured *The Texan* that there were no hard feelings. Mr. Bible says that "he goes with our best wishes," and that Mr. Robertson declared he had considered that matter closed until "the boys raised this noise."

"But it's good to know they're loyal," he added.

What ever the nature of Tex's departure, he was able to pick his successor. Hank Chapman, an All-American diver for Tex, became the Longhorns' coach in 1951. As for Tex, he turned his attention to Camp Longhorn, his little piece of property in the Texas Hill Country which would grow into the largest privately owned summer camp in the nation.

"Best decision he ever made," Gilbert said.

Afterword

by
John Robertson

I was born in 1944, the middle of World War II, and traveled with my mother to join Tex as he moved from duty station to duty station. The first trip, however, occurred just before I was born. Tex was in Dallas for a brief visit in February of 1944 to be present when I was delivered. As the time for him to return to duty approached and I showed no signs of arrival, Tex loaded Pat into the Pat's parents' car and drove back and forth over the railroad tracks that crossed Lover's Lane. This was to no avail, as I was born soon after Tex rejoined his unit.

Pat and I later joined up with Tex in Florida where he was engaged in training the early Navy UDT members. He had secured a small off-base dwelling for his new family. From Pat's description, it wasn't much, but it did have one outstanding feature; in the yard next door was a large orange tree. Tex devised a device consisting of a long pole, a basket, and a knife with which to reach over the fence and liberate oranges from that tree. The same can-do attitude and inventiveness has served him well as he completed his Navy time, as a coach at UT, and at his life's work at Camp Longhorn.

When Tex and Pat – yes, we have always called them that – left Austin to live all year at Camp, Sally was two years old and I was seven. As it was necessary to move out of the temporary summer apartment over the chow hall, Tex and the Longhorn crew began construction of a new home. The house had many unique features such as a fireplace in the center of the living room and a longhorn steer shoulder mount hung on the wall to the dining room; Tex would invite visitors to come around the wall to "see the rest of the longhorn." The feature that I remember best and with less than fond memories was the "Big Bathtub."

It was a tub, eleven-foot long and three-foot deep, located in the front bathroom. Tex never missed a day working out in the tub attached to one end by an elastic band of surgical tubing known as a torture belt. I spent many memorable hours in that tub with Tex moving the mark for me to reach farther and farther up the tub.

Few days passed without those workouts, the coach never quit, and few that worked for the coach quit either! As hard as he pushed his team and us, he pushed himself harder.

BOOK 3

ATTAWAYTOGO
THE FOUNDING OF CAMP LONGHORN

7

Chapter

Mary laid by the pool at the Dallas Country Club with her friend, Nancy. It was 1939 and the recent graduates of Highland Park High School were catching some late summer sun before they started college at Southern Methodist University in the fall. As they talked of fast-approaching college life, two young men walked out of the clubhouse and stood at the edge of the water. Mary's speech trailed off, setting aside whatever point she was making to look at the new arrivals. She was watching one in particular. He was young and fit, his six-foot athletic build topped by a gentle face and waves of curly, light brown hair. He smiled broadly with his sharp blue eyes as he boisterously explained something to his friend and gestured with his wide wingspan. The friend departed and the young man prepared to enter the water, removing all but his short wool swim trunks.

Mary sat up.

"Look at that guy. He's the best-looking guy I've ever seen," she said.

Nancy smiled and nodded once in agreement.

Mary thought for a moment and then flatly stated, "I'm gonna marry him."

"You're gonna marry him?" Nancy asked, incredulously, still lounging in her sun chair.

"Yeah."

"You don't even know who he is."

"No, I don't."

"Well, I do."

Mary turned to Nancy. "You do?"

"Yeah, I know who he is. He's a coach."

"He's a *coach*?"

"Yeah he is. He's a coach."

"Where?"

"University of Texas."

"Oh my God," Mary said, watching Tex swim laps in the Dallas Country Club pool. She thought a moment then looked at Nancy and said, "You know, I don't care. I'm gonna marry him anyway."

"You still don't know who he is," Nancy said.

"No, but I'm gonna go meet him right now."

Mary stood up from her chair and walked over to the pool.

As Tex swam back and forth through the water, she laid down by the edge of the pool and then called out to him to get his attention. Tex broke stride from his freestyle and swam to her.

"Hello, I'm Mary Agnes Hudson and I'm a swimmer."

Tex smiled and said, "Well what do you swim, Mary?"

"Oh, you know..." She then started mimicking the freestyle while laying on her stomach at the edge of the pool. Tex started laughing.

Well, I gave him an answer, Mary thought. *Stupid. Should have known better than to answer like that to a coach.*

When Tex stopped laughing he said, "Alright. Why don't you try doing that in the water?"

"MOM, DAD, I just met the man I'm gonna marry."

Robert Hudson, Sr., tipped the newspaper he was reading and stared blankly at his daughter.

"What are you talking about? When did you meet him?"

"Today. I kind of introduced myself and told him he'd come here for dinner."

The Hudson household was only two blocks from the country club and after the impromptu swim training Mary had invited Tex to eat that evening at her parents' house.

"Pat, honey, you've never even gone steady with anybody. What are you acting this way for?"

"I tell you, Dad, I'm going to marry that man."

"What does he do?"

"He's a coach."

"Honey, you just got out of high school. He's coaching?"

Her parents were concerned about their daughter Pat – the nickname most knew Mary by – inviting this stranger over; a stranger she was apparently set on marrying. But the invitation had already been extended and there was little that could shake Pat's resolve when she set her mind.

Tex made an immediate impression on the Hudsons, especially Pat's mother, Lucile, who found him as charming as her daughter did. It was also apparent this wasn't a passing fancy by their teen-aged daughter. She was serious. She'd decided she was going to marry him.

Any time she was able to get away from classes at SMU, Pat would travel to Austin, stay at a friend's sorority house, and go on dates with Tex. They took a grand total of three dates. It seems that's all that was needed. Pat invited Tex to return to her parents' house for Thanksgiving dinner. Though neither said it during the meal, it was apparent to Robert Hudson that an engagement was fast-approaching.

"Honey, you be careful," he told her that night.

"I know, Dad, but I said I'm going to marry him."

"When are you going to get married?"

"Well, I haven't told him yet."

"I can't do anything to stop this, can I?"

"Nope."

He was not only concerned about his daughter so quickly marrying a man ten years older than her. He was also concerned for Tex. Fully aware of his daughter's strong-headed personality, he wanted to make sure Tex knew what he was getting into.

"You sure about this?" he asked Tex in a private moment, as they both knew Pat would soon ask Tex to marry her.

Tex was sure. The mile-a-minute Mary Agnes Hudson was exactly his speed.

"We decided to get married at Christmas," said Pat, remembering her wedding day. "Well, *I* decided, and that's what we did."

Pat's parents were Catholic and the original plan was to get married in a Catholic church. But Tex didn't want to go through the conversion to Catholicism. So they were instead married in the priest's house behind the church.

On December 21, 1939, at the home of Rev. James F. O'Dea,

Julian William Robertson and Mary Agnes Hudson got married. Tex wore his one suit. Pat wore an ice blue crepe dress with a street-length skirt and high neck. Her hat and gloves were dusty pink. It was a short, simple ceremony followed by a celebration at Pat's parents' house.

The honeymoon was in Monterrey, Mexico, at the Gran Ancira Hotel, owned by the father of one of Tex's swimmers. The trip to Mexico included Tex rolling their car into a ditch in Leander, Texas, and driving the rest of the way with a crushed roof. Pat quit school at SMU, and the couple moved into a house in Austin on Speedway Boulevard, just north of the UT campus.

Not long after their nuptials – and once the roof of the car was fixed – Tex took Pat on a drive west into the Texas Hill Country. As he drove he told her of his dream. He'd already accomplished one of his two life goals, becoming head coach of the Texas swim team. He wanted to show her where he was going to accomplish the second.

They passed through the small Hill Country town of Burnet and arrived at a granite outcrop overlooking Inks Lake, a reservoir created by Texas' Lower Colorado River Authority about sixty miles northwest of Austin.

"You know, when I was at Michigan as a swimmer, I helped at my coach's camp in the summer," he told Pat. "What we're gonna do is we're going to have a boys camp and call it Camp Longhorn and you're going to be the camp mother."

"I'm not anybody's mother," Pat replied. "I'm eighteen years old and I am not going to do this."

"Oh, yes you are."

Pat was not sold on the idea, at least initially. But Tex was going to start his camp anyway. Coaching swimming and teaching campers encompassed the whole of his life's goals. Camping, both organized and disorganized, had been a part of his life from near the beginning. There were his traps, his trips to Cottonwood Creek, the West Texas Council Boy Scouts on a muddy North fork of the Concho River, nights on Mt. Wilson, and Camp Treasure Island in Los Angeles. After he told Michigan swim coach Matt Mann of his plan to create a place just like Mann's Camp Chikopi, he began to spend most of his time out of the pool at organized camp sites and doing some organizing of his own.

Camp Longhorn was not the first summer camp created by Tex

Robertson. The first was Camp Wolverine. During the spring semester of his first year at Michigan, Tex moved out of the boiler room at the ΔKE house where he washed dishes with Gerald Ford and into the home of one of his physical education professors, Harold D. Copp, to serve as a sitter for Copp's grade school children. The following fall he and Copp created a Saturday swimming camp using university facilities. With the moderate success of the weekend camp, together they built Camp Wolverine on the ten acres of property Copp owned along the Huron River. Even after becoming head swimming coach at UT in 1935, Tex would still return to Michigan during each of the next two summers to work at Camp Wolverine.

Using his title as the coach at Texas, he would send letters to several summer camps around the country with the offer of creating a swim program for them. He would then use those camps for trial and error, shaping his teaching style and lesson plans into exactly the right balance of work, reward, and fun. Along with returning to Chikopi for another summer, Tex worked at Camp Hampshire in New Hampshire, Camp Lincoln in Minnesota, and Camp Cheley in Colorado.

Program plan in hand, he set about combing the state of Texas for the perfect camp site. Since it was Tex, that meant any plan would involve a network of contacts, allies, supporters, and all manner of associates he had met through every back channel, front channel, or side-to-side channel. A notable example of this is the first job Adolph Kiefer received when he came to Austin to swim at UT. Tex told Kiefer that a portion of his "scholarship" would be paid by a part-time job that he had lined up.

"My first job was as a page boy at the state legislature for Senator (Rudolph) Weinert," Kiefer said. "After I got the job, Tex wanted me to talk to the senator about finding property for a camp. So I went to Senator Weinert and I said that my coach, Tex Robertson, wants to start a camp."

In the Forty-Fifth Texas Legislature, Weinert served as Chairman of the Game and Fish Committee and the Vice Chair of Public Buildings and Grounds Committee. With Kiefer as Weinert's page boy, Tex had the connection he needed in the legislature.

With Weinert's help, Tex began searching primarily along the Guadalupe River in south-central Texas, having decided that East Texas was "too weedy, mossy, and hot." He met with the owners of five different camp sites and started physically scouting locations. None met with his specifications. There wasn't a spot on the Guadalupe that allowed for swimming, skiing, and sailing – all of which he wanted to include in his new camp.

The root of his problem started 21,000 years ago when the Wisconsin Glacier receded.

"I soon realized that the great glacier that made thousands of camp type lakes up north didn't get to Texas," Tex once wrote.

If he was going to find a lake where breezes could fill sails, it would have to be man-made. The solution came from a friend of Weinert. He represented Seguin, a town along the Guadalupe River, and he introduced Tex to its mayor, Max Starcke. In the spring of 1937, Starcke called Tex and asked if the UT swim team could help celebrate the opening of a new pool in Seguin. Tex loaded up two of his divers and four of his swimmers and they put on a truncated version of the Aqua Carnival. While down in Seguin, Starcke showed Tex a few more potential camp sites, but none were what he was looking for.

A few months later Starcke called Tex to let him know he had left the office in Seguin to become the new general manager of the Lower Colorado River Authority. The LCRA was in the process of completing several dams along the Colorado River, and a series of reservoirs, now called the Highland Lakes, would soon be available. Starcke felt he had the perfect location for Tex to build his camp.

The largest lake in the chain was Lake Buchanan. Located about twelve miles west of Burnet, the over 22,000 acres of surface water could provide all the room Camp Longhorn would need. Tex and Max drove out to the lake together and traveled to the far side, near the small unincorporated community of Tow, where Starcke showed Tex twenty-five acres of land he could use for the camp.

The property was fine. The problem was the waterline. The massive, two-mile long Buchanan Dam was nearly finished and when Tex asked Max about it, Max informed his friend that Buchanan would not be a constant level lake. A shifting shoreline based on flooding, power-generation, and drought is not what Tex had in mind. Still, it was the most promising location he had seen. But while the two were driving back, they crossed the Inks Lake Bridge. Tex looked down at the pristine water and unoccupied shoreline and asked if Inks was like Buchanan.

"No," Starcke said. "Inks is a constant level lake."

They turned off the highway onto a dirt road used for construction of another of the dams being built along the Colorado River and arrived at a granite outcrop overlooking Inks Lake.

"The lake view was love and 'Wisconsin' imagination for me," Tex wrote.

When they got back to Austin, Tex and Max went to the LCRA offices and discovered the state owned 2,200 acres on the Burnet County side of the lake. Over the next several months Tex would explore the property and meet with Weinert, Starcke, LCRA Board President Roy Fry, local booster Edgar Seidensticker, and Dr. Joe Shepperd, the Mayor of Burnet. They decided on a thirty-seven-acre strip of land along the water's edge. Max leased the property to his friend for one dollar a year.

In the summer of 1939, Tex brought the entire University of Texas swim team out to his property on Inks Lake. They camped on the edge of the lake and engaged in the longest workouts most of them had ever undertaken. Twice a day the sprinters would swim across the width of the lake and back. The distance swimmers would head up to the bridge and back. The Divers would use the Inks Lake Bridge to practice high dives. Part of the "training" included clearing rocks, brush, and cedar for the camp site and building the first cabins using lumber "borrowed" from a UT building project.

When he brought Pat to the camp the following spring, they walked down to the water and to the few cabins they had built, and he talked of how he found the perfect spot for Camp Longhorn. But he wasn't speaking of the spot where he was standing. The lake itself would do nicely, but while training his swimmers he discovered that the Llano County shoreline on the far side had deeper water and prevailing breezes. He had investigated that shore the previous January while working the LCRA land with his swimmers. Richard "Cactus" Pryor, who would go on to become a legend of Texas broadcasting, was a swimmer for Tex's Austin High team and remembers diving into the frigid lake.

"It was so cold," Pryor said. "Billy Bob Williams – big ol' boy; he was six-foot-four and weighed about 200 pounds then – and Tex and I went to look at the camp site. We were on the east side, the opposite side from where Camp Longhorn is now. Tex said, 'Let's go take a look at it.' So we start walking for the car. Tex said, 'No, we're going to swim.' It's January. Tex is a man of action."

The property had everything he was looking for in a camp site. But the LCRA did not own that land. It was owned by Albert Murchison. Tex, Pat, and Max each approached Murchison and eventually he agreed to lease a ten-acre strip along the water for ten years at ten dollars a year. New land in hand, Tex gathered up all his swimmers available, both from UT and from his Austin High swim team, and brought them back out to the lake. This time the "training" exercise would involve tearing down the cabins and swimming across the still winter-chilled lake, dragging equipment and planks of wood behind them.

"Babe Papich swam across the lake holding a sledgehammer," Bill Johnson said. "You try doing that. That's a long way."

With a soft breeze to mitigate the sweltering Texas summer heat and the sun setting behind Long Mountain to the west, Tex was happy with the property and Albert Murchison was happy with the ten-ten-ten lease agreement. None involved realized the rental was prelude to a land feud that would last fifty-one years.

"BOY, THIS IS GOING TO BE EASY," Tex said to himself, hanging up the phone.

Thanks to Pat's friends, he had acquired the contact information for every member of the Dallas Country Club, a roll call of monied parents with athletic kids to fill the roster for the first year of Camp Longhorn. He had just got off the phone with the first person on the alphabetical list, Fred Alford, who enthusiastically agreed to send his son, Ferdinand, to Camp Longhorn. With his UT swimmers scheduled to join him on Inks Lake for training that summer, he had all the counselors he would need to handle the plethora of children sure to come.

Over the next several days he proceeded to call all the remaining names on the list. Every family said no.

"Mom and dad's neighbors had a boy named Bill Miller," Pat said. "So Tex says to his parents, 'I'll take him for free. It'll give us more than one camper at camp this summer.'"

Camp Longhorn started in the summer of 1940 with one paid camper, one volunteer camper, and seventeen counselors. (Tex always counted that first summer with just his swimmers, so the camp flag and

Camp Longhorn merchandise all read "Est. 1939," though the first youth camper actually arrived in 1940.) With only two campers to look after, the "counselors" spent much of their time clearing the land, cutting away brush, rat-tail cactus, and ash juniper trees in-between hard swimming in the lake every day. Chow was typically oatmeal cooked on a wood stove. (Meals improved when Pat started canoeing down to Steve Stevens' Fishermen Store to stock up on supplies.) It wasn't long before four swimmers had quit and returned to Austin, but the remaining thirteen stayed.

The camper-to-counselor ratio stayed under one the next year. Ferdinand was joined by Pat's young brother John, Louie Stayart, and Tommie Height. But in 1942 the camp had enough kids to call itself a real boys camp, with the total jumping to thirty-five. Tex got campers in various ways, but most commonly it was traveling to towns across the state. When he wasn't coaching or working one of his jobs in Austin, he would drive to small towns and meet with friends of friends of friends, asking each to give him a list of families nearby who might be interested in sending their boys to a summer camp.

Those early campers learned plenty about roughing it in the wild. There was no electricity and no running water. Instead there was a hand pump with a line leading into the lake. In order to get enough water to the chow hall for cooking, the counselors had to give it fifty strokes each day to fill the big tin tank Tex had found on the side of the road. The pump system was one of a number of early engineering projects overseen by Dr. Zarkov.

"Dr. Zarkov figured out how to get water out of the lake, and he ran it through a glass thing that had blue lights on it that disinfected the water that everybody drank," Johnny Crawford said. "Nobody got sick. Zark was a genius. He was really brilliant. He could build anything or figure out anything. Chemistry, physics, you name it."

Dr. Zarkov was actually a cousin of Tex named Frank Withers. Since Withers had a natural talent for engineering and electrical work, swimmer Bob Tarlton nicknamed him Dr. Zarkov after the scientist and inventor from *Flash Gordon* who created the rocket that sent the story's hero to the planet Mongo. While Zark was attending UT, he handled the lights and other technical aspects of the Aqua Carnival. When Tex created Camp Longhorn, he asked his cousin to help him build it.

Zark designed everything. He drew up the plan for every building and every dock, designing each to be easily disassembled in case Tex's lease on the Murchison land didn't last past those first ten years. He built the camp's first sailboat from scrap wood and canvas. He handled all the plumbing and all the electricity, once plumbing and electricity became available.

"I guarantee you that Camp would not have survived its infancy without Zark," Bill Johnson said.

Thanks to Zark's filters, no one got sick from drinking the lake water. If anyone got sick for any other reason, Tex would canoe them across the lake to the state park and drive them to Burnet to see Dr. Joe Shepperd. Burnet was a small community, with Mayor Shepperd also serving as the town doctor. With no telephone, Tex would let Dr. Joe know a sick camper was on the way via homing pigeon.

At Tex's request, the Austin Racing Pigeon Association donated nine birds to Camp Longhorn, all the offspring of "speed champions." Once the birds got familiar with the camp, Tex took the pigeons to Dr. Shepperd's office to train them. Four of the nine flew back to their original home in Austin, but five made it back to camp. A feature in *The Houston Chronicle Magazine* in 1948 described Tex's five feathered friends: "Now the birds are a definite part of the camp, and the campers regard them each as a personality. Each has a name, and by the way, all carrier pigeons' last name is Pigeon. Casanova Pigeon is the largest of the group, and one of the favorites; Walter Pigeon (the most photogenic) has registered the fastest time – 9 ½ minutes from Burnet; Homer Pigeon is the tamest; Dodo Pigeon is consistently the fastest; and Rojo Pigeon is a red thoroughbred."

Before construction of a road leading to camp and before telephone lines went up, all information entered Camp Longhorn by air.

"We got a newspaper once a week by airplane," Johnson said. "They'd drop the newspaper from the air as they went by. We worked on building the road into camp. There was no road into camp. We had to pick up kids at the state park. That was alright unless the wind was blowing or you had too many in a canoe or someone didn't know how to paddle the canoe."

Along with building the physical foundation of Camp Longhorn, the early '40s were also when Tex built the foundation of people who would be a part of the camp for decades. A few of his swimmers decided to continue to help Tex even after their graduation. Two of those, Bob Tarlton (or just "Tart") and Bill Johnson, so believed in Tex's vision they would make Camp Longhorn into a career. Joining them was Pat's brother, Bob Hudson, a sailing expert and talented landscaper who proved to be very popular as a counselor. These original few became legendary characters in Camp Longhorn lore, thanks mostly to Tex's ability to build anyone working at camp into a mythic figure in the minds of campers.

"Everyone at camp is bigger than life," said Tex's son Robby. "He named Bill Johnson the Strongest Man in the World. Bob Tarlton was the World's Greatest Story-Teller. Zark from Mars. His mastery was in making ordinary not ordinary. It shows in his Aqua Carnivals, where there was a Barnum and Bailey-like atmosphere. It showed in camp."

With the number of campers jumping from four to thirty-five in 1942 and fifty-five in 1943, Tex finally had some momentum.

"In the early days of Camp Longhorn we were operating with no money in the bank. It was a matter of survival," Tex said.

But immediately following the summer of '43, the camp had to be temporarily shut down. Tex, Tart, Zark, Bob, and Bill all went to war.

8

Chapter

While Tex trained his Frogmen in Florida, the other four went overseas, with Tart and Zark in the European theater of war and Bob and Bill in the Pacific. Tart was a radio operator in North Africa and Italy. Zark crossed Europe on foot in the Army and was in the middle of the Battle of the Bulge. Bob fought in the Philippines with the Army, and Bill on Iwo Jima with the Marines. Each was fortunate enough to return home, with a portion of Bill Johnson's hand the only body part left on the battlefield.

War changed Camp Longhorn. When the camp reopened with sixty-six boys in 1946 it had a very different tone. It was run by a group of veterans who had just returned from World War II. Campers marched to chow and saluted the counselors checking them in to each activity. The boys would stand at attention for daily inspections, which checked fingernails, ears, and teeth. Bunks were made and all clothing stored away in footlockers. Older campers learned Morse code from Tart. Tex started a "Frogman Club," where campers passed underwater swimming challenges, such as successfully spearfishing a catfish in murky Inks Lake, to move up in rank.

Everything at camp was war surplus. Campers ate off of GI metal trays, paddled yellow rubber lifeboats, and stored equipment in army trailers. A six-wheeled, six-wheel-drive Burma truck cleared boulders and trees to make room for an air strip and a road leading to camp. At the end of the term the boys, if they'd been good, earned rifles, bayonets, gas masks, canteens, and foxhole shovels to take home.

"(Tex) would go to the army surplus store and he'd pick out all these things and we had no idea what he was going to use them for. He didn't either. It was so cheap, he'd just buy and then figure out a use for it," said Wilson Cozby, a pre- and post-World War II camper.

Tex had the money to buy all the army surplus items that fueled the camp thanks to an old source of income. Remembering his days as a lifeguard in Santa Monica, he spent a portion of his time in California doing some illegal abalone fishing.

While Tex dove for the molluscs, Pat would sit on the beach and keep an eye out for the authorities. The two developed a variety of signals, such as Pat hanging a towel on a nearby post if a California Fish and Game warden was near. Similar signals would be used at the fish market; a red flag typically indicated to smugglers that it was ok to bring in the illegal haul. It proved profitable. There was high demand for abalone, particularly because many of the fishermen who had been providing abalone before World War II were Japanese Americans who were taken away to internment camps.

"We came home with $6,000 but we didn't realize that it was going to cost a lot more than that to restart Camp," Pat said.

With Camp Longhorn shut down during the war, Tex and Pat left the property in the hands of a woman from Burnet just to keep up basic maintenance. But in addition to taking care of the camp, she also turned the cabins into chicken coops, which made a mess of the floors.

"Believe me it was pretty deep," Pat said. "Every floor had to be pulled out and every cabin had to be rebuilt."

The $6,000 disappeared quickly and the camp was back to operating as cheaply as possible. Zark's ingenuity allowed Tex to find less-expensive solutions to every problem, such as providing enough cold drinking water for the campers and counselors.

"Regular drinking fountains were terribly expensive," Zark said. "My father gave us some old refrigerators. I laid them over and put in a water coil and put some hydrants on it and we called them Old Facefuls."

Tex was also a master of squeezing free labor out of everyone he encountered. Even with paid counselors on staff, during the late '40s Tex would still bring his swim team from the University of Texas out to the lake for training; training which inevitability involved some manual labor related to Camp Longhorn.

"Tex piled us all into the Burma jeep and he said he was taking us to a 'picnic,'" Wally Pryor said. "When we got there we got out of the Burma jeep and he handed us a couple of picks and said 'Here's the picks, now go nick those rocks.' We constructed roads; we built houses; we cut bee-brush. It was hard work, but it was fun."

Pryor is not the only one to comment on how much "fun" it was to do things for Tex with no compensation. His encouraging personality

– combined with putting you to work without you knowing what was in store – gave him all the free labor he would need to get his camp running.

"For Tex to start Camp Longhorn with nothing, that took imagination, ingenuity, and being a con artist," Johnson said. "He got us to all to work for him free. He told us how much good fresh air and how much water we had and how that was worth a million dollars and how we were overpaid. He could get you to do anything."

Some of the money used to sustain camp in the early days came in the form of loans that would extend indefinitely.

"We borrowed some money from some citizens of Burnet that we never paid back. Those turned into gifts," Tex said.

He would also use the campers themselves to change the face of the land. Along with their regular activities, campers had a work period where they would pick up rocks or learn a basic engineering skill. Each cabin would have a section of grass they had to keep green in the unforgiving Texas heat in order to pass inspection. Camp counselors would also provide additional labor, typically while the kids were resting.

"We didn't have a lot of tools. What we had was a lot of manpower," Emory Bellard said. "During the rest period, one counselor would stay in with the kids and the other would be a part of the workforce."

Bellard was a football player for Texas in the late '40s and years later would invent the "Wishbone" formation while serving as the Longhorns' offensive coordinator. Swimmers were not the only athletes Tex brought to Camp Longhorn. He was able to convince a significant number of football players to include a trip to Inks Lake in their training and he got many of them to stay on as counselors.

Included in the group of players who taught athletics at Camp Longhorn in the '40s and '50s were Carlton Massey – a Pro Bowl defensive lineman for the Cleveland Browns – Rice quarterback LeRoy Fenstemaker, and Texas quarterback John "Bunny" Andrews. (In 1951, Andrews gave a young Duke Carlisle the award for Best Athlete at Camp Longhorn. "I couldn't out-throw Duke Carlisle when he was nine years old," said Andrews. Carlisle would go on to lead the 1963 Texas Longhorns to a national championship.)

"(The football players) could lift those wheel barrels full of cement. It was wonderful to see the power," Johnson said.

This power was best put on display when one of the floating cabins broke free of its mooring. To add some extra square footage to his ten-acre strip of land, Tex came up with the idea of building cabins that would float on the water, and they became a popular place for campers to sleep. One exceptionally windy day the ropes holding a floating cabin in place broke.

"I was struggling with a rope trying to reach a tree in order to tie up the cabin," Johnson said. "Suddenly I was pulled off my feet as the cabin lurched to shore. Carlton Massey had got a hold of the rope and he was able to pull the Sea Hawk Cabin in by himself."

The famous names served as a draw, but it was a short-term gain. Tex eventually moved away from working to secure big names he could use for advertising purposes.

"He attracted the greatest counselors through the years, All-American football players. But inventive, strange people were the best," said Tex's son, Bill. "He learned through the years that the well-known figures didn't make the best counselors. He ended up going after the counselors that focused on kids. That's how you got them to come back."

No one at camp was more involved with the individual campers than Tex and he demanded a detailed level of work from each of his counselors. Every day after lunch Tex would meet with one counselor from every cabin and ask them about each camper by name.

"Tex would want to hear about every cabin, and every camper in it was discussed. Every day. 'How they doin'?' 'Were their ears clean?' 'Did they get to sleep?' 'Did they make their bed?' 'Did they sleep well?' He was so dedicated," Crawford said.

With the war, the ubiquitous army surplus, the professional and collegiate athletes, and the work period for the kids, Camp Longhorn had a toughness about it. In addition to swimming, activities like riflery, football, and boxing were added.

"That was my first introduction into boxing and I ended up boxing in some Golden Gloves after that," said Jeff Heller, a camper in the '40s who later became a Marine pilot. "The less tough kids weren't used to suffering a little pain. Nobody got real hurt, but some of them the first time they got hit they'd start crying."

For all the changes, it hadn't become a boot camp. Fun was still the primary focus. But discipline became a significant part of Camp

Longhorn, which added a new appeal for parents, and the restructuring of camp led to a post-war boom. Two years after it reopened there were 167 campers attending.

"Right after war we had maybe two or three cabins, but after that it took off," Zark said. "We couldn't build cabins as fast as we were filling them up for a while."

More and more of Tex's time was being spent on camp, which he had originally intended to be a small, 100-child operation he ran in the summer. During the winter months Tex would visit every camper in their home town. The travel, which was both for maintaining relationships and attracting new campers, began to make his coaching schedule unsustainable.

Unable to get full-time pay from the University of Texas and still working multiple jobs on the side, in May of 1950 Tex officially resigned as head coach of the UT swim team. Camp Longhorn would become his full-time job for the rest of his life. The camp was already a full-time job, but Tex quit primarily because he knew the number of campers was about to rise dramatically.

In 1950, Camp Longhorn for Boys dropped the "for Boys" part of its title.

During the early days of the camp, sessions lasted four weeks and in the middle of the term there would be Visitors' Day, when parents were allowed to watch their sons participate and compete in various camp activities. Mid-term V-Days were later canceled because so many kids would cry, as the visit reminded them of home, but V-Day did allow for sisters to visit Camp Longhorn. While there were some boys who wanted to go home with their parents, there were plenty of little girls who wanted to stay. Pat wanted them to stay as well.

"I told Tex, 'I love the boys, but I'd really like some girls, too.' He was tickled to death with the idea," Pat said.

The staff set about recruiting sisters and building new cabins. Tex asked Pat's brother, Bob Hudson, to run the girls camp. Bob was not thrilled with the idea, initially. He loved working in the boys camp and had no experience working with young girls.

"He didn't want to do it, he really didn't," Pat said. "But once he got in there he loved it."

He would end up being director of the girls camp for twenty-seven years. He couldn't get enough of it. And they couldn't get enough of him.

"Bob Hudson's spirit and heart was enough to fill all of girls camp," said Margret 'Trigger' Butler, one of the first female campers. "If we had the opportunity to spend time with Bob, whether we were Wrens or counselors, we all wanted to be close to him. He had this heart that extended to all of us."

To help Bob with the task, Tex hired Mary Pryor, mother of swimmers Cactus and Wally.

"Tex Robertson recognized in my mother a woman with a talent for handling children," Cactus said. "He'd been our neighbor and had watched the manner with which mother rode herd on her wild herd. So when she became widowed in her '50s, he offered her a job with the girls camp at Camp Longhorn and for over thirty years she proved his choice had been a wise one."

In 1952, thirty-two girls and twelve female counselors came to Camp Longhorn. (Much like the boys camp in "1939," Tex would always give the date of the girls camp founding as 1950, the year he decided to have it rather than the year it actually started.) The experience for a female counselor at Camp Longhorn was the same as that of a male: hard manual labor.

"Don't forget that we cut bee-bush and we laid pipes too. We had work detail," said Helen Frady, who was a counselor in the '50s and still works at Camp Longhorn as a coordinator. Helen met her husband, Ray Frady, at Camp Longhorn. Couples at camp were common. Needing more counselors to handle both a boys and a girls camp, Tex would ask those already working at camp for the summer to bring their spouses.

"That whole concept of being married and being counselors at Camp Longhorn was incredible. 'So, you're married. Come on,' Tex said and he built Jell-O Courts for those who were married," Butler said.

The "Jell-O Courts" were a group of small cinder block homes, each one painted a different color (hence, "Jell-O"). They served as homes for married counselors, who would alternate between staying in the cabin with their campers and in the courts with their husband or wife.

"That eventually went away," Butler said. "But in those early days we had to have a place for those married counselors to spend the night every other...The two camps were very separate."

The boys and girls camps were separate from each other, but the activity schedule was nearly identical. The girls played baseball and got muddy and a bit bloody playing tackle football on the rocky field covered in more dirt than St. Augustine grass. Minus boxing, they also went though the same military procedure as the boys camp.

This was a shock for some.

"Away from camp we would not have these kinds of rules and regulations in our families," Butler said. "Families who came to camp early were very well to do. So coming to camp and having rigorous inspection was very different from anything we knew at home. But Tex, Bob Hudson, Bob Tarlton, Zark, Mary Pryor made us feel like this was good for us to learn how to take care of ourselves."

The girls marched, saluted, learned to operate firearms, and could pick from the same army surplus items as rewards at the end of camp as the boys. There were few places the girls could get an experience like this in the 1950s, and there was a tremendous amount of pride in that first group.

The names of most can be found on trees at the camp. Getting a dedicated tree at Camp Longhorn is one of the organization's highest alumni honors. The tradition started when every one of the girls that summer got a bronze plaque – poured and molded at the camp foundry – nailed to a tree at the height of the camper at the time. Most of the nameplates are gone, taken away by wind, rain, and rust. But one can still find weather-beaten, greenish-gray names such as Becky Crouch, Sue Barnes, Martea Reed, Becky Love, Suzanne Kline, Sally Bagby, Nancy Burt, Shannon Harrison, and Janie Maxfield. The center of the group was Bob Hudson. Tex was the one who created girls camp and he was deeply involved with the day-to-day operation, but he was also seen as a more distant, patriarchal figure. For the three decades he spent as director, Bob was the star. After Bob's death, in a letter to Pat that best captures the central figure of girls camp, Butler wrote:

Not one of us from 1952 to 1979 will ever forget Bob Hudson!

In his quiet, gentle way, with a smile unlike any other, he made us feel very special.

He made us laugh, told us stories, took us for rides in his BEAUTIFUL cars and on his sailboats; he guided us through difficult spots on land and in the water.

Bob Hudson stayed close to us, choosing to live among us above the Wren Cabin and at the top of a giant slide.

He taught us to sail and shoot a rifle. He took us on overnight, cooked pancakes in the morning, and threw rocks on top of the overnight cabin to awaken us.

Bob knew how to play; he chased us, teased us, and when we couldn't hit the baseball during those after-dinner ball games, he found a way to our bat with the ball he pitched, and we got a hit anyway!

Bob took us to the movies (and we all wanted to sit next to him) during those early years; he visited us in our homes during the winter, and we felt like "royalty" had come.

He opened and closed every campfire in the girls' camp, and we loved him. How we all did love him!

Bob Hudson was our first "boyfriend"; he was our mentor and close friend; even when he gave us a "demerit" – why, we felt so bad because we had disappointed him!

We all wanted to be next to him – at the table in the chow hall, sitting at campfire, on church mountain, wherever! Bob made room for us all, too.

Bob Hudson loved animals and birds; always there was a special dog. He had a special communication with them just like with us.

He grew flowers and planted grass where once was only dirt, rock, and rat-tail cactus; he mowed that grass and moved sprinklers; he taught us about the beauty of the earth.

Bob Hudson, to us, never aged; he seemed forever young!

If you've ever wondered why Bob never married, just ask one of us who loved him between 1952 and 1979. There were just too many of us to choose from, and he wouldn't dare to hurt all of us save one!

Surely, this epistle could go on and on, but I shall close with a final moment of gratitude, a final prayer of thanksgiving for Bob Hudson, a man whose heart was big enough to love us all.

This was the same Bob Hudson making the girls march, salute, and make their bunks tight enough to bounce a nickel off. Girls camp was a curious mix of military discipline and heart. But that was how Tex intended it. It created an environment where the girls wanted to march and wanted to help clear granite boulders and cactus. The swimmers who came to the camp for "training," the counselors who got more manual labor than they bargained for, and the campers defending their patch of grass so they could pass inspection, they were all the same. Tex didn't simply tell them to work; he got them to *want* to work for him.

Camp Longhorn survived and flourished because of it.

Chapter

It started with a rare sight: a rancher with clean shoes.

While on an off-season trip visiting campers in 1967, Bill Johnson stopped in Hamilton, a small town on the plains of north-central Texas about sixty miles west of Waco. He was getting a bite at a cafe when he met Seth Williams, a local cattle rancher wearing pearl white sneakers. Bill couldn't help but comment on Williams' footwear and he discovered that Seth was a decent tennis player on the side and had just finished a game with his daughter. They began discussing eclectic hobbies and Bill discovered that, along with tennis, Seth's present addiction was buying bargains at military surplus sales. He was buying so much surplus that he was running out of barn space to store all of his acquisitions. Given that for years Camp Longhorn was run on army surplus, Bill was happy to take a trip out to Williams' ranch.

He found more than he expected. It was a massive collection that included, for example, roughly 1,000 six-foot ladders. Camp was good on ladders, but a constant problem was rain-soaked mattresses under leaky tarps covering the judo/tumbling slab and the riflery range. All the sprinklers Tex would set out to encourage the grass added to the problem. Bill found what he thought was an answer in Seth Williams' forty-foot long, 10,000-gallon rubber storage tanks. He decided he would buy the drab, olive-colored, deflated behemoths from Williams and cut them up into a set of new tarps. Johnson paid his new tennis-playing, cattle-ranching acquaintance a hundred dollars and loaded the tanks into his truck – which folded into a relatively small bundle when not filled with 10,000 gallons of gas.

When he returned to Camp Longhorn, Johnson unloaded his acquisitions at the canoe bay to store them until he found the time and equipment to cut them into proper rain tarps. But when he arrived, Bill found two camp employees working with an air compressor. Given that the tanks were tough enough to maintain a seal when being rolled out of cargo planes into the Gulf of Tonkin, they were able to stay taut when he used the compressor to fill them with 1,337 cubic feet of air. This occurred for no other reason than to serve Bill Johnson's curiosity for what would happen if he took a giant military oil bladder he had purchased from a barn outside Hamilton, Texas, filled it with air, and then put it on the water.

Tex encouraged constant innovation from everyone at camp. He wanted there to be a new activity to surprise campers with every year they came back, despite a limited budget. Often he would buy a large amount of random surplus items just to see what he and those working with him could create. A five-ought gauge steel wire became a zip line into the water. Oil drums with no bottom became tunnels for the frog-boys and frog-girls to swim through.

The result of Johnson's experiment with the air-filled gasoline tank turned into the most popular activity at Camp Longhorn, the Blob, where campers jump from an overhanging tower on to the heavy-duty vinyl monstrosity, bouncing other campers off into the water. (The tower proved much more effective than the original idea of using a trampoline to jump from the shore to the Blob.) Even old Blobs would be recycled into new inventions. When one of the first Blobs tore open and wouldn't hold air, Tex cut it into a long tarp and strung it between two parallel poles to create a suspended slide he called the "Water Soc."

Some ideas were better than others. Letting the campers drive all-terrain vehicles proved dangerous and too costly to maintain. The "Gum Drop," which involved dumping pieces of gum from a small plane passing over campers worked marvelously, but attempting to drop a watermelon via parachute just resulted in a two-foot crater in the ball field. It's also impressive that nobody was ever injured by the "Ski Wheel," a long, horizontal, rotating pole powered by an outboard motor that would swing a skier (or non-ski-wearing camper) in circles at a tremendous rate.

"Now we wouldn't think of doing that because of the risk and the liability and the health of the kids. So we've tamed down a bit," Tex said in 1999.

But some ideas that took root at Camp Longhorn became popular at camps across the country and in some cases across the world. The Blob – an idea thrown together at camp while looking for something new to do – is now a sport. The International Blobbing Battle – where three-man teams face off in competitive Blobbing – debuted in Austria in

2011. The most widely distributed invention to come from the mind of Tex Robertson, though, is a plastic flying disc.

"We had very little equipment. So we adapted my childhood habit of saving discs and we called them Sa-Los," Tex said.

Frisbee as a sport has its beginnings with Tex, as recognized in *The Complete Book of Frisbee* by Victor Malafronte:

> In 1922, an eleven year old Tex Robertson always looked forward to playing the game of throw and catch. But not with a baseball or football! He and his buddies preferred to sail a metal cover from a one gallon container to Jewel Shortening. From his home town of Sweetwater, Texas, Tex traveled to Los Angeles in 1931 [sic], and introduced the "flying cover game" to the Los Angeles Junior College Physical Education Department. Unfortunately, all three metal can covers he brought were destroyed within 30 minutes, from striking the ground too many times.
>
> Two years later, in 1933, Tex Robertson established the first organized "flying disc games" at the Wolverine Day Camp, then located in the vicinity of Ann Arbor, Michigan. Tex Robertson added some new twists to the camp activity menu: the flying disc games of Pitch-n-Catch, Hit The Runner, and Keep Away. Discs consisted of paper covers from ice cream containers, attractive no doubt by sweet association in youngsters' minds. Coaching his charges in disc throwing techniques, Tex would repeatedly urge them to "sail it low and level," good advice for any beginning disc thrower. This saying, distilled down to Sa-Lo, became the name both for Tex's flying disc, and the games he invented utilizing it. Therefore, Camp Wolverine truly has claimed the right to be called the birthplace of organized frisbee playing.
>
> By 1935, Tex had moved from Michigan to Austin, Texas, where he became the swimming coach for the University of Texas, a position he held until 1951 [sic]. In 1937, he and student friend Jack Nendell performed the perhaps first ever large scale flying disc demonstration before a capacity crowd at a University of Texas basketball game. The crowd

was introduced to a game of Sa-Lo utilizing a cardboard "disc" reinforced around the rim with tape. A round piece of felt was glued to the top of the disc to add extra weight and stability.

Tex was also the announcer for the very popular and consequently always crowded swimming meet known as the Texas Aquatic Carnival. In order to receive the results of each swimming match more quickly, (there was no room for a runner), the scores were written on a Sa-Lo disc; then head judge Bob Tarlton with a flick of his wrist would "air mail" the results to the stage!

In 1939, Tex and his wife Pat started Camp Longhorn at Inks Lake located in Burnet, TX. Part of his plan to recruit new campers was to ask youngsters in the neighborhood to take the "Sa-Lo challenge." This was a test of skill in throwing a Sa-Lo through a three-foot hoop that Tex would place in the prospect's front yard. His fascination with flying disc games resulted in the Sa-Lo becoming an important part of Camp Longhorn's summer activities. Soon, Tex introduced the game of Sa-Lo golf by laying out 5 hoop holes around the camp grounds to which the children tossed metal and paper Sa-Los. In addition, campers could choose from a menu of Sa-Lo tennis, distance competitions, and the catch and throw skills event.

Camp Longhorn only slowly caught on in the beginning. Some children even had to be "borrowed" for photographs in the first camp brochure. Although most of the campers enjoyed the thrill of playing Sa-Lo, some of their parents thought the game to be a little out of the ordinary. However, Tex stayed the course, and thanks to this southern gentleman, Sa-Lo represents the oldest organized flying disc game as an institutionalized activity offered to other people. Tex's Sa-Lo games continue to be played at Camp Longhorn to this day...

Novelty flying discs were first sold to the public by inventor Walter Frederick Morrison in 1938. He patented the idea in 1957 and sold it to the Wham-O toy company, which changed the name to its modern nomenclature, "the Frisbee." Tex taught students how to play Sa-Lo years before Morrison was selling his discs on the beach in Santa Monica. But Tex never sold the Sa-Lo and never applied for a patent. He never applied for a patent for anything. If fact, he was opposed to the idea of patenting any of his inventions.

Gardner Parker was more responsible than anyone else for managing Tex's finances in the latter half of the 20th century – which was necessary because Tex had no desire to manage his own money. Parker said:

> Tex cared more about good camps for kids. Later, when I was on the board (of directors), the Blob was taking off and people were wanting it. I told Tex I was going to patent it and he said, "What's that mean?" I said, "Well I want to patent it because every time it gets sold Camp Longhorn will get part of the proceeds." He said, "That means it will cost more." I said, "Well possibly. That is true. If someone's going to pay for the Blob and there's a patent or royalty fee you're going to pay that." He said, "Ok, then no. I'm going to go the other way. Any camp that can't afford one, I want us to buy one for them." So instead of this great business idea for Camp, he said he was going the other way. Of course I already knew by then he didn't care about money.

It was all about the camp. The invention was secondary. Tex had an opportunity to create a sturdy, marketable frisbee instead of reconstituted lids when he went to a plastics company in Austin and asked them to make a mold for a durable Sa-Lo.

"The guy wanted $500 to make a mold to make the flying discs," said Tex's son, Robby. "Tex said he could either build a cabin or have a mold for the Sa-Lo. So he said, 'I've still got potato chip can lids; we'll just keep using those,' and he built another cabin instead."

All of his inventions were off-shoots of a desire to improve the camp. If it became famous outside of Camp Longhorn it was a side effect.

"ATTA-WAY TO GO."

That little piece of encouragement is likely the most common phrase uttered by Tex during his life. At Camp Longhorn, though, it's not a phrase but is instead considered a single word: attawaytogo. When a camper or counselor intones it to another, it is often coupled with a hand sign. Both hands are clasped with fingers interlaced and thumbs pointed skyward, creating the image of a longhorn head. While it is used to encourage campers, saying "attawaytogo" to someone at Camp Longhorn represents an idea that Tex wanted to be central to CLH: self-improvement. There is plenty of competition between and within cabins, but none of the competition is structured to rank one group as better than the other. It is structured to encourage competition with the self, to better one's time in, say, the mile swim.

Of course, he created more incentives than just verbal confidence boosters. The most notable is his merit system, which he first used at Camp Wolverine. When one of his campers on the Huron River in Michigan did something positive, such as saying "yes, sir" or properly cleaning up, Tex would put a check mark next to the camper's name in a notebook. When they did something negative, such as showing disrespect to a counselor or fellow camper, Tex would put down an X. At the end of the camp, the final score of checks minus Xs was the camper's merit total and he would be rewarded with prizes based on his score. Tex kept the system for Camp Longhorn, but soon the checks and Xs were replaced with plastic orange discs the campers collected. Merits could then be exchanged at the Merit Store for various prizes. Merits could also be saved from one year to the next, with honors received for passing milestones of 500 and 1,000 total merits. Some impressive totals have been gathered by those who, for example, went to camp every year from second grade to high school.

"Everything at camp was on a friendly competitive basis and the merit system molded behavioral training," Heller said.

The expectation of a reward is an effective way to control behavior, but it also gave great value to simple respect. There is no individual action that will gain a camper more than a single merit. "Yes, sir" is one merit. Successfully swimming a mile is one merit. The athletic feat and the basic pleasantry each have the same purchasing power in the Merit Store. This naturally inspires a high level of courtesy at Camp

Longhorn. One year at the end of a term – back when the Merit Store still sold guns – a camper's father asked if he could buy a .22 rifle that his son wanted, since the camper had not yet earned enough merits. When he was refused, he stormed off to go find Tex. When he did find Tex, he received the same answer.

"You don't understand," Tex said. "Your son's *wanting* that is a great thing."

However the "highest honor" for a camper, as it is described at Camp Longhorn, is to receive an Early Bird. An Early Bird is just an invitation at the end of the term to return to camp the next year, accompanied by a single feather, typically from one of Tex's many pigeons. The camper's parents may be paying customers, but Tex set up a system where being a paying customer is treated as an honor to be earned.

"Kids can't just pay their tuition. They have to contribute to the camp," Tex said.

This also allows for an easy dismissal of a child who Tex decided should no longer be a camper. You aren't told you can't come back. You just don't get your Early Bird.

"Ninety-nine percent of the people who went to Camp Longhorn became a better person," Parker said. "That's even true of the ones who didn't get Early Birds. Probably impacted them more."

WHILE PROPER TREATMENT OF FELLOW HUMANS is a central focus of Tex's camp, animals have played a big role in Camp Longhorn. As early as his childhood in Sweetwater, running his trap lines every morning, Tex always had a fascination with nature. One of the results of this fascination is the notably well-stocked camp zoo. Along with the expected petting zoo animals, Camp Longhorn often features animals found in actual zoos. This began with a trade. As Bill Johnson explained:

> One time we had too many diamond-backed water snakes in the boys swimming bay. Joe Demmer was an old pro with animals. I learned from Joe how to catch snakes. We ended up in the zoo with a whole lot of these snakes. The

Fort Worth Zoo had a giant cobra that would eat nothing but water snakes. I called up Lawrence Curtis, the director in those days and he said, 'Please bring them up here! I'll give you anything.' I thought that was a pretty good trade, so I went up with a laundry bag full of water snakes and he said, 'What do you want?' I said, 'I want one of everything, but I don't want it until the middle of May.'

Johnson brought back a potpourri of creatures from Fort Worth, such as prairie dogs, parrots, and several small monkeys. Included in the haul was a small, young American alligator, which over the years has become a very big, old American alligator – and as of this writing is still alive. Ali the Alligator (who Tex would sometimes refer to as "Muhammad") was one of Tex's favorites and he aided its longevity by keeping it well fed and putting a fan in its pit in the summer and a heater in the winter. Along with animals purchased or traded for at zoos, there was always a big collection of local wildlife captured around Camp Longhorn, such as possums, squirrels, racoons, deer, and "black eagles" (buzzards).

The animals also gave Tex a chance to play his favorite character. Campfire is the nightly gathering of all campers for awards and entertainment, usually in the form of skits and routines put on by the campers. Once a term it would be interrupted by a grand entrance. Sometimes it would simply be him stepping onto stage in the middle of a counselor's speech. Sometimes it would be a vehicle arriving at campfire. Once he crashed a station wagon into the stage at a relatively low but still dangerous speed, leaving a large crack in the concrete.

"Hello, I am Dr. Schwartz from West Germany Institute of Wildlife!" Tex would shout in an over-the-top German accent as he climbed out of the vehicle. Wearing a coonskin cap, thick glasses, clothes shredded by apparent claw marks, and covered head to toe in bandages, the bumbling Dr. Schwartz would saunter on to stage with full cages and squirming bags. From that point the act became a constant assault of puns about animals.

"Now a lot of people think I'm a hare-brain," he'd say, removing his coonskin hat to reveal a small white rabbit sitting on his head. He'd open one bag to reveal a ten-foot boa constrictor, which he'd string across the front row while warning the campers, "Be careful, he'll love you to death."

Out of another bag would come a series of non-poisonous hognose, coachwhip, and ribbon snakes, which he would casually wrap all over himself. Ignoring the continual bites from the aggressive but ultimately harmless ribbons, he'd grab another bag and fling the snakes into the crowd, eliciting screams from the younger campers before they realized that this bag only contained rubber snakes. He'd tell a tale of braving the snowy tundra and capturing the "Great White Wolf." At the end of the story he'd bring out the dread wolf: Pat's miniature American Eskimo dog, Glory, which he'd taught to stand on its hind legs. While feeding an armadillo from his hand, he'd tell the story of this particular rascal, "Arnold Dillo."

He kept very little control over the animals during the act. By the end there would be snakes, racoons, possums, dillos, and rabbits all over the stage. The surrounding counselors could usually wrangle most at the end of the show, but Tex didn't care if the local wildlife disappeared into the woods. He'd just go out the next day and catch more.

The act changed each term depending on the animals available and because many of the jokes were comprised of whatever pun came to mind on stage. Outside of the persona of Dr. Schwartz, Tex would still tell stories at campfire about animals, though after an incident in the early days of Camp Longhorn he avoided intentionally frightening tales.

"We told the campers that Hugo, the gorilla from the San Antonio Zoo, had escaped and he'd been seen in Marble Falls," Tex said. "We told them be sure and lock your cabins. We had a kid who was in on it and we put some ketchup on him."

Sight of the supposedly blood-covered camper sent kids shrieking to their cabins.

"One of the older brothers was in there standing behind the door with a broom and he hit me on the head and knocked me down to the floor," Tex said. "We got about five or six cars together and turned on the lights and said, 'Come on out. The gorilla is dead. We got him.' Nobody came out. And six or seven campers didn't come back the next year."

WHILE INSPECTION AND GI TRAYS REMAINED, many of the military aspects of Camp Longhorn faded over the years. But there remains a single program at the camp that is explicitly military in origin, a program started by Parker following his return from the Marine Corps.

There are few people who were more loyal to Tex Robertson than Gardner Parker, and that loyalty started very early.

"As a child, when Tex was visiting campers at their homes, I'd come home from school and I would sit out on the curb in front of my house every day until dark just waiting for him," Parker said. "I don't think there's any other person in the world I would have done that for. I lived and breathed it twenty-four hours a day."

A camper, then counselor, and later financial adviser and board member for Camp Longhorn, Parker was one of Tex's few close confidants. As much as Tex loved interacting with people, there weren't many people who could be called his friend. He kept people at arm's length when it came to personal matters, typically turning attention away from himself to the other person or whatever project he was promoting. Parker's relationship with Tex more resembled a mentor-student or father-son kinship, but he's one of the few people outside his family who Tex truly trusted.

"We developed early on a very special relationship," Parker said. "He allowed me to do things he didn't allow other counselors to do and create lots of new things at camp. He only told me this once, but he said 'You remind me of me.' I think that's why he allowed it."

Parker was a counselor in the '60s and left camp for six months to join the Marine Corps. Soon after his return, Tex asked him to invent something new for the fourteen-year-old campers. There was very little difference between the program for a thirteen-year-old and a fourteen-year-old camper and Tex told Parker the similarity was the reason for a significant drop-off in thirteen-year-olds returning to camp the following summer. Parker's solution was called the "Marines." Like the rest of Camp Longhorn it was all for fun, but unlike the rest of Camp Longhorn a "general" could wake you up from an afternoon nap with an air horn and scream in your face. There was plenty of marching, saluting, and dodging of water balloon hand-grenades. For an infraction, push-ups were added on to the standard relinquishing of a merit. At the end of the term, the whole camp would watch the Marines dive into a pit full of mud, followed closely by their generals, signifying their completion of the program.

Much has changed with the program since its inception. The most notable difference is the lack of explosives. Utilizing UDT techniques taught by Tex, Parker, and Tarlton, the Marines would swim out into the lake with a mayonnaise jar containing three sticks of dynamite and plant the explosives on a derelict sailboat deemed no longer usable by the camp. The other campers sat on the shore and watched as Parker and his Marines set and lit the three-minute fuse. But the Marines were not allowed to leave at this point. They instead had to nervously wait for Parker's signal as the fuse burned down.

"When I finally said 'go,' they were breaking mile-swim records getting out of there," Parker said.

The tradition of dynamiting a sailboat ended in the early '70s – not long after it began – due to extremely obvious danger concerns.

"Looking back, it was crazy," Parker said. "I've had former Camp Longhorn Marines tell me on the street they've never in their whole lives been more scared than when they were watching that fuse and waiting for my signal."

Initially the Marines were male fourteen-year-olds, but as it is with all other activities at Camp Longhorn, the girls soon got involved with the "Marinas," which was introduced by Tex's son John, a Vietnam vet, not long after Parker created the Marines.

While there were a large number of activities created by Parker at the camp, Tex pushed everyone working for him to be creative and he had a very unique balance of pressure and encouragement, but always with a smile.

"He kept the pressure on you the right way," Parker said. "He expected more. When you think you've finally done enough for Tex, he's going to say, 'This is the greatest thing in the world.' Then he'd shoot a little hole in it and say 'You can do better.'"

Tex had no desire for an explicitly religious camp. There is no religion spoken of in promotional material. There is no religious restriction to admission. However, each Sunday night campers walk to the top of Church Mountain for a service. No denomination is promoted, but it is a part of an underpinning spirituality to Camp Longhorn.

It is representative of the religious duality of Tex Robertson. He cared little for particular denominations, marrying Pat in the priest's home behind the church because of his refusal to convert to Catholicism. He was consistent in writing letters back to any person or organization that wrote him, but in the files he left in his office every letter from a religious organization still sits unopened.

Yet he would begin every board meeting with a prayer. On Church Mountain he would speak not of a particular way to worship, but would still display devotion to the idea. "Attawaytogo, God," Tex would say, raising his clasped hands to the sky in his signature hand sign. Keeping his hands clasped, he'd then turn his thumbs downward, bring them together, and crook his index fingers, forming the image of a heart. "And we love you."

His personal religious belief more resembled nature worship than church-based religion. He loved the trees, the rocks, the air, and the water and would speak often of the "Spirit of Camp Longhorn." He didn't love structured religion; he loved ideas.

And he loved his camp. It was also important to him that the two men he most wanted to emulate both approved of what he'd created. His father and his coach died just a year apart from each other: Frank in 1961 and Matt Mann in 1962. Shortly before they passed, each visited Camp Longhorn.

Frank found financial success in Los Angeles but always thought of himself as a "country man." He loved what Tex did on Inks Lake and was proud that for all his son's time in Los Angeles and Michigan that he stay true to his wild Texas roots. In a hand-written note to his stepsister Nancy while at the camp, Frank wrote: "We have no telephone; no electricity; no baths, except the lake; no mail delivery, and nothing modern under the Sun. But it is a most beautiful natural setting on a clean lake margined by green trees and all kinds of wild flowers and millions of pretty song birds."

As for Mann, Tex's life path mirrored his own. With no money to start with, Tex became a swimming coach and ran a summer camp. More than anything else, Tex wanted to be Matt Mann, and indications of that loyalty can be found all over Camp Longhorn. The song sung at the beginning of campfire each night, "Hail to That Campfire-Lighter," is sung to the tune of Michigan's fight song, "Hail to the Victors." In fact, the idea of campfire itself came from Mann's Camp Chikopi. Mann was impressed with what his swimming champion had created, especially because it went so far beyond what even Tex had envisioned. On that quiet afternoon in 1933 at Camp Chikopi, when Tex told Mann that he was going to build Camp Longhorn, Tex said his camp would have a hundred kids. When Mann arrived in the early '60s, Camp Longhorn had more than a thousand.

The unique nature of the camp reflects the unique nature of Tex. It was a combination of everything that made up Tex – swimming, coaching, and camping – and it was where he constantly poured the best of himself.

Camp Longhorn is Tex.

Afterword

by

Sally Robertson Lucksinger

My dad was a romantic. Not in the traditional sense, but in a quirky, endearing way unique to him. And you saw it in everything he did.

When you were with him, you felt like the most important person in his world; he was such a singular person, you almost couldn't help it, but it was his way of expressing his love and affection that, more than anything, convinced you he was a special person, and that you were just as special as he.

I remember every night he would come to our beds and ask us merit questions. It made each of us feel special, and we always looked forward to it. Then he would wake us up for school with a loud, silly song. The words were often made up or nonsensical. He just kept singing until we got up. My favorite was "skeety weety weety woe."

And he loved our mom in the same odd, wonderful way. It was a love affair that lasted sixty-eight years – through Camp's lean beginning, five children, eighteen grandchildren, and seven great-grandchildren and counting. My mom and dad had completely different personalities: he was patient and persevering; she was fiery, independent, and always in a hurry. But it worked.

On any special occasion there would be a sweet message written with soap on mom's bathroom mirror. He called her 'Muv' – a combination of 'mom' and 'love'. The dinner table was their comedy show, with him as the comedian and her his unwitting straight man.

It was the same with anyone else he encountered; he gave them that extra bit of personal attention that left everyone eternally endeared to him. I never even remember him buying a greeting card. He would just cut the names off of cards given to him and scratch out the printed words and write his own messages.

And he was funny – really funny. He could find humor in most any situation. And almost always did.

But he was also always the coach. He knew how to get us to do most anything and think it was fun. Every quiet time (the campers' nap time during the summer) he would put on his big hat, get in the motorboat, and we would swim across the lake and to Inks Dam and back. He had the best whistle and would use it while we were swimming. You could hear it underwater. He used that whistle for ending all games at Camp, calling his pigeons, and calling us home when it started to get dark. Everyone loved and remembered him for things like that. He used his talents as a people person to interact, love and form bonds with others. That was what truly mattered to him.

He never cared about possessions or money; he loved nature and people. In fact, he could hardly have cared for possessions any less. He had an old orange Cadillac, and it was the messiest car inside and out that I have ever seen. It was usually full of bird seed, zoo supplies, or an occasional snake that escaped in transport from the New Braunfels Snake Farm. Grass grew on the floorboard. A clipboard was screwed into the dashboard with a light over it. The clipboard always held a yellow legal pad with pages and pages of ideas, letters to politicians, and swimming news – all in his nearly indecipherable handwriting.

He understood, perhaps better than anyone I have known, what was important to him in his life and what he wanted to do with it.

My dad was unique. A special man who influenced so many lives, and made everyone he met feel special – but especially me.

Tex's father, F.G. Robertson, and his two oldest brothers, Frank and LaClaire, in Sweetwater, Texas. (Estimated year – 1906)

Tex's mother, Nancy, with Frank and LaClaire.

Tex's mother, Nancy.

Tex's father, F.G. Robertson, and his two oldest brothers, Frank and LaClaire.

Julian (foreground) and his brothers on a family trip to
the beach in Corpus Christi, Texas. (Estimated year – 1911)

Tex (in white) and his 1936 UT relay team.

Tex (left), his wife Pat, and UT swimmer Mike Sojka. (Estimated year – 1940)

Tex as a swimmer at Michigan.
(Estimated year – 1934)

The 1936 University of Texas swim team, with coach Tex Robertson in the center.

The 1937 team, and a duck, one of a myriad of the team's live mascots, which included Ralph Flanagan's live alligator.

The first cabins at Camp Longhorn. (1942)

Tex and his father at Camp.
(1942)

Tex and Pat at Camp. (1942)

Inks Lake in 1942.

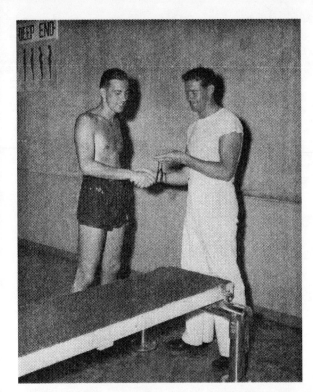

Tex (right) shaking hands with
one of his sailors in San Diego.
(1944)

Tex (front row, left) and a class of sailors he taught to swim in San Diego. (1944)

Drawing from a 1946 Camp Longhorn pamphlet, following Tex's return from World War II.

Wally Pryor inspecting campers' ears at a disciplined
Camp Longhorn following the war. (1946)

The UT swim team travels
to Mexico City for a meet.
(1946)

Tex coaches a group of his swimmers, including gold medalist
Skippy Browning, Olympian Eddie Gilbert, and UT's first
scholarship swimmer, Johnny Crawford. (1950)

Aqua Queen Candidates, 1950

Adolph Kiefer on the cover of the program for the 1939 Aqua Carnival, also known as the Aquacade. The Longhorn doodles on the left would eventually become the logo for Camp Longhorn.

One of Camp Longhorn's founders, Bob Tarlton.

Tex and Pat at the gates of Camp Longhorn.

Campers jumping on the original Blob.

Tex and Pat in 1960.

Pat, Tex, and their five kids – John, Sally, Robby, Nan, and Bill – at their home.

Tex raises the flag at a Texas
Age Group Swimming
meet in 1966.

Camp Longhorn Indian Springs, shortly after its founding in 1975.

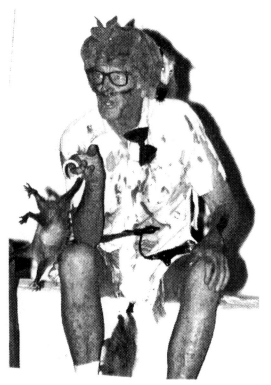

Tex as animal expert
"Dr. Schwartz" at campfire.

A group of the founders – Bob Tarlton, Tex, Dr. Joe Shepperd, Pat, and Frank "Zark" Withers – at the 50th anniversary of Camp Longhorn.

Tex (left) and his age-85+ relay team.

Tex giving his "attawaytogo" hand sign as he receives one of his many Masters swimming medals.

Tex wearing goggles and nose clips during his speech at the International Swimming Hall of Fame.

Tex and Pat with then-Governor George W. Bush.

Adolph Kiefer, Jane Dillard, Tex, and Pat at the
International Swimming Hall of Fame.

Speaking at Church Mountain.

Tex at the dedication of the
Tex Robertson Natatorium
in Burnet, Texas.

He often carried an animal or two with him wherever he went.

Tex and campers feeding his pigeons.

Tex on Church Mountain, holding his hands in the shape of a heart to the sky.

Tex (submerged) and Pat.

BOOK 4

POLITICAL BULLDOG
TEX AND POLITICS

10

Chapter

Attack, attack, attack, attack, but always with humor. I never
saw him get angry at anyone. He'd say: "They just don't see it
the way it's supposed to be, so I'm going to stay with it until
they understand how it's really supposed to be, because I'm
right and you're not." That was his way. He was a bulldog.
If he saw something and he thought it should be a certain
way he would continue, he'd write letters, he would promote,
recruit, he'd do anything he could.

-Tex's son, Robby

The state capitol building in Austin was a second home. Walking
the halls of the seat of the state's government with Tex was to be greeted
with a constant stream of "Hello, Tex – Hello, Tex – Hello, Tex" to
accompany the clatter of dress shoes on marble. The guards at the gate,
the bustling aides and secretaries, the custodial staff, and the legislators all
knew him. More important, they knew he wasn't going away until he got
what he wanted.

"There was no giving up," his daughter Nan said. "'No' was not an
answer to him. I'd go with him to the capitol and if someone wasn't going
to see him or didn't have time to see him or didn't want to listen, he would
walk those halls and hand out those candy cigars of his and eventually
they would give in and listen to what he had to say. We'd spend all day
there. I was exhausted. And he'd go back the next day. It was amazing."

Senator Rudolph Weinert and LCRA manager Max Starcke
were not Tex's only friends in the state government. Any time there was
a legal issue to be tackled, a coalition of people organized by Tex would
suddenly appear. He always had the ear of someone of influence in Austin
and, more important, would make sure that their kids went to Camp
Longhorn. Once the camp gained size and momentum, Tex approached
lawmakers and industry leaders from around the state. One of those
businessmen was a Midland oilman named George H.W. Bush, who sent

his sons George, Jeb, and Neil to Camp Longhorn.

"I came to Camp Longhorn from Midland, Texas, in the mid-50s," George W. Bush said. "We were in a drought in Midland, Texas. I remember how wonderful Inks Lake looked when I first saw it. 'There actually is water,' I said to myself."

Along with the friends he made at camp – including some future Yale classmates – Bush stayed in contact with people associated with Camp Longhorn, especially considering he wasn't the only Texas politician to attend.

"I know a lot of people who went to Camp Longhorn," Bush said. "There's a certain camaraderie with Camp Longhorn people whether they were in your cabin or not."

While he attended, his father would come visit the camp and meet with Tex. The V-Day visits went well, even when the elder Bush once ended up in the lake in his clothes. As Bill Johnson told it:

> George [H.W.] Bush came to see little George SCUBA dive.
> So Mike Holland was driving the riff-raft [a mobile dock
> with an outboard motor]. We used various methods to make
> it float and we had two wing tanks – they looked like bombs
> and they had a bung hole at the top and that didn't matter
> except that Mike Holland overloaded the riff-raft. People kept
> jumping on, including George; they want to see where the
> Boys were out diving. Water started going into the holes in
> the top of the tanks and in the middle of the lake the deck of
> the riff-raft sunk to right on the water level. I'm standing on
> the shore and it looked like Bush was walking on the water.
> What a picture that would have been, publicity-wise. Who
> says George Bush can't walk on water?

The Bushes became legacy campers, with both of George W. Bush's daughters attending Camp Longhorn, as did the daughter of Rick Perry, who succeeded Bush as Governor of Texas when he became president.

"Laura and I were thrilled to send (Jenna and Barbara)," Bush said, "particularly during the teenage years when there's a lot of swirling hormones that send contradictory signals to children. And in the age of

TV, which sends a lot of conflicting signals, it's wonderful to have them go to Camp Longhorn. It's such a wholesome experience. We're really pleased they enjoy Camp Longhorn as much as I did."

Through his camp, Tex established an extensive network of political connections, though many also came from his coaching days. A swimmer for UT in the 1930s, J.J. "Jake" Pickle, was elected to the U.S. House of Representatives in 1963, where he would serve for the next thirty-one years. (During his first term, Pickle became one of only six southern congressmen to vote for the Civil Rights Act of 1964.) When there was national legislation in any way related to camping to be passed – or to be fought – Tex had Pickle's ear.

But the connections most frequently relevant to Tex's concerns were those with the state's Lower Colorado River Authority, starting with his friend Max Starcke, the general manager. It would prove invaluable during his fifty-one-year land feud with "East Germany."

ALBERT MURCHISON didn't make it to the end of his ten-year lease agreement with Tex. He died in 1948, leaving his property on Inks Lake in equal-sized strips to his six sons and one daughter. This meant the specific area of land leased to Camp Longhorn was broken up into four sections owned by four different people.

Looking to take ownership of the land his camp was located on, Tex was able to purchase three of the four pieces of property that covered the lease. But Albert's daughter Lola and her husband Lee McCarty refused to sell. While in negotiation for the final piece of property, Lola suddenly withdrew, saying that she didn't believe her father would have wanted her to sell it. This land had been in the Murchison family for a long time. They originally acquired the property in a land grant predating Texas independence. The problem for Tex was that Lola's thirty-eight acres cut through one side of Camp Longhorn, separating the boys cabins from the swim bay.

Initially campers would walk directly to swim bay, but that stopped when Lee built a barbed wire fence down to the water's edge, effectively bifurcating Camp Longhorn. Campers and counselors began calling the property "East Germany," with Boys Swim Bay "trapped behind enemy lines."

Tex's seemingly ideal spot on Inks Lake had been split in two.

"I was distressed and for the first time my dream was a nightmare," Tex wrote in a 2005 letter to LCRA manager Joe Beal, retelling the story. "I advertised in the Austin newspaper, the camp was for sale."

Camp Longhorn has since become one of the largest camps in the nation, but in the early 1950s Tex came very close to selling his beloved camp.

He did not, because a friend from his coaching days at UT came to the rescue. Joe Greenhill became friends with Tex while he was attending the University of Texas Law School in the late '30s and, like Tex, served as an officer in the Navy during World War II. After his return from the war, Greenhill was named First Assistant Attorney General of Texas, a position that would put him in the middle of one of the biggest civil rights cases in Texas history.

Soon after being named to his office, the state asked Greenhill to defend Texas in a U.S. Supreme Court case brought by Heman Sweatt, a black man who sought admission to the University of Texas Law School. At the time, no law school in the state of Texas would accept "Negro" students, so Sweatt sued. In response, the state district court in Travis County initially ordered a six month continuance to allow for the passing of Texas State Senate Bill 140 to establish "Texas State University for Negroes" in Houston, which would later be renamed Texas Southern University.

This was still eight years before *Brown v. Board of Education.* The Travis County court told Sweatt that a "separate but equal" facility had been created and he would not be allowed to attend UT Law. Sweatt and the NAACP appealed and eventually the case reached the U.S. Supreme Court.

As the state's counsel, it was Greenhill's responsibility to represent the UT Law School. This put him in a difficult situation. Greenhill maintained that throughout his life he was "no segregationist," but he decided to go forward with defending the state's position because it was "the law and it was my job." His opponent was NAACP lead counsel and future Supreme Court Justice Thurgood Marshall.

Greenhill, much to his own relief, was not successful. Sweatt won his four-year fight in a unanimous decision after Marshall successfully showed that the facilities at the single black law school were woefully unequal; one of many precedents that would lead to segregated facilities being declared inherently and intolerantly unequal in *Brown v. Board.*

Texas Southern University's law school is now known as the Thurgood Marshall School of Law. The courthouse in which Sweatt was first told he would have to attend a segregated law school is now called the Heman Marion Sweatt Travis County Courthouse.

Following the case, Greenhill and Marshall became good friends. In 1954, Greenhill stood with Marshall when the verdict was handed down in *Brown v. Board of Education.* Greenhill was the first to congratulate Marshall and in celebration Marshall picked up Greenhill's son, Joe, and ran up and down the Supreme Court's halls.

In 1957, shortly before Greenhill would be named to the Supreme Court of Texas, he heard of his friend Tex's legal trouble and offered to take up the case. Greenhill took a break from state and national litigation to represent Tex's side in a land feud in Llano County court. Greenhill was joined by Charles Herring, a state senator and former U.S. attorney, who would also argue for Tex.

Tex sued to have the McCartys' barbed wire fence moved off the waterline to allow for passage. Both sides wished to go to court anyway, since by this point Bill Johnson had angrily taken matters into his own hands and pulled down a section of the McCartys' fence with a tractor.

Sim Gideon, who had replaced Starcke as LCRA general manager and was also a friend of Tex, served as the primary witness for Greenhill. Gideon noted that a property owner can't build a fence to the water's edge since all lakefront land below an elevation of 890 is owned by the LCRA. Judge Tommy Ferguson ruled in Tex's favor. All fencing below 890 had to come down, giving campers plenty of room to walk around the McCartys' property.

"(Greenhill) walked into the courtroom and turned that country lawyer inside-out," Robby said. "The judge was not about to rule against Greenhill."

Angry at the decision, Lee leased part of the property to Karl Pearl's Fishing Camp, which failed after less than a year when Pearl sued McCarty for not keeping Camp Longhorn from using half of the bay and McCarty sued Pearl in turn for not making a payment on the lease. Pearl shut down his camp, leaving five unused cabins behind. Undeterred, Lee did his best to be in Camp Longhorn's way, in part by putting forty head of cattle on the land. But much of it was simply through fence location. Over the years each side called for multiple surveys that would move the property line back and forth, as if fighting for inches in a trench war.

After Lee's death in 1973, his son Lee, Jr., took up his father's banner, replacing the original barbed wire fence with an eight-foot wooden wall. (The location of this wall, including how close it could be to the water was again arbitrated in court.) Lee, Jr., then took the matter a step further, attempting to remove Camp Longhorn's access to the waterfront by submitting an application to the LCRA to build a marina.

The LCRA rejected his application as "incomplete plans." This caused the McCartys to go public with their complaints, writing to every local paper with criticism of Tex, Camp Longhorn, and the LCRA. Taking his actions to yet another level, Lee began walking the fence line with a rifle and firing it into the air when campers would approach. Concerned for the well-being of the children attending camp, a Llano County sheriff was posted at edge of the McCarty property to prevent Lee, Jr., from firing his rifle.

Years passed. More surveys were made by each side. Tex made more offers to purchase or lease the land. All were refused. Lola lived to the age of 102, refusing to sell or rent, even with a friend of hers, former Detroit Lions lineman Ox Emerson, trying for years to convince her to sell the property to Tex. (Coincidentally, Emerson was a cousin of Tex via his mother, Nancy Robertson née Emerson.) Lee, Jr., died in 1998, and there was still no deal.

At this point Tex was dealing with the great-grandchildren of the man who originally leased him ten acres for ten dollars. But it was a feud over land, not between families. Not all of the Murchisons opposed Tex. Those who sold him their sections of the land remained happy with the sale.

"Tex got along great with some of the Murchison family and some of the Murchison family were horses' rears. Just the way it was," said Tex's son John.

Ox continued his friendship with the next generation of McCartys and tried to convince Lee McCarty III and Debbie Slangal until he became ill and died in November of 1998. Lee III refused and told

Camp Longhorn to stay off the shoreline. Tex wrote a letter asserting the long-time established right to traverse the shore and offered to buy just the half-acre closest to the shore for $25,000 and $100,000 for the rest of the property. Lee responded by suing the LCRA for allowing campers in front of his property. The LCRA provided a mediator, and Tex's children, who were on the Camp Longhorn board of directors, met four times with the McCartys, but each meeting was fruitless.

Another, larger, fence was built.

Lee then advertised his property, looking to sell it as a marina and housing project. According to Gardner Parker, Tex's longtime financial adviser, the McCartys got no real offers. Camp Longhorn was the only buyer. The residents of nearby Inks Lake Village became concerned about the possibility of a housing project and voted to restrict use of their entrance. Boxed in and out of options, Lee McCarty III began to bargain. McCarty accepted Parker's offer and the rest of the board approved.

Fifty-one years after Albert Murchison died and the land split first occurred, Tex officially bought the McCarty property on the first day of camp. A massive celebration was held with all of Camp Longhorn present for the "tearing down of the wall." After the wall fell, Pat drove a golf cart across the wreckage and planted a flag in the middle of "East Germany" and proclaimed that it was now "West Camp Longhorn."

Tex enjoyed himself at the festivities, though he still grumbled that he paid too much.

GREENHILL WAS CHIEF JUSTICE OF THE TEXAS SUPREME COURT and a man who had been involved in one of the U.S. Supreme Court's most important civil rights cases. Charles Herring had been appointed a U.S. attorney by President Truman and was a sitting state senator. They both argued for Tex in local court over a fence.

"It was always something like that. Greenhill would do whatever (Tex) asked him to," Robby said. "That's what's bizarre – the kinds of things he would ask people to do and they'd go, 'Oh, sure.'"

He had plenty of friends in the LCRA, even if he wasn't always on the best terms with the agency. For all the headaches the organization went through during the East Germany land feud and his standoffs with LCRA over water rights, in 1999 Tex was inducted into the Lower Colorado River Authority Walk of Honor. He grew his political connections throughout his life and he was not shy about using them.

"Dan Boren, a (U.S.) Representative from Oklahoma, he's a camper," Robby said. "He proposed to his wife up here on Church Mountain. Need a favor? Call Dan. Need a favor? Call Kay Bailey (Hutchison). Hey, George (Bush)? Can you help us? He always had a foot in the door and wasn't bashful about it either."

However, for all his national connections, his focus was on local politics. He cared little for the goings on in Washington, D.C., and was happy to apply his influence to state and county matters.

That changed in 1972 due to Mitch Kurman and Senator Abraham Ribicoff.

In 1965, Kurman's son David died at the age of fifteen in a whitewater canoe accident on a YMCA-sponsored trip in Maine. David's family said the boy did not have a life jacket and the group used canoes with flat hulls designed for lakes, not rivers, and a counselor had ignored a forest ranger's warning not to take that particular branch of the Penobscot River. After receiving a $30,000 settlement, Kurman, a Connecticut-based furniture salesman, became a safety regulations advocate. Lobbying efforts throughout New England by Kurman resulted in safety regulations laws passed in Connecticut, Maine, New York, and New Jersey, and his son's death was the driving force behind the Federal Boat Safety Act of 1971.

Through Kurman's efforts a number of new safety regulations were on the books, but his primary goal during the entire process was a national camp safety bill. In 1972, Senator Abraham Ribicoff of Connecticut got the Senate to pass a bill establishing federally mandated safety standards for camps. This meant that summer camps, such as Camp Longhorn, would be regulated at the federal level as opposed to the state level, an idea Tex vehemently opposed.

With the bill passed in the Senate and a vote approaching in the House, Tex contacted his closest friend in Congress, former UT swimmer Jake Pickle, and asked him to block the bill's passage by any means necessary. Pickle successfully delayed the bill by getting the House to agree to a study by the Department of Health, Education, and Welfare on the safety records of camps around the country. When the study came back saying that campers were on average safer at camp than they were at home or at school, momentum for federal regulation died. In addition, Tex's lobbying efforts went beyond Pickle. Rather than going to Washington alone, he had constructed an organization to fight passage of the bill: Camping Association for Mutual Progress.

"Tex went to Jake and concurrently with that was the formation of CAMP, which was originally formed with Tex and Larry Graham (Camp La Junta), Spike White (Camp Kanakuk), Carl Hawkins (Camp Rio Vista), and Si Ragsdale (Camp Stewart) to battle this youth camp safety act," John said.

Many more youth camps soon signed on. One of Tex's most impressive skills was his ability to organize people. When Ribicoff first proposed his bill in the Senate, Tex was on the phone with the directors of other camps the next day.

He also created an organization that would continue to grow, even after his regulation fight in Washington. Rather than dissolve CAMP after its original goal was accomplished, Tex then used it to strengthen connections between summer camps.

"That got the camps to open the doors to each other," Bill Johnson said. "We found out that rather than protect our secrets, if we could share them and make better camps, that it would help us all. That's the same theory that if we helped Baylor, Rice, and SMU get good coaches then we'll have better competition and it'll make our swimmers better."

Using the organization to influence policy, Tex stayed in the middle of its operations. For sixteen years he printed a small newspaper, *CAMP News*, and wrote most of its articles. Knowing that federal regulation would eventually come up again, Tex and CAMP then turned around and got the state of Texas to pass its own set of safety standards for summer camps.

The front page of a 1973 issue of *CAMP News* features a picture of Tex dressed in a pinstripe suit – standing out from the other, more conservatively dressed, attendees – next to Governor Dolph Briscoe as he signed a bill giving the State Department of Health the responsibility to provide safety and health guidelines for Texas camps. As Tex wrote in the adjoining article: "This new law was requested by the Camping Association for Mutual Progress representing all types of youth camps in Texas to prove their claim of excellent health and safety records thereby helping to prevent unneeded federal legislation being threatened in Washington."

Several other states followed suit. State-level regulation of camps was quickly becoming a trend.

Kurman was undeterred. He again convinced a congressman, this time Representative Dominick Daniels of New Jersey, to introduce a national camp safety bill. In May and June of 1974, a House subcommittee held hearings on H.R. 1486, a bill "to provide for the development and implementation of programs for youth camp safety." The pages of a transcript of the hearings in Tex's office are filled with his notes and comments on the proceedings.

"We have discovered that there is often a credibility gap between camp literature and the actual facts relating to whether or not a camp is a safe place for youngsters," Daniels said at the hearing. This quote in Tex's copy of the transcript is covered with a large question mark. There is also an arrow pointing at the paragraph from where Tex wrote, "Maybe you're wrong – Jus maybe."

Tex was also called out in the hearings for his efforts to stop the bill. During the proceedings, Daniels' congressional colleague, Peter Peyser of New York, held aloft the above-quoted copy of *CAMP News*:

> I have just received a copy of a newspaper called "CAMP News," which is published in Burnett, Tex. [sic], and this paper points out the results of this survey, and incidentally, Texas was one of the States that gave us the major, in fact, led the opposition in defeating this legislation, and here they say, "HEW [Department of Health, Education, and Welfare] results show we don't need any Federal regulations on camp safety." ...And I see the comment involved here is that they hope that we get off the issue now and let the States take care of it themselves. Believe me, we are not going to get off the issue and we are going to stay with it.

Next to this, Tex wrote the word: "propaganda."

Kurman testified using anecdotal evidence of injuries and fatalities that had occurred at camps throughout the country. But Dr. Kenneth Cook, vice president of the research corporation that had been contracted by the House to study camp safety, testified that federal regulation was not necessary because "responsible agencies and organizations and camp operators have for years been improving their own rules and regulations to protect the health and safety of campers." In an exchange with Representative Ronald Sarasin of Connecticut, Cook argued that aid to the states was preferable:

> Dr. COOK. Let me say, if you were going to have Federal legislation, I would assume that the best kind of legislation to have would be the kind that you are proposing, aid to the States, and we would suggest that as Dr. [John J.] Kirk and the National Safety Council did yesterday, for example, that there be a provision for education. We would go further and suggest that aid for education should be directed to camp operators and directed to counselors...
> Mr. SARASIN. The legislation proposed would provide for minimum safeguards and yet in your conclusion, you are saying that if the Federal Government became involved, the answer would be "no, we would not see a significant reduction in illness and injuries"?
> Dr. COOK. Yes, I believe that in terms of percentages, you already have a fairly decent kind of picture and, therefore, any improvement can only be a very small one over that. You know, it is essentially, if you start at 98 percent of perfection, then, you can only get up 2 more percent.

Along with CAMP, Kurman also suspected the Boy Scouts of America as having a hand in blocking his repeated attempts to create national safety regulations, as quoted in the June 16, 1975, issue of *People Magazine*:

> Part of the reason, Kurman suspects, is that the Boy Scouts, while paying lip service to the ideal of safety, have opposed any interference in their camping domain. "I'm convinced," he fumes, "that if they really wanted that law, there wouldn't be five votes in the damned Congress against it." (The Boy Scouts deny Kurman's suspicions.) Earlier this year a bill

was passed by the House of Representatives and is expected to come up in the Senate soon, but even if approved there it faces a possible presidential veto.

The bill died in the Senate. But even if a law had reached the President's desk, it would likely have been vetoed. The U.S. President in 1975 was Tex's old Michigan roommate, Gerald Ford.

ONE OF THE TOUGHEST PARTS of Tex's fight with Kurman is he didn't disagree with the main points of his opponent. In Tex's mind, it was a matter of state-level vs. federal-level regulation. He respected Kurman and his desire for a safer environment for campers.

Tex, for his part, had doubts about his own position, though he never showed it outwardly. When Tex fought for something, he did so without hesitation and without reserve. But his old copy of *CAMP News* with the picture of himself and Governor Biscoe signing a state safety bill in 1973 contains a comment from Tex written in pencil. Dated as April of 1997, it simply reads: "Did we do the right thing?" April of 1997 was around the time Tex was writing his own eulogy and reflecting on his life. (The lengthy self-penned eulogy would stay on the shelf for a while; Tex lived another decade after writing it.)

But he was largely vindicated by the safety record at youth camps in Texas, especially at his own. The most serious injury of a Camp Longhorn camper did not occur at Camp Longhorn.

In June of 1999, while on a half-day trip to nearby Longhorn Caverns, a van driven by a camp counselor rolled over on Park Road 4. There were eleven campers in the van. Ten escaped serious injury, but one suffered head and neck injuries that resulted in some paralysis and a lengthy recovery.

In a letter to parents of campers, Tex wrote: "With 58 years of operation, an average camper stay is 4.5 years, and the average length of term is 20 days, which equals 6.5 million camper days without an accident like we just experienced, but when it comes to taking care of your child, 1 is too many." Tex then canceled all future camper trips.

Even more than camp safety, the political issue that would most frequently draw his attention was the possibility of year-round school in Texas, which would have delivered a devastating economic blow to summer camps. In addition, Tex passionately defended the value of summer camp in a child's life, often quipping that "school shouldn't get in the way of a kid's education."

"The one issue that I remember specifically that would draw him (to the state capitol building) was year-round school," said his daughter Nan. "He built, with several senators, a coalition that ended that. From there he fought to legislate a start-date for schools. When year-round school was defeated, some schools came back with the idea that they'd start earlier and earlier, some reaching back as far as late July. Here comes the coalition again."

His ability to quickly create a coalition of people allowed him to successfully fight year-round school. This ability came from the constant contact he kept with those who could potentially help him in the future. Tex's office at Camp Longhorn contains piles of hand-written notes from national politicians, such as George H.W. Bush, George W. Bush, Kay Bailey Hutchinson, and Gerald Ford, as well as an array of relevant state politicians. Many were responses to the steady stream of letters Tex had going out to his contacts in power.

When, as Governor of Texas, George W. Bush was asked if he frequently got notes from Tex, Bush responded: "Do I ever, particularly any issue that involves the Colorado River Authority. He's quite anxious to make his opinion known. He is a man who does not hold back. For that I'm grateful. It's good to have somebody straight forward."

FOR ALL OF HIS MANEUVERING, organizing, and lobbying, laws that related to camps encompassed the whole of Tex Robertson's involvement in politics.

He typically supported Republicans, but only because the Republican Party in Texas tended to match up with him on the select few issues he cared about. Due to the effectiveness of his influence, two of the most powerful members of the G.O.P. came to Tex to urge him to seek election to public office and offered a significant amount of financial support. Anne Armstrong was Co-chairman of the Republican National

Committee and in 1972 became the first woman from either major party to keynote at the national convention. John Tower was first Republican Senator from the state of Texas since Reconstruction. Both traveled to Burnet to meet with Tex.

"They wanted Tex to run for office," Bill Johnson said. "Anne Armstrong, John Tower, and a bunch of others came to ask him to run for something, anything, and he said no. He said he was doing what he was trained and destined to do. That was a hard group to say no to."

Given his ability to influence, maneuver, motivate, organize, and mobilize, Tex could have been a dangerously powerful politician. But he turned down an offer from the Republican Party of support for a major office and instead ran for Burnet school board. He didn't care about political parties; Jake Pickle was a Democrat. All he would lobby for was his camp, and he did so relentlessly.

"I shudder to think if Tex would have chosen politics instead of camp life," Cactus Pryor said. "But he'd have gotten things done."

Chapter

Zark, Bob Tarlton, and Bill and Mary Francis Johnson sat in the Camp Longhorn office, discussing the upcoming summer session. It was the late '50s. Tex was no longer coaching and the girls camp was up and running.

Suddenly Tex flung open the door and interrupted the conversation by dropping a large map of Texas on the table with a flourish. There were lines drawn on the map, splitting the state into different regions.

"Let's organize swimming in Texas," he said. "I propose we divide up into seven districts."

There was very little youth competitive swimming in Texas. It's why when Tex was head coach of the Longhorns, his swimmers had either taught themselves, like Hondo Crouch, or were from another part of the country, like Adolph Kiefer.

To build a base of talent in the state, Tex created another of his acronym-bearing organizations: Texas Age Group Swimming, or TAGS. The state would be divided into seven different regions and the winner of each region would advance to a state meet. The regional system was specifically designed to spread interest in the sport to as many locations as possible.

"If you had a state meet and you had eight lanes and you had the eight fastest swimmers in the state, they'd all be from Houston," Bill Johnson said. "They were further along. His idea was that you have to get the people from Pecos, Texas, and Clarendon up in the Panhandle and El Paso and Brownsville. You have to get them involved sooner or later, so why not start off and have districts? Then you have your big meets in the head towns in these districts."

Tex got many of his employees at Camp Longhorn involved in his side project. Mary became his "leg-man," as Bill put it, ordering jackets, patches, and ribbons. Tex, while on the road recruiting Camp Longhorn campers, would stop at swimming centers across the state to set up the local swim meets. He contacted coaches Art Adamson at Texas A&M and Hank Chapman at Texas and set up a TAGS championship meet that would alternate between College Station and Austin. He furnished information for prospective coaches, encouraged coaches of other sports to start swim teams at their high schools, and spoke with Texas colleges from outside the Southwest Conference about starting swim programs. Once Tex had a group of potential coaches together, he organized them into the Texas Interscholastic Swimming Coaches Association, or TISCA.

Tex loved acronyms. He also loved the contacts his various organizations would create and the impressive-appearing letterhead it would give him. Some of his organizations were far-reaching political committees; others were just a few people. But Tex, ever the artist of persuasion, understood the legitimacy a letterhead could give him.

A state or national representative wouldn't just be hearing from a business owner named Tex Robertson. He or she was hearing from Camping Association for Mutual Progress, effectively the entire industry within the region. Even the school board in Burnet, Texas, received letters from COBS (Citizens Of Burnet Schools), as opposed to a single parent.

Tex also made use of his former swimmers. Along with encouraging each to become a swim coach, he got several directly involved in his new organizations. Wally Pryor, the original voice of the Aqua Carnival, was Tex's first meet director. Wally Hoffrichter, the Michigan transplant who had roomed with Hondo Crouch, became the first president of both TAGS and TISCA. Both organizations were tied together by *Splash News*, yet another newspaper printed at Camp Longhorn, with Mary Johnson serving as editor and photographer. From 1962 to 1973, Tex wrote three issues of *Splash* a year and sent it to every coach and school that would take it.

There was plenty of confusion at the beginning, but by 1963 Tex had created the first TAGS state championship, the first high school girls swimming meet in Texas, and the first state college meet for non-Southwest Conference schools.

"Tex played a bigger part in swimming in this state than most people know," said UT swimming coach Eddie Reese. "The battles he fought, those were many."

By 1968 TAGS was out of the development stage and running, holding swim meets across the state. But it was still a separate organization from high schools. The University Interscholastic League, which organizes all official high school sports in Texas, did not recognize swimming as a varsity sport. Tex applied a great deal of pressure to the UIL, calling in favors from his various political connections. It was the same as his coaching days at UT, when he fought a constant battle with administration forces for each resource and scholarship.

"Texas, as you know, it's a football state," Johnson said. "Swimming had to make an inroad by fighting, by cheating, by stealing, by everything in order to get your foot in the door."

In 1969 swimming officially became a UIL sport. Though Tex's goal of recognized high school swim teams was accomplished, TAGS continues to hold swim meets and provide competition for youth swimmers in Texas. In addition, there were more fights to be had with the University Interscholastic League, such as how the sport was operated and how the dates were arranged, both for meets and for collegiate visits.

"I took over his UIL fight," Reese said. "When I first got here (in 1979), the UIL would not let an athlete visit a college until their season was over. Swimmers finish early March. Everybody had already made up their mind by then. Slowly I got them to go to December, then finally they let them visit anytime they want. They were trying to keep everybody the same, and everybody's not the same. Luckily I played racquetball with (former UIL director) Bailey (Marshall). He's married to Becky. Becky was a trainer here and played racquetball. I gave her all of my arguments. Women win arguments. Men don't win arguments. They finally changed it for the betterment of the athlete."

Tex kept a fresh rotation of people running his organizations, even if they didn't realize what they were going to be doing. Former UT swimmer Dotson Smith ran the Austin Aquatic Club and at Tex's invitation would bring his swimmers out to Camp Longhorn for competition. Tex slowly got Smith more and more involved with TAGS and TISCA. Within a couple years Smith was the new president of TAGS. He wasn't quite sure how it happened:

(Tex) got me in more trouble. He'd hand some job off to me, as president of TAGS, something I didn't know beans about. All of a sudden he'd have me working. That was the biggest thing about Tex. He got you involved and you didn't realize it until it was too late. All of a sudden you're trying to build Noah's Ark without any wood. He was the Tom Sawyer of swimming. "Here's a paint brush and I'm not going to let you do this. Ok, here you try it." Just like his camp. Every time I went out to camp there was something new and I thought, oh, that's the way it's supposed to be. You figure out something new, like my swimming camp. But everything that was done with TAGS or TISCA or anything else had Tex's name on it. It didn't really dawn on me, but everything I injected into the program, it had Tex's name over it. But you'd just keep plugging away because he'd keep telling you you can. "Well Tex, I can't do that." "Sure you can. Attawaytogo."

Tex was like that with everyone. One day he walked into the office at Camp Longhorn and said to Mary Johnson, "Hey we're going to a swim meet." Mary replied, "That's great," and they both got in Tex's car. When they arrived at the swim meet, Tex said, "Oh by the way, you're the meet director."

Mary was confused. "I don't know what that means."

"It means you're the meet director," Tex said. "Start directing."

Having organized a great deal of TAGS, Mary did a fine job as meet director, but she didn't know she was going to be doing the job until she got there.

That's how it was with Tex. He'd just ask you to come with him. By the day's end you're trying to build Noah's Ark without any wood.

MOST OF WHAT TEX DESIRED to create he created. His swimming career, his coaching career, and his camp all came about by his force of will. One of the few things he wanted to create that never occurred was Camp Longhorn Mexico.

Tex loved Mexico. He spent a great deal of time in the country during his life. He and Pat honeymooned in Mexico and took almost all of their vacations there. While he was the coach at UT, Tex would take his swim teams south of the border for dual meets with local teams and Aqua Carnival performances. More so, he wanted to establish youth swimming in Mexico nearly as much as he wanted to in Texas.

"Tex was a missionary for swimming and here was a fertile ground," Bill Johnson said. "The leaders in swimming were good people and they sent their sons to camp. Pepe Santabañez, his father was a good backer of swimming. He was an Olympic swimmer in Mexico. I still have his notes from water polo. 'When the referee isn't looking, put your foot in the man's suit and send him to the bottom and hold him there.' He was fun, and very fun for the kids. Kids like to horse around."

His strongest push to develop youth swimming in Mexico came shortly after the creation of TAGS. Following the second state championship meet in 1964, Tex brought the top TAGS swimmers to Mexico City for a competition he had arranged with the top youth swimmers in Mexico.

The Texas-Mexico Games were born. The next year Tex reciprocated by inviting the top swimmers in Mexico to come to Austin. It being the spring and Camp Longhorn not in session, Tex offered to give lodging to Mexico's swimmers at his camp. As Johnson wrote in his book, *My Memories of Camp Longhorn*:

> The following year the Mexican Age Group Swimmers came to the big meet in Austin and stayed at Camp Longhorn. Our staff, including new resident staff man G.P. Parker, was ready, we thought, for the invasion. A Mexican team "on vacation" didn't really care about schedules, rules, or sanity, but just came to have fun. Parents and swimmers drove every boat, jeep, golf cart, or truck until the vehicles died or ran out of gas. I have never seen G.P. as frustrated, trying to control people in English who chose to understand only Spanish. Hondo Crouch tried to "help" one "very relaxed" parent start a jeep on the girls baseball field. Turning the toggle switch (which replaced the key which would get lost) to OFF he ran the battery down and the jeep stayed put for 3 days, in safety. Good thinking, Hondo.

One of the reasons Tex was successful in building excitement in Mexico about swimming was the approaching 1968 Summer Olympics in Mexico City. The Texas-Mexico games ran for four years ('64 in Mexico

City, '65 in Austin, '66 in Mexico City, and '67 in Midland) leading up to the Olympics.

For the 1968 games, Tex was selected by the IOC as a stroke judge, where he watched the U.S. take home twenty-one gold medals in swimming (the next closest was Australia with three) and fifty-two swimming medals overall (the next closest was again Australia with eight). Mexico had one gold medalist, Felipe Muñoz, who won the 200-meter breaststroke. After the Olympics, Muñoz committed to the University of Texas and was an All-American for the Longhorns in 1972.

During his travels in Mexico, Tex searched coastal cities for the right location for Camp Longhorn Mexico. He visited Mazatlán, Manzanillo, Las Estacas, Zihuatanejo, Isla Mujeres, San Blas, and Puerto Marques. With Mexican school vacations occurring from December to February, Tex would be able to bring equipment and staff from the camp on Inks Lake and be able to live in Mexico during the winter while running his second camp.

That plan fell apart when Mexico lined up its school vacations to match those in the United States. However, though he could still have a summer camp in Mexico, during his search for a location Tex had become increasingly concerned about land rights and governmental stability. Down south he continued to promote swimming, but Camp Longhorn Mexico was no longer in his plans.

It was one of the few institutions he wanted to create and never did.

AS EARLY AS THE 1950s Tex was organizing free swim classes for the local kids in Burnet. He would meet them at the state park across Inks Lake from his camp and teach both basic swimming and advanced techniques to the more experienced kids. It was staffed by Camp Longhorn counselors who weren't paid. (Tex told them it was "practice" for when the paying campers arrived.) Soon after he began formulating his plan to build a public swimming pool for the town.

Tex loved spreading the skill of swimming and he loved children, but the Burnet pool – and most of the other improvements he brought to Burnet – came about primarily out of a love of his own children.

"Anything in Burnet seemed created for us," said his son Robby. "We were going to swim, and the only way he knew of to make us swim, which he'd learned with Johnny more than anything, is you've got to have friends. If you're going to have friends, you've got to make a program. If you're going to have a program, you might as well have a good program. So he started the swim team in Burnet."

After successfully getting a pool built in Burnet in 1963, he began hosting a yearly Aqua Carnival to raise money for the local swim team, utilizing many of the same tricks he used in the Aqua Carnival at the University of Texas. (For example, he did the bulkhead trick with a pair of twins, making it appear as if a single swimmer was smashing a record.) The Burnet pool also hosted the small high school state swimming championships for thirty years. In addition, the first girls' high school and college state championship meets were held in Burnet's pool in 1968.

The pool was one of several public institutions created in Burnet because of Tex.

"Kids needed something to do, so he bought the old town club and created the community center," Robby said. "He saw some great people in town who weren't getting recognition, so he created the Honor Citizen Award. He created another group, COBS, Citizens of Burnet Schools, and led a big campaign to improve the schools in Burnet, because they weren't good enough for us. What he did for us as a family was what he did for everybody else. It just brought everybody else along."

He borrowed the idea of the Rattlesnake Round-Up from his hometown of Sweetwater and picked up some extra cash by selling the rattlers the community had gathered to a snake farm in San Marcos. Tex also brought to the festivities his pet gator, Ali, who had grown to nine feet and 217 pounds. Ali's jaws were shut with duct tape and a local woman, "Butch" Allman, wowed the crowd with her alligator wrestling skills.

Tex also supported public institutions in Burnet other than the schools. Lumped in with his personal medical records in his office, Tex kept extensive documentation on the state of local hospitals. He hosted multiple Highland Lakes Medical Center fundraisers to ensure residents got the best medical attention available.

"He was working for our children as well as his and Burnet to get established a better school system and better hospitals," Johnson said. "He led us into one worthwhile project after another – not for his glory, he didn't give a hoot about that, in my opinion. There may be people who don't appreciate him like we do."

Tex saw in his mind the local community he wanted to live in and continually applied pressure to create it. And just like with the larger community of swimming in Texas, his coaching career, and Camp Longhorn, the world that existed in his head would typically become reality.

12

Chapter

"Golly! Just think of the bales of hay I could store in here!"

Tex could only smile at his old friend Hondo as they stood together admiring the newly constructed 880,000-gallon pool on the University of Texas campus. The relationship between the swimmer and coach had been strained at times, especially when Hondo left Camp Longhorn to start a competing camp on nearby Lake LBJ, but through it all they remained friends. They were joined by other former swimmers in 1977 for the opening of the Texas Swim Center, a mammoth structure housing one of the nation's premier pools. It is still considered one of the fastest tanks in the world due to its depth, gutter system, high filtration rate, and lane width.

Tex was the driving force behind its construction.

He left the university in 1950 and in 1965 was elected to the Longhorn Hall of Honor for his accomplishments as a coach. But his impact on Texas swimming had just begun.

In 1968, soon after TAGS was off and running, Tex created WETS, Working Exes for Texas Swimming. Hank Chapman (the diver who replaced Tex as coach), Shorty Alderson (UT's first swim coach), and two hundred other alumni were present for the founding of Tex's latest organization.

Tex, as Tex did, quickly organized people and events for WETS. Due to an increasing time demand on collegiate swimmers, the Aqua Carnival had gone away shortly after Tex's departure from the coaching ranks. After the creation of WETS, the Aqua Carnival became an alumni-operated event to raise money for the program. Wally Pryor, who would serve as president of WETS for thirty-five years, reprised his role as announcer of the Aqua Carnival. Along with getting old-timers to come back for the show, Tex made sure to get a maximum number of alumni to his fundraising WETS banquet.

"To earn the WETS Award you have to show up at the banquet," former UT women's swimming coach Jill Sterkel said. "I think that was

Tex's way of saying, 'Come back. It's important that you come back and you're here and you're a part of things.' It was his philosophy and it was a good one."

Fundraising apparatus in place, Tex set in motion his plan to build his state-of-the-art swim center.

"He was really a promoter to get that all together," Tex's old athletics ally Denton Cooley said. "The result was the best facility of any swimming program that I know."

In 1970 his fifty-meter pool plan was accepted by the UT administration thanks to one of Tex's most influential political connections, Frank Erwin, chairman of the University of Texas regents. Erwin and Tex knew each other during Tex's coaching days. Erwin enrolled at UT the same year that Tex Robertson became the Longhorn swimming coach and both joined the Navy. When Tex returned to coach, Erwin returned to Texas to get his law degree. Shortly after graduating, Erwin became president of the Longhorn Club, which funded the university's first swimming scholarship (split between Skippy Browning and Johnny Crawford). In 1963 Erwin sat on the UT Board of Regents and in 1966 he was named chairman.

Like Tex, he always got what he wanted. Unlike Tex, he typically did so in undiplomatic fashion.

"Erwin was one of these guys that didn't go through the process asking everybody what they thought and taking a vote on it," said Jeff Heller, a former Camp Longhorn camper who is on UT's fundraising Development Board. "If he decides to do something, he did it. He had a lot of enemies, but he had a lot of supporters too."

Frank Erwin was not known as a sympathetic person. When Texas was expanding its football stadium in 1969, about fifty students and non-students climbed into the branches of the pecan and elm trees on nearby Waller Creek to protest the removal of the trees. Erwin showed up on site and ordered the bulldozers to push over the trees with people still in them, telling police officers, "Arrest all the people you have to. Once the trees are down they won't have anything to protest." The machines advanced. Protestors jumped. Police arrested twenty-seven.

Control over projects was paramount to Erwin, saying, "I don't fund anything I can't control." In this case he wanted to control the direction of UT swimming under coach Hank Chapman. Erwin refused to go ahead with plans for the new swimming center unless Texas won a SWC swimming title or got a new coach. It had been a long time since the Horns were conference champions.

One of the reasons Tex had become so heavily involved with UT swimming was because UT was no longer the dominant program he coached. His desire to create tougher competition in the Southwest Conference had worked, but Texas was unable to keep up with that tougher competition. Starting in 1958, Red Barr and his SMU Mustangs won twenty-three consecutive SWC championships. With SMU's streak in full force, a new coach would have to be selected to appease Erwin and ensure the new pool was given the go ahead. Chapman was moved to a non-coaching position in the administration, and a search began.

Tex knew exactly who he wanted. Texas A&M head coach Melvin "Pat" Patterson was a former president of TAGS and a former UT swimmer. Given that the Longhorns hadn't won a championship since Patterson was a swimmer, his arrival was eagerly anticipated.

Erwin's coaching concerns dealt with, WETS could move on to the financial phase of the project. But thanks to Tex's connections donations were not necessary.

"That was paid for with state money," said current Texas men's athletic director DeLoss Dodds. "It wasn't a donated athletic building. It's still technically not an athletics building because it was paid for by available fund money."

Through Jake Pickle in congress, Tex was able to convince the state legislature to fund the project and in 1973 construction began, just five years after WETS was founded. Tex was involved in many of the specifics of the project, but it was Patterson who did most of the designing.

"They traveled to Mexico City; they traveled to Tokyo; they traveled to Montreal to look at swimming pools," Reese said. "Then they went to Munich and decided to base it on that pool."

The Olympia Schwimmhalle in Munich hosted the swimming, diving, and water polo events at the 1972 Summer Olympics. It was heralded as the fastest pool ever built. This proved accurate. During the games, Olympic records were broken in all twenty-nine swimming events and world records were set in twenty events. Mark Spitz won his then-record seven gold medals, setting a world record in all seven events. The

Texas Swim Center was designed based on the Olympia Schwimmhalle, incorporating new advances in swim technology made after the '72 Olympics.

Five years later, Tex, Pat Patterson, Hank Chapman, Hondo Crouch, Wally Pryor, Wally Hoffrichter, Bob Tarlton, Shorty Alderson, Bill Johnson, Johnny Crawford, Eddie Gilbert, and the rest – an assemblage of great swimmers and coaches from the program Tex brought to national prominence – witnessed the opening of the Texas Swim Center.

Making sure that Alderdson (who actually coached the first Texas swim team) got his name somewhere in the building, Tex suggested the Alderson Conference Room. The diving well was named for diver Skippy Browning, Texas' first individual national champion and a Navy pilot who died when his plane crashed.

In thanks to his friend Frank for the help getting the new building constructed, Tex created the Frank Erwin Award to signify outstanding achievements and contributions of individuals to Longhorn swimming and diving. The first recipient was, of course, Frank Erwin.

A few years later Tex received the award he created. That happened a lot with Tex.

PATTERSON WOULD NOT STAY TEXAS' HEAD COACH long enough to see the Longhorns break SMU's streak of conference crowns.

The Longhorns had a top-flight swim center but didn't have the swimmers to fill it. The athletic department was not burdened by the center since the building was funded with state money, but funding of the swim program had not increased to match the facility. After eight years of suggesting, asking, and pleading for adequate program support, head coach and diving coach pay, and scholarships equal to that of SMU, Texas A&M, or any of the top NCAA programs, Patterson told UT officials that he was resigning.

His sudden departure came as a shock. Patterson spent seven of his eight years coaching at Gregory Gym Pool, experiencing only one year of the fruits of his designs for the Texas Swim Center. But without the number of scholarships offered by his competition, it was an upstream swim.

A meeting was called between Patterson and the other WETS directors, Wally Pryor, Hyl Karbach, and Jose Gilbert. And Tex, of course. They formed an unofficial coaches search committee, and Patterson provided them with a list of recommendations for his replacement. However, there was one name Patterson had circled as his top choice: Eddie Reese of Auburn.

Reese was responsible for the fastest program turnaround in the country. When he took over at Auburn in 1972, he inherited a team that had not qualified a single swimmer for the finals or even consolation finals of the Southeastern Conference Championships during the previous season. Six years later, the Tigers had finished in the top ten nationally for four consecutive seasons, culminating in a second-place finish in 1978.

Texas athletic director Darrell Royal called Reese and made his offer. Reese agreed to come to Austin and take a look:

It was February when they called me and we'd moved into our new house at Halloween. It was our dream house. Two and a quarter acres that ran into a five acre pond. I had to break ice sometimes to catch fish but I always caught fish. Even before we got into the house, I said, 'Don't get too settled in the house. We're going to Texas.' It was 100 percent kidding, because I'd never looked to leave anywhere. I never wanted to be an Olympic coach, never worried about winning NCAAs. I wanted to work hard and get people to go faster.

We finish the NCAAs that year; we were second. After that was over, I visited Texas. I came in on a Sunday about one or two in the afternoon, Darrell Royal picked me up. I said, "Y'all are pretty serious about this aren't you?" He said, "Yeah, why do you ask?" I said, "Wouldn't you rather be on the golf course?" He said, "Without a doubt." He showed me around, took me to Cisco's (Restaurant and Bakery), East Sixth. The pool and Cisco's cemented it.

But I actually turned the job down the first time because they offered me the same salary I was making at Auburn. I'd done that going from Florida to Auburn. I had two daughters and I wasn't going to do that. I turned them down and Darrell Royal went back to Don Gambril, who was my mentor and the Alabama coach at the time. "Who else do we go get?" He said, "Go get Eddie. Do whatever it takes." That was back when Texas had two sports: football and spring football. It was a leap of faith for them to do it and come through with what they needed for the program to make it grow like it grows.

Royal was initially hesitant to give a swimming coach a significant salary. But Patterson and the WETS directors were certain Reese was the man for the job.

"Tex was a big part of that because he was seeing everybody from the governor to Darrell on it," Reese said. "If he got a no from Darrell, then he'd go to the governor."

Reese got to winning in a hurry. As his assistant coach, Kris Kubik, explained:

The first year we were here, the spring of 1979, the conference meet was held at our pool and SMU had won that unbelievable amount of times in a row. Tex was in the stands. When we finished the free relay, which completes the meet, and SMU's about to pick up their trophy, the team wanted to go to the locker room and Eddie said, "No, I want you to stay out here. I want you to listen to them cheer, because I don't want you ever to hear that cheer again." They did a cheer which was a countdown from the beginning of their conference streak all the way to 1979. Then Texas won from '80 all the way through the end of the Southwest Conference and now has won every Big 12 championship. Kind of neat Tex was there for that too. And, again, fitting.

In 1980 the Longhorns would also finish second at the NCAA Championships and their first national championship would come just a year later. More importantly, it would not be the only national championship won by a Longhorn swimming and diving team in 1981.

With women's swimming finally getting momentum thanks in

large part to Title IX, the Longhorns would also need a women's coach. Patterson became Texas' first women's swimming and diving coach in 1973 and coaching duties for the women's team were then split between Patterson and his diving coaches – first Olympic gold medalist diver Bob Clotworthy and then U.S. national diving champion Mike Brown.

The WETS committee recommended the hiring of a dedicated women's swimming coach so Reese could coach the men's team and Brown could focus on the divers. Patterson recommended Paul Bergen, coach of eight AAU national championship teams. The move paid dividends. Under Bergen, Texas won the final two championships held by the Association for Intercollegiate Athletics for Women (1981 and 1982), the governing body for women's sports before the NCAA finally offered women's championships.

Though he orchestrated the first national championship for any women's team on the UT campus, Bergen returned to the club ranks in 1982. But Texas would not be crippled by the departure, because it coincided with the hiring of the most successful coach in the history of women's swimming, Richard Quick.

An All-Southwest Conference swimmer at SMU, Quick helped establish the women's programs at SMU, Iowa State, and Auburn before coming to Texas. Starting in 1984, Quick led the Texas women to five straight NCAA championships, giving the Longhorns five of the first seven NCAA women's swimming titles. He left immediately after for Stanford, where he would extend his national championship streak to six. He was a six-time U.S. Olympic coach. At Texas, Stanford, and Auburn, Quick coached thirteen teams to NCAA titles, the most ever by a swimming coach, men's or women's.

As for Tex, he was also interested in Texas swimming because his kids were on the team. When Reese and Kubik arrived at Texas, Tex's son Robby was a senior and Bill was a sophomore on the men's team and his daughter Nan was on the women's team.

When asked what it was like coaching Tex's kids, Reese joked, "It's a lot better coaching his grandson."

Reese has been at UT long enough to coach two generations of Robertsons. The second generation showed up in 2006. Bill Robertson married fellow 1981 national champion swimmer Carol Borgmann – who was also a three-time individual national champion – and their oldest son, Jim, became a UT swimmer like his parents.

"Jim reminds me a lot of Robby and Bill," Reese said. "He came in, redshirted his first year, and he was voted the most improved. He works every day as hard as he can. There are not many like that."

A Big 12 champion in the 1650 freestyle, Jim made the 2008 Olympic trials and was a member of the Longhorns' 2010 National Championship team, Reese's tenth in his time at Texas. Jim came to Texas fully aware of the lineage to live up to.

"Lot of Robertsons through here," Jim Robertson said. "Coming here was really a dream come true. My parents' bathroom is decorated with all of their UT awards. My mom's NCAA medals. My dad's team spirit award. My mom's most improved award. All their national championship pictures in front of the tower in a bathroom. Kind of nice to know maybe I'll get my picture somewhere in the house. Maybe a closet or something, if I'm lucky."

"DARRELL ROYAL paid him maybe the highest compliment I've ever heard an AD pay an alum," Reese said. "He said he'd never run across anybody who cared about his sport as much as Tex."

For the rest of his life Tex continued to show up to practices and meets, hound alumni for donations, hound administration officials for funding, and stay involved in Texas swimming.

"He'd come on deck and he'd bring his little candy sticks that had his WETS sticker on them. He was like a father or grandfather," said Sterkel, who swam at Texas and won a pair of Olympic gold medals before becoming the women's head swimming coach at UT in 1992. "When you're feeling dead and just getting out of the pool he'd be there to say 'Attawaytogo.'"

He was a regular attendee of Texas practice and made plenty of suggestions to the current coaches, solicited or not.

"Tex had a way of just appearing," Kubik said. "We started noticing that probably once a week he'd pop through practice with his candy cigars and his big smiles and ask the boys why they weren't working a little bit harder and occasionally tell us 'so-and-so's stroke technique would improve if he was swimming downhill instead of uphill,' which was an apt way of describing exactly what so-and-so was doing wrong in the water."

Despite Tex's frequent advice, inquiries, and unannounced sojourns to the Texas Swim Center, the coaches never felt like he was looking over their shoulder too much.

"Never. Never," Reese said. "But every once in a while the AD would say, 'Well, I saw Tex again today. He never gives up.' I said, 'Good, then I don't have to.' He helped a lot of ways. A lot of ways I don't know about."

Reese may have been perfectly comfortable with Tex's constant influence, but athletic directors were another matter.

"He butted heads with Darrell," Reese said. "I'm not saying he's wrong, but Darrell's attitude was as football coach and AD. There's none of those out there now. It can't be done. It's not best to be done that way. Because those guys, when they quit football and are AD, they'll come in at nine o'clock and be playing golf by noon. You can't do it now. Now you get in before eight and you're there until seven."

The athletic director who Texas hired after Royal's retirement was much friendlier to swimming. He also felt Tex's presence the moment he arrived in Austin.

"Oh, it was immediate," DeLoss Dodds said. "We'd meet three or four times a year and talk about swimming. He always had something on his mind when he came in, something he wanted us to do or something he wanted us to know... Persistent is what I'd say about the man. He was persistent. If he had a thought or an idea, if you didn't do it the first time he came to see you about it he would come back with the same plan and the same thought the next year."

Most of the meetings went well. Dodds, whose grandson attended Camp Longhorn, supported most of the projects put forward to improve Texas swimming.

"There's never been a question of, 'You need what or why?' It's been a question of 'What may we do to help you and help your program to be the best it can be?'" Kubik said. "I wasn't around seventy some-odd years ago, but I doubt that's exactly the way it transpired for Tex. He's somebody who we're forever indebted to in terms of athletics. There's not a swimmer, including this current generation, who doesn't know of Tex and doesn't understand his contributions to this program."

In 2001 the Texas Swim Center (which was renamed the Lee and Joe Jamail Texas Swimming Center) received a three million dollar upgrade and renovation, which included new seating, an aluminum bulkhead that runs on a track – allowing for the lane lengths to be changed on the fly – a new sound system, and a new entrance to the building.

But even Tex and Dodds butted heads. The first fight came when Dodds attempted to fold WETS and have all fundraising handled directly by the University of Texas Athletic Department.

"I think the tension with DeLoss' regime was when the NCAA started cracking down on these programs and blaming the university," Heller said. "(Dodds) was afraid all of the clubs and things like WETS and so forth could get in trouble and it's beyond their reach. That was a contentious thing for a while."

Because of NCAA fundraising rules, most independent organizations have been phased out. When Dodds arrived at UT in 1981, there were six organizations that raised money for a campus sport. Only WETS remains. It has made changes to the way it runs itself and where the money goes to comply with the requirements, but it has survived. Dodds has tried, repeatedly, to bring WETS into the athletic department. The directors of WETS have always refused.

"When I came I was concerned about that money being outside the department and changing hands between coach and the donors. We pulled all of it inside," Dodds said. "We started with football and then basketball came. They all came in but one. WETS stayed out and they're still out there today. That was always an issue on his agenda, talking about WETS and them raising money and him doing things for swimming. I was the bad news guy because I wouldn't let him spend his money on things inside the department. And he was very good about it."

WETS was a constant disagreement, but the most contentious issue between Tex and Dodds was the outdoor pool.

Years after successfully guiding the construction of the swim center, Tex laid out a plan for a professional-level outdoor venue for Texas swimming, which would also provide additional recreational aquatic facilities for students. Every time he met with Dodds, Tex would bring up the pool or show Dodds his new design for the facility. Dodds would always say no. According to Dodds, there was, and still is, a significant financial gap.

"That's the only facility, the *only* facility, that we wanted to build that we haven't built," Dodds said. "We've done golf, we're doing tennis, and the reason we were able to do those, versus swimming, is the money was there. If the money's there we're going to do it. But it's not there yet."

But whether or not the money was "there" was always a point of disagreement between Tex and the UT administration. Tex attempted to raise the money for the building separate of both the university and WETS. He called up his friend Heller, who was working in Dallas for Ross Perot.

"Tex called up one night," said Heller, "and he said, 'I need you to be the financial guy for the money we're going to raise for the new swimming pool at Texas.' I said, 'Tex, I've got a day job.' He said, 'I know that. This won't be anything. We'll send you a list of people and stuff.'"

Like most things with Tex, the project was more difficult than he sold it, but Heller was successful at gathering significant donations. Over two years he compiled checks, some of which were for more than $50,000, from more than 500 people.

Then, out of the blue, Tex tells Heller to cancel the entire project.

"He calls me up one day and says, 'We can't get the politics worked out at UT to get the pool built. So shut the that thing down and give all the money to the athletic foundation.' I hung up the phone, but I started thinking about it and I called my lawyer," Heller said.

Heller's lawyer informed him that, given that the donations were for a specific project, he would need to contact each donor individually to ask them if they were willing to give that money to the general athletic foundation or if they wanted it back.

"Well, most of them did give it to the foundation," said Heller, "but my lawyer said, 'Don't screw this up. You could get sued for you don't know how much.' I said, 'Don't tell me that.'"

Tex canceled the fund Heller had been working on for two years because he was at an impasse with Dodds and the UT administration over the pool. According to Tex's son Bill, the athletic department refused the money. The issue was the number of donors. If the pool couldn't be built with internal athletic department money, the administration wanted to keep the number of donors attached to the project to a small handful. Tex offered to have the money donated to WETS and then WETS act as a single donor. Again, the athletic department refused.

Given Dodds' stated desire to have the outdoor swim center built, and the athletic department's financial windfall in the form of a dedicated television network, the pool is likely to be built someday. But, like Camp Longhorn Mexico, it was one of the few things Tex wanted to create and never saw.

And it was the only aspect of UT swimming he didn't have go his way. He had the top swim center in the country built, scholarship numbers increased, and top-level coaches hired for a sport that previously received little attention from the athletic department.

"He never understood any part of the word 'no,'" Reese said. "You need people like that. You've got to have them, otherwise we'd still be in horse and buggy and using candles."

Afterword
by
Robby Robertson

Dad always had a way with getting people to go along with his silliness – either by presentation or just wearing you out until you gave in.

My favorite example is the "attawaytogo" hand sign. Like many nights, about 9:30 one night during the winter off-season I went to the office for something and heard a slow, grumbling "attawaytogo" come from his office. I looked around the corner and he was sitting at his desk hands clasped together, saying "attawaytogo," and smiling with pure joy.

Then he had to sell it and let us all know this was the new CLH symbol. He said it would be like the hand signs used in college sports by the Aggies, Horns, Raiders, and of course Bears. He paused, letting us wonder why "of course" the Bears, before saying that it was "because you do it bare-handed."

We were all reluctant. But the master wore us out and now you see it all over Camp.   Attawaytogo, Tex.

BOOK 5

IT ONLY TAKES A SPARK...
THE LEGACY OF TEX ROBERTSON

13

Chapter

Tex was the only one who wanted to create Indian Springs.

All the directors at Camp Longhorn were opposed to creating a second camp. In 1975 the company was barely turning a profit. They didn't have the personnel. Where Tex wanted to build the camp was too wooded, too rocky, and too far from any large body of water.

All voted against it. Tex did it anyway. That was how most decisions at Camp Longhorn went.

"Any time there was a big decision to be made, at Tex's request I'd poll the group, see what they want; then he'd do what he wanted to anyway," Tex's long-time financial adviser Gardner Parker said.

And Tex was right. Despite the initial cost, expanding Camp Longhorn to a second location became an overwhelmingly successful financial move. Due to a sizable waiting list amongst the younger cabins, there was a group of customers ready to fill the roster.

"We had too many young campers," Tex said in a 1999 interview. "We'd had a place where we'd leased across the lake for our horses. We found out there were wonderful springs – artesian – flowing slowly. We found out we could make a small lake out there to have swimming and Blobbing."

But money had little to do with Tex's surprise decision. He had a long view of what he wanted Camp Longhorn to be after his death, and central to that plan were his children. No matter who else was involved in the business, Tex planned for Camp Longhorn to be solely a family-owned and operated company.

His plan was to create a structure where each of his offspring would be a director. With five kids, there would need to be more than one camp. So in 1975 he created Camp Longhorn Indian Springs, initially just known as the "Ranch Branch." But he could not hand the business to his children yet. In 1975 Billy was sixteen. Twins Robby and Nan were twenty years old and in college. Sally was twenty-five and working as a teacher. The oldest, John, had just returned from his second tour in Vietnam. Sally and Nan were signed up as the first counselors, but to run the new branch of his camp, Tex turned to Frank and Mary Patt Everest.

A South African from Kimberley, Frank met Mary Patt while in Spain. Mary Patt was a Camp Longhorn counselor and former camper. She convinced Frank to join her on Inks Lake for the summer. Impressed with their leadership, Tex asked them both to take over the Ranch Branch.

"After one summer there, Tex approached me and said, 'Would you like to go to the Ranch?' and I said, 'I'd love to go to Ranch and see what you guys have been talking about,'" Frank said. "We drove over with Bob Tarlton and looked around and saw this pile of rock and this little steam. A camp? Here? Crazy. But it turned out that after a lot of rock throwing and a lot of fun we turned it into a camp."

For the first few years Indians Springs resembled the pure outdoor camping seen in the early days of the Inks Lake camp. According to Frank, when the fifty-four kids signed up for the first summer arrived, "the lake wasn't up, the cabins weren't really screened in yet, the doors weren't on, the shutters weren't on, the mattresses weren't in."

In true Tex fashion, the campers themselves were heavily involved in building the camp. "Rock pick-up" was a daily activity, as the land was slowly cleared by a combined effort from both employees and customers. Rather than feeling burdened, many campers took pride in changing the land, and the initially rough-it style of Camp Longhorn Indian Springs proved popular.

"A lot of the value of Camp Longhorn is what we don't have," Tex said. "We don't have electricity in the cabins. Of course we don't have a TV, which most kids seem delighted to sacrifice. No furniture, not even a bathroom in the cabins."

The number of campers nearly doubled the next year. Just like the Inks Lake camp in the 1940s, Indian Springs grew quickly and the camp staff grew with it. Frank and Mary Patt were joined by former counselor Don Wilhelmi and his wife Susan. Raul and Antonia Valles' work behind the scenes was instrumental in keeping the camp running.

"We had to build those cabins fast enough," Frank said. "Zark and Barney (Baker) and Francisco (Ontiveras) would seem to appear out of the ground. Tex must have had quite a vision to turn a pile of rock into one of the United States' finest camps."

The overflow at Camp Longhorn Inks Lake was in the younger age groups, but when those new campers got old enough to return to the original branch, they didn't want to. With the campers so heavily involved in the building of the camp, it became the place to experiment with new activities – some successful, some deemed too dangerous and scrapped. As opposed to the Inks Lake camp, the "Ranch Branch" had horseback riding.

"They loved riding horseback and loved the features and building the camp," Tex said. "The next year they didn't want to move. Pretty soon it became a full-fledged camp."

The new camp also allowed Tex to further engage in one of his favorite activities: contriving elaborate legends. For example, at the Inks camp he would have counselors take kids out on a trail ride into the woods, where they came across the remains of a graying, weather-beaten, burned-out cabin. There the head counselor would tell the story of "Ghost Town," based primarily on this story Tex wrote and printed out for them to memorize:

Long ago, when "Ghost Town" was a thriving, rip-roaring mining camp, none of the 89 inhabitants dreamed there would be a Camp Longhorn or even an Inks Lake.

The mines produced almost every known mineral and the occasional "strike" of small quantities of gold caused frequent celebrations and great promise. The digging was so hard that the Comanche Indians, from a village across the river, where Indian Springs is now, were given the jobs to "scratch out" the ore.

There was a joy, romance, and adventure during the short life of the town, but the silver, lead, and gold veins were soon bled off and the expected gold in the pan didn't pan out. Unpaid Indian workers became fewer and those who did remain grew increasingly rambunctious, and desperados made bold raids on the settlement, causing the formation of vigilantes who hung the worst offenders from a branch of the hanging tree, which has since died, but the old rope still remains – an ominous warning. As the miners continued to overwork and mistreat the Indians, any friendships between the two groups disappeared. One night, the Indians banded together and left Ghost Town, taking with them a small boy. He has not been seen for generations, but he is believed to be the hermit who was living in the hills around Camp Longhorn. As with all hermits, he is timid and scared and now roams farther back from camp since it has gotten larger.

It's just a story. But there are natural limestone caves near the Indian Springs camp that are called the "mines" and counselors would scatter arrowheads around some of the more common hiking trails for kids to "discover." Having a camp closer to those caves allowed for expansion of the tale and similar stories were told at the Indian Springs involving the "Ghost Wagon" and "Hangman's Tree." On his visits to Indian Springs, Tex would tell kids that there was a tribe of natives still living in the woods near the camp and that he was only able to create the camp with the permission of Chief Peta. (The details and pronunciation have changed over the years, but the name "Peta" comes from a real historical figure, Peta Nocona, the father of Comanche chief Quanah Parker.) He'd then tell stories of his adventures in the woods and rocky gorges with Peta and his tribe, encouraging campers to raise their right hand in a sign of peace if they ever encountered one of the Comanches.

Tex loved mysticism. Maybe there was gold still under your feet. Maybe you could get dragged off in the night like the old hermit. This was reinforced by a counselor, or Tex, occasionally playing the old hermit or a Comanche and passing through the nearby trees just close enough to be barely seen by the kids. It's an old trick, but an effective one.

"Fundamentally, (children) are the same as they were in 1940," Tex said. "Youngsters respond to the same sort of thing. We thought maybe the traditional camps would go out when all the sports camps and specialty camps and dance camps and all that came in. But there's more and more and all the camps are growing."

Aspects of the business have steadily adjusted with time, but the fundamental structure and goal of the camp has stayed the same over its seventy-five years of operation.

"It's about as good of a people-run business as I've ever seen," Jeff Heller said. "They stick to the same formula and it still works. Probably always will." And he added, in a hilariously accurate impersonation of his boss, Ross Perot: "One of Ross' sayings is, 'Computers don't change anything, people do.' It's true."

TEX DREADED THE DAY Camp Longhorn would start making money. Dreaded it.

"Tex would tell you that the '60s were the most fun for him," Parker said. "The reason it was a good time is until after the '60s Tex was truly financially struggling."

There were many counter-intuitive qualities of Tex Robertson, perhaps none more than his approach to money.

"Money meant nothing to Tex," Parker said. "He never knew how much he was worth; he never cared. Once he knew he could keep Camp going, that's all he cared about. He achieved that about '60. Then by the '70s it started becoming bigger and became about money. The '60s it was still not a big business."

Until the 1970s Tex was accumulating nothing. The price of attending camp wasn't determined by market demand but rather by what would get him financially even. Instead of avoiding it, he desired to live paycheck to paycheck, a straight-forward life that would just let him run his camp in peace.

This also resulted in a frugal nature that many around him would describe as extreme. He never bought shampoo, since he had hundreds of bottles he took from each hotel while visiting campers in their home towns. He demanded this same level of meticulous conservation from those working at the camp. He never tried to make a great deal of money, but he wanted to know where every cent he put into his camp was going.

Often he would walk the grounds with those who worked for him and ask about minute details of the operation. If it was costing him money and he didn't see a value in it, he wanted it removed. Clem Love, who worked in maintenance at Camp Longhorn for many years, would walk with Tex around the two man-made lakes at Indian Springs and listen to his boss ask questions about each item:

Tex said, "Clem, that building across from chow hall, where that big pump's running, what does that do for me?"

I said, "Tex, it does a lot for you you can't see by eye. The pipeline on it, I designed it, but they didn't do it exactly the way I wanted it. You clean the lakes every year and the water's going. You can clean one lake and pump it back over into the other one and save a lake of water."

He said, "Oh, ok, good. Well what's that do for me?" and pointed at something else.

When Love wanted to buy lumber to build a wind screen for the animals in the camp zoo, Tex told him "Pig City" had all the wood he would need. Pig City is an embodiment of the frugality of Tex Robertson. It's a junk yard (one at each camp) where everything that could potentially be reused is dumped. It's where Zark would get materials for his experiments, building drinking fountains out of old refrigerators and a sailboat out of scrap wood and tarp. Instead of going to a building supply store in Burnet, Clem sat in Pig City working nails off old boards until he had enough lumber to build his wind block.

Despite the relatively low price of attendance, in the early '70s the camp began to make a significant profit. The massive purchase necessary to build Camp Longhorn Indian Springs helped bring Tex back to being comfortably in the red, but Indian Springs expanded and both camps started to bring in wealth. Tex found himself in over his head. He called Parker and asked for help.

Parker had been a camp counselor in the 1960s and had wanted to work at Camp Longhorn the rest of his life. Tex fired him in 1969, telling him: "You can achieve so much more than being a camp director. You can't come back."

Tex had a point. After becoming a CPA, Parker would later serve on the boards of a number of oil industry companies, including Triangle Petroleum, Hercules Offshore, and Carrizo Oil & Gas. In the late '70s, Tex phoned Parker with a proposal.

"I read in magazines about boards of directors," Tex began. He told Parker that he wanted to create a board of directors for Camp Longhorn, that he wanted Parker to serve on it, and that the first meeting was in two months. Parker was thrilled:

I was back to being a kid sitting outside on the curb. The next two months I was so excited. I'm a grown man and I'd get to be back with Tex. Then I started visualizing who else would be on the board. I put so many combinations in my head. Four hours driving up there I didn't think about anything else but who was going to be there. So I showed up, he was at the house, and I thought I was early because no one else was there. After ten minutes after the meeting was supposed to start, I said, "Who else is coming? Who else is going to be on the board?" He said, "Oh. Just you and me."

For about fifteen years the "Board of Directors" was just Tex and Parker. Parker spent much of that time arguing with Tex over the price of tuition.

Once I was on the board I started looking at the books. He set his price where he'd write his last check when he started collecting money the next year. He wanted no more than break even. I compared other camps and the fee at that time for camp was only $600 or $700. He was $150 or $190 behind other camps. I said, "Tex, you need to go up $100 on tuition." He was driving and I thought he was going to run off the road. I said "You got to do it, Tex. It's only fair." He thought the more he increased tuition, the more campers he would lose. He cared more about having fun and if he lost one camper by going up $100 he wouldn't do it. He and I negotiated on the phone for literally three months. He'd say, "How about $50?" I held to my guns. I think he did $60 or $70. We're a superior camp. It's fine to be five or ten percent below, but we can't be thirty.

The board remained limited to two people because Tex was waiting to put all five of his kids on the board at the same time. Along with wanting his children to run the camps, he wanted them to make up the whole of the board of directors and represent the whole of ownership.

"He didn't put the kids on the board until they all could be on the board," Parker said. "He didn't want four of the five. Everything gets treated equal. If you really think about it, he was the perfect communist.

Don't take that wrong."

As opposed to the finances, the actual experience of Camp Longhorn was all that mattered to Tex. Once all five of his children were directors at Camp Longhorn and full board meetings were being held, only a small portion of each meeting was actually spent on money. Tex preferred spending that time talking about the operation of the camp, such as the length of quiet time – the camp's afternoon rest period.

"When we started accumulating money, we had to make a million dollar investment decision," Parker said. "We were allowed two minutes in the board meeting to talk about that million dollars. But we'd talk for three hours about whether quiet time should be an hour or forty minutes."

"HE WAS A LITTLE BIT OF A CONTROL FREAK," Parker said.

Not about money, certainly – Tex turned that over to his "consigliere," as Tex once called Parker – but Tex wanted to be in complete control of his camp and his family. His daughter Sally spent much of her career outside of Camp Longhorn, something that visibly frustrated Tex because it didn't fit with his design. When the board invested his money, Tex paid little attention. But when anything was going to change with the operation of the camp, he wanted to be in control of it.

"Just getting him to buy off on Longhorn Rangers was a major ordeal," Robby said, in reference to the Colorado trip he takes tenth grade campers on as a part of counselor training.

But in the end, I had to go in there and convince him we needed to do that for these guys. Because it was totally off of what we'd ever done, he'd say no and no and no.

"Is what we're doing now anything like what you thought camping would be?" I asked him.

"No."

"Well, this is another opportunity. I really think we can make this be something."

I finally got his blessing and we went ahead with it, but when it came to things like that I couldn't just walk in and say, "I want to do this." He had to be convinced. At the end of it I told him, "I need something that's my own. I need to create. I need the chance to create something. This is it." It worked out, I guess. We're successful and making money and it's still going.

Camp exists as Tex wanted it. The board of directors is still his five kids and Parker. But it can't stay that way forever.

"There's going to have to be an enlargement because of the family traditions that have established," Tex said. "And we're embarrassed with a long waiting list."

Tex and Pat had eighteen grandchildren. It's no surprise that a third branch of Camp Longhorn is on the way.

14

Chapter

Tex revived his swimming career forty-four years after he left Michigan. At the age of seventy he joined Masters Swimming, which organizes age-group championships. With a heated, indoor swimming pool at his home, he continued to swim regularly, but Tex decided to make the leap and become a septuagenarian competitive swimmer.

At the 1980 U.S. Masters Championships, Tex finished second in the 500-yard freestyle (age 70-74 bracket), earning him his first Masters medal. He was immediately successful in the longer distances because he had maintained tremendous health. Even before returning to the competitive ranks he had continued his routine of swimming a mile every day; a schedule he maintained into his early nineties.

"I once asked him if he still swam a mile a day," said Eddie Reese, "and he said, 'Yes, and that's about how long it takes me to finish.'"

Tex had several top-ten finishes nationally while in his seventies, but his first big splash at the senior level came in 1986, when 3,444 swimmers from twenty-nine countries met in Japan for the first FINA World Masters Swimming Championships. The seventy-seven-year-old Tex qualified with a top-five finish in five events at the swim trials in Fort Paris, Florida.

Tex made his first trip to Japan and thoroughly enjoyed himself, commenting that Tokyo is "just like New York City, except for the hieroglyphics on the buildings." Perhaps the swimming would be secondary to the trip. Given his times in Fort Paris, he was not expected to win any medals at the world championship.

He won seven. At Yoyogi Olympic Pool in Tokyo, Tex bested all his previous Masters marks, winning three bronze medals (50-meter freestyle, 100 free, 200 free relay), three silvers (200, 400, and 800-meter freestyle), and his first gold medal as a member of the 200 medley relay team, setting a Masters world record of 2:51.98. He had finished fifth in his own country in the 50-meter freestyle and the 100-meter freestyle, but jumped to third in the world at the championships. He finished second in the U.S. in the 200, 400, and 800 and managed to finish second as well at the worlds. His toughest competition, though, didn't come from another American, but rather an old friend he had not seen in a very, very long time.

At the 1932 Olympics in Los Angeles, fifty-four years previous, Tex met a Japanese swimmer named Terao Toshio. At the 1986 Masters World Championships, Terao dominated the 75-79 age group. In the five individual events where Tex won bronze or silver, Terao won all five, setting five world records in the process.

"No matter how well I seemed to do, he always beat me," Tex said. "But we became very good friends. I met his family and he presented me with a nice t-shirt before I left."

The medley relay gave Tex his first gold, but despite owning seven world championship medals he still had no individual titles, even at the national level. But as he got older, his standing relative to his competition increased significantly. Tex's most impressive accomplishment in Masters swimming was his longevity. As his competition faded with age, he just kept going.

From age eighty to eighty-four, Tex won nine national championships. He then won three gold medals (200, 400, and 800-meter freestyle), a silver (100 free), and a bronze (200 backstroke) at the 1992 Masters World Championships in Indianapolis. Terao was back and Tex bested him this time, but he was kept from getting two more golds by Masters world record-holder Shogoro Azuma.

Tex was one of the fastest old swimmers in the world (or one of the oldest fast swimmers). He won championships, but it wasn't until after 1993 that he moved into unprecedented territory. As a former coach, he had been training himself. He made a huge leap in performance after he began working with the husband and wife team of Keith Bell and Sandy Neilson-Bell.

Keith was one of the early practitioners of sports psychology. A former collegiate swimmer who was at the University of Texas getting his B.S. in psychology, he began thinking about the benefits of a dedicated psychologist for a team.

"It wasn't like the coaches were just going to let me into their teams," Bell said. "So I made an appointment with Pat Patterson and I told him I had these ideas and I wanted to bounce them off him as an expert in the sport and see what he thought. I met with him for an hour and talked passionately about my ideas. About an hour into it he said, 'Can you do that with the team?'"

After becoming the UT swim team's first psychologist, Bell was eventually hired as an assistant coach and later the head coach for the women's team. And if he was coaching UT swimming, that meant he was going to meet Tex.

"My first contact with Tex was he would come around and give everybody candy cigars," Bell said. "I had no idea who he was. I knew nothing about him; I had no idea he was the coach and started the program and had done such great things at UT and started TAGS. He seemed like just some weird guy."

The team would make regular trips out to Camp Longhorn and, as with each coach at Texas, Bell became friends with Tex. While coaching at Texas, Bell started the UT Masters swim program and got older swimmers involved in national and international competition. But it wasn't Keith who convinced Tex to join the team; it was his wife Sandy.

There are few swimmers who are as fascinated with pushing the age limits of athleticism as Sandra Neilson-Bell. She won three gold medals at the 1972 Summer Olympics (100-meter freestyle, 4x100-meter freestyle relay, and 4x100-meter medley relay). But twelve years later she managed to beat her Olympic record time in the 100 by more than a second. As U.S. Swimming's "Comeback Swimmer of the Year," she competed in the 1988 and 1992 Olympic trials and missed the 1996 trials by .09 seconds – twenty-four years after her gold medal swims in Munich.

They are the king and queen of Masters swimming. Keith became the only male to win eleven gold medals in a single Masters national championship event and Sandy the only woman when they combined for twenty-two golds at the 1998 U.S. Long Course Championship.

"That's probably the largest gold medal haul by a married couple in any sport at any level," Keith said.

Sandy had taken over the UT Masters program from Keith and she recruited Tex to join the UT Masters team. Specifically she was looking to put together a relay team to compete in the oldest age group.

"I started coaching the team in '93," said Sandy. "Keith said 'You should recruit Tex.' We were at one of the alumni meets and we got them together and it was great. They were the most fun to coach."

In Masters relays, it is not required that every member of the team be over a certain age. Instead, age groups are broken up by the cumulative ages of each of the four swimmers. The oldest age group at the time was 320+ (average of at least eighty years old). Realizing the talent she had to work with, Neilson-Bell got together her team of four – Gus Clemens (75), Jesse Coon (83), Bennett Allen (79), and Tex Robertson (84) – with the goal of being the top relay in the world. Later that year, as "Team Lone Star," they broke the 320+ world record in the 200-meter freestyle relay (2:59.21) and the 200-meter medley relay (3:22.86). Their free relay was fifteen seconds faster than the next closest time.

Five years later, they still timed as the top 320+ relay team in the world. An impressive accomplishment considering only a single member of the team had changed and the rest had continued to age. (Gus Clemens left and was replaced by seventy-six-year-old Allen Hellman.) That changed in 1999, when their record was smashed by the Juei Club Team from Japan by a ridiculous twenty-five seconds (2:34.38).

Both Tex and Jesse Coon were in their nineties, but their relay team was still top ten in the world in the 320+ group. With Tex and Coon at such an advanced age yet still so effective, they realized they could add a pair of youngsters, relatively speaking, and stay over a total of 320. With the addition of sixty-five-year-old Bob Bailie and seventy-four-year-old Frank Campbell, it gave the team exactly the number it needed to stay eligible (65 + 74 + 90 + 91 = 320).

With the widest split on the planet between oldest and youngest member of a relay team, their time improved by sixteen seconds in 2000. They jumped to the number one spot in the U.S. and the number three spot in the world, behind Manly Aussi from Australia and Juei, which had improved on its world record time by yet another five seconds. (In an impressive feat of consistency, Juei would hold the number one world ranking for seven consecutive years, with Tamura Isamu swimming on each of those seven teams.)

As for individual swims, Tex continued to make leaps relative to his competition. After winning nine championships in the 80-84 age bracket, he won ten Masters Championships in the 85-89 bracket. He was stacking up golds at an ever-increasing rate. Under Sandy and Keith's tutelage, he actually increased in speed as he approached ninety. At the age of eighty-nine, just as he was about to leave the 85-89 age group, he set the American record in the 100-yard backstroke.

The next year, unsurprisingly, he became the number one-ranked swimmer in the world over ninety. He set records in the 50-meter freestyle (54.46), 100-meter freestyle (2:15.10), 200-meter freestyle (5:03.14), 50-meter backstroke (1:23.69), and the 100-meter backstroke (2:44.90).

He credited his record-breaking to a paucity of opponents.

"The average age of my competition in the 90 to 94 age group is 'deceased'," Tex said.

In fact, I did not know until I began researching for this book that I was indirectly responsible for preventing him from winning two more. He won three of his gold medals at the U.S. National Senior Sports Classic in 1995. An article on his performance in San Antonio appears in a June 7, 1995, edition of *The Citizens Gazette*, a newspaper in Burnet: "Robertson was scheduled to compete in two other events on the final day of competition, but the events were running behind schedule and Robertson was forced to scratch from those events so he could attend the triple birthday celebration of his grandchildren Matt Manning, Mark Manning and Ross Lucksinger. Robertson said he hated to leave early, but 'first things first,' and that gave him four firsts."

I remember him attending my thirteenth birthday. I was not aware until this writing that he'd given up an opportunity for gold to be there. But that's what mattered to him.

TEX AND HIS RELAY TEAMMATES had reached the point where they could set records just by trying events no one in their age class had attempted. They set such a record in November of 1999 at the North vs. South High School All-Star Meet in Midland, Texas. They had been competing in the 320+ age group, but there had never been a relay team with all four members over the age of eighty-five. The organizer of the meet, Steve Emmanuel, wanted to add some history to the event by setting that official time.

The eighty-six-year-old Bennett Allen returned to the group and seventy-four-year-old "greenhorn" Frank Campbell was replaced by eighty-eight-year-old Roy Bodine. Tex and Coon swam the last two spots in what they dubbed the "Dinosaur Relay." Sandy made the arrangements and picked the four of them up in Austin.

"It was just like a kids travel trip," Sandy said. "I made the plane reservation, picked them up, and got them in the hotel. We did a little swim meet trip. And this was with a group of amazing people. Ben, he was the youngest at eighty-six. Roy was actually a POW in the war. Jesse's an astrophysicist. Tex is a legend. And here they are cracking these jokes that had me laughing the entire time."

At the end of the all-star meet the four of them got ready for their freestyle relay. Rather than leave, the kids were curious about why these four old men were disrobing next to the pool. Each of the four of them were announced, along with their accomplishments in swimming. Tex's announcement took the longest, as it went back all the way to his invention of the flip turn. Sandy was amazed by the high school kids' reaction:

> The guys take off their clothes and they start announcing them. Here are these old men and the kids are like, "What's going on?" The kids were getting their bags and could have gone. Everybody got up, everyone was watching the whole thing. The whole relay everybody was screaming for them. Tex anchored, and he did the flip turn and the crowd went wild. The kids were so thrilled. It was very, very cool. They were excited enough and when he did the flip turn they were twice as loud. After the meet the kids were coming up to them and asking them for their autographs. It was wonderful.

Tex was one of the few who would still execute a full flip turn at ninety years old, though certainly not as crisply as in his youth. Once during Masters competition it caused him to end up in the wrong lane, according to Sandy:

> There was a zone meet at UT. Tex was swimming the 200 backstroke and he was swimming in the second to the wall lane. There's an empty lane and here's his lane. He swam 100 and at the end he pushed into the end lane. He swam a 50 and realized it and pushed off and got back in his original

lane. The referees looked at each other and said, "Did he just switch lanes and switch back?" Normally you're supposed to be disqualified. But who's going to disqualify Tex for something like that? We said something to him about it after he got out and he just gives you this wonderful mischievous grin. He knew. Who the heck's going to disqualify him? He said: "I started and finished in my lane."

For a year Tex, Jesse, Roy, and Ben were the world's only 85+ Masters swim team. Their old rival, Team Florida, could not stand for this.

As Tex's relay team had been setting records and winning championships in the late '90s, a Masters team from Florida had been right on their heels, once losing to Team Texas in the 200 free relay by one second, 3:23 to 3:24.

To compete for the title of top 85+ relay, Team Florida got together a group comprised of Dave Malbrough (86), Frank Starr (89), Frank Tillotson (85), and Art Holden (88). U.S. Masters Swimming officially created the 85+ relay event for the two-team race, and in 2000 Tex, Roy, Frank, and Jesse faced off against Team Florida in both the 200 freestyle relay and the 200 medley relay.

The freestyle relay was neck-and-neck the entire way. But on the final leg, Tex out-swam Holden to get the win. In the medley, with Tex the sprint freestyler at the end, Team Texas won by more than a minute.

They were no longer the only 85+ relay team, but retained their title of the fastest. Their times of 3:38.91 in the free and 3:46.43 in the medley are yet to be broken.

But it would prove to be the end of Tex's long swimming career. His days of swimming anchor leg ended when his leg became an anchor.

PRIOR TO NATIONAL COMPETITION in 2001 – after already getting hip and knee replacements – Tex fell and broke his femur. The reconstructive surgery put enough metal in his leg to halt his assault on age-group world records.

He had a support harness built in his swimming pool so he could continue to exercise, but his competitive swimming days were over. He could reflect on an incredible career in the sport. Even if he didn't, many, many more did it for him.

At the end of the twentieth century, *Swim Texas Magazine* hosted a banquet titled "Legends of Texas Swimming." The greatest and most influential swimmers in Texas were honored and almost the entire list was comprised of people who have appeared in this story: Wally Hoffrichter, Jane Dillard, David "Skippy" Browning, Alfred "Red" Barr, Adolph Kiefer, Art Adamson, and Hank Chapman. Also honored at the event was Jane Kneip – who married Pat Patterson – one of the pioneers of women's aquatics in Texas, and Danny Green, an AAU champion and All-American for Texas A&M before and after World War II.

Each was presented a plaque as a Legend of Texas. But the banquet itself was for Tex. He was honored at the end up the night as the "Texas Swimming Man of the Century."

Along with giving him the Texas Masters Swimming Lifetime Achievement Award, Keith and Sandy named their annual swimming competition the Tex Robertson Highland Lakes Challenge.

"It's a competition where you swim in three lakes," Sandy said. "We put on these events because Keith wants to swim them. He's like, 'You know what would be fun?' It's kind of like Tex."

Tex also had a swim center named for him. The Galloway-Hammond Recreation Center in Burnet is an impressive facility, especially considering it's in a town of only 5,000 people. Naturally, Tex was heavily involved in the agencies responsible for its construction.

"He had that thing funded from about eight different entities in bits and pieces," Texas assistant swim coach Kris Kubik said. "It originally was going to have an outdoor pool because whoever was the agency that was funding that could only fund an outdoor pool, but he had this other agency in his hip pocket that could put a roof over it, because they were going to put a gym next door and the roof could just extend over the pool. He was an incredibly wise man who knew how to work the system."

What Tex did not know is the facility's swim center was to be named for him. In February of 2003, shortly after the center's opening, a high school swim meet became a surprise party for Tex. He arrived at the event to find family and friends, including a number of the swimmers he coached. There was a sign marking the entrance to the "Tex Robertson

Natatorium." He was genuinely surprised, which did not happen often with a man so in control of any project he could get his hands on.

It was also in 2003 that he was honored by the International Swimming Hall of Fame, where he donned the gold sash, goggles, and clips and tossed around water on stage. Tex was honored for the ways in which he changed the sport, the institutions he created, the lives he changed, and his accomplishments as a swimmer, which included becoming the best swimmer in the world over the age of ninety.

While Tex was at Michigan, his coach Matt Mann predicted Tex would soon be the best swimmer in the world. Mann was right, albeit sixty-five years early.

15

Chapter

It seemed as if Tex would live forever.

As he left his mid-nineties, he was still in shockingly good health. The metal in his leg slowed him significantly, but he was still moving around well enough to operate the nation's largest private summer camp. And, amazingly, his mind was as sharp as ever.

There were a lot of factors that contributed to his unusual longevity. His mother may have died young, but his father's long life was a good sign. Francis Garland Robertson, Jr., was born two years after the Civil War and was still running Robertson Brokerage Company during the Vietnam War. But those who knew Tex claim his swimming had the greatest impact on his lifespan. Tex and his contemporaries in the sport lived well above the average age of his generation. When most were dead, he was breaking world records.

"He swam so much," Eddie Reese said. "There's a connection between aerobic exercise and all the brain diseases that are attributed to age. Much of it is attributed to a lack of movement. He'd swim a mile a day and then when he couldn't do that he'd swim thirty minutes. You live until you die, and that's what Tex did."

Tex's old student Adolph Kiefer is the same. My interview with him was delayed because he was in the hospital with a bout of pneumonia. A week later he was back at work. A ninety-two-year-old man got pneumonia and in a week he was at work.

"I don't know why the hell I'm still here," Kiefer said, "but it probably has something to do with swimming. I swim every day. If I didn't swim every day, it would be a little different. Tex, he swam up until ninety-eight. Of course he had a perfect set up for that. Just walk out of his back door."

Tex's mind remained perceptive, his enthusiasm never faded, and he got all he could from his body, but eventually it gave out. While he was ninety-seven years old he could still move, still work, and still swim. At ninety-eight, there was a sudden and precipitous drop in his health.

But it was in this time that he, in a way, was his strongest. As his son, Robby, explained:

> I think of all the things he did in his life, I think it was the final year of his life that was so amazing. You'd help him out of that chair and the bones would crack and creak and, my God, it had to hurt like hell. He'd fall and he'd break that leg. He'd have a broken leg and his leg would be sticking out to one side. And always with a sense of humor. He never, never, not one time when we were rolling him over to change him, rolling him over to bandage his sores, never, never, never did he bitch or complain about the fact that this was happening to him. Ever. He never said, "Why me?" If there's anything I could ever do in my life, it would be able to take things in stride the way he did.

Humor was how Tex taught and inspired during his life. Humor was also how he coped with his toughest times, including the end. Not only did he somehow avoid senility, he would make light of people thinking he was senile and take advantage of it for a joke. Sometimes this would take the form of running over someone in his motorized cart and getting them to apologize to him when he acted spacy – before giving a grin and a wink to someone else who was in on the joke. Other times it would take the form of intentionally confusing nurses at the hospital.

Parker went to visit him while he was in the hospital and he was stopped on the way in by a nurse. "Before I went in the nurse said, 'Now, he's gonna say some weird stuff because he's lost his mind. He's crazy.' He had told them I was Abraham Lincoln. The nurse said, 'See?' And I said, 'You don't know Tex. We don't know what the shit that means. He's always been like this.'"

If there was a joke to be made, Tex would find it. He couldn't move around much, but he still kept tabs on many of the details of his business. He called George Lillard, a local veterinarian who helped with the camp zoo, and said: "I need you to weigh this fifteen-foot boa constrictor." Lillard responded: "Tex, I can't weigh a boa constrictor." There was silence for a beat. Then Tex said: "Well why not? He's covered in scales."

"That's just the way it was to him. 'I'm going to make the best of it and there's bound to be a damn good joke in there somewhere,'" Robby said. "In the hospital, they didn't know whether he was senile or trying to be funny. You would have to explain to them, 'You have to understand. This is a joke. There's no such thing as senility in him. His mind does not work like yours does.'"

HE WAS A LEGEND to many, an infallible patriarch of a Camp Longhorn family 100,000 strong. But he was human and he had his flaws, as all do.

Tex Robertson was a tremendously complex man. His flaws came as a part of the unusual dualities of Tex. He was a good man. He cared deeply for his family, for his swimmers, and for the thousands and thousands of youngsters who attended his camp. But those outside of his created circles could often be pushed aside.

His approach to money was both consistent and counter-intuitive. He didn't appear to care at all about making money. He didn't attempt to patent the Blob or the Frisbee though he obviously could have profited greatly from each and for years kept camp fees lower than competitors. He genuinely feared the day camp would make money. There is nobility to that unique perspective, but keeping profits as low as possible often meant keeping wages for many of his employees low as well.

There was no advertising for Camp Longhorn and no vanity to the product. But relying on word of mouth meant that for many years a majority of campers were from families in the same social circles.

"We've had the luxury of our campers recruiting other campers," Tex said.

Those who actually did come from outside of the same community were typically able to do so because of the influence of their families, such as the children of President George W. Bush, Governor Rick Perry, and Heisman Trophy winner Earl Campbell to name a few. Building connections and political influence mattered to Tex so that he could control his domain: camping.

His ability to create came from his determination and certainty of his rightness. But this often caused the exclusion of other legitimate perspectives. He was never arrogant or aggressive in his dealing with those who disagreed with him, but in most situations he had little ability to see things from others' perspective. There was only his way, and that was that.

"We would take a vote and it would sometimes be five to one, the one being Tex," Bill Johnson said. "And he'd say, 'Ok, we're going with my way.' He was always going to get what he wanted. But he did it in interesting ways. He was patient, but he was going to get his way."

Yet there were clearly defined situations and roles in which he easily yielded control. His lifetime of accomplishments as a coach didn't cause him to treat his Masters coaches as anything other than his coaches. He was the swimmer; Sandy and Keith were the coaches. He did everything they said and was loyal, just as he felt a swimmer should be to his or her coach.

"He was a good friend, and yet he looked up to us as coaches," Keith said. "He would take the swimmer role in the coach-swimmer relationship and treat it with that vertical distance and authority. It was a really cool relationship."

He defined himself, perhaps more than any other way, by his love of his family. The entire structure of the camp was built around his family. Such love is an exceptionally positive quality, but it sometimes came at the exclusion of some others who felt as much a part of Camp Longhorn. He drove off many talented people because of it.

"Bill Johnson and Bob Tarlton, they always felt like they owned part of Camp Longhorn," Parker said. "They always sensed, and Tart did too – he admitted before he died – that was their being naive. Where they got that from was Tex saying, 'We need to build something for us here.' The definition of that meant something different to Tex than them. But eventually they reconciled."

Much of it was through a failure of communication. He was designing the camp from very early on to be a solely family-run business and some found themselves continually frustrated by that.

All that he created through his camp and coaching made him a father-figure to many, but this caused a separation from his true self for most whom he called friends.

"Tex, he was my father," Kiefer said. "When I was fifteen, my father was dead, my mother was out of it, and I was growing up a gypsy. Fully gypsy. The Depression was on. I would gravitate to him."

Even the person outside of Tex's family that he trusted most had more of a father-son relationship than that of a best pal.

"He made you feel like he loved you," Parker said, "but you were still afraid of him."

"You are not dying during camp."

Pat had put her foot down. It was summer of 2007 and Camp Longhorn was in session, but Tex was clearly in his last days. However, Pat told him in no uncertain terms that it would be too traumatic for the kids to have him die while the camp was going on.

So he didn't.

Once Tex was convinced he was in the right, there was nobody who could convince him otherwise. Nobody, save for one.

"Tex wouldn't override her, even if he wasn't convinced it was the right deal," Parker said.

Few people outside of his family ever saw the sensitive side of Tex. The fastest way to reach it was to ask him about his wife.

"When I'd talk to Tex, if I ever wanted him to slow down and quiet down – which was a hard thing to do with that man – I'd ask him about Pat," Kris Kubik said. "He'd get a little teary eyed and quiet. They were really special together."

He trusted her completely. Political forces of any level of power could oppose him and he would be unmovable in his opinion. But he always listened to Pat.

"I learned a long time ago if you could get on the good side of Pat, to hell with the rest of them," Clem Love said. "If she liked you, he liked you."

When it came to Tex's longevity, Adolph Kiefer gave a great deal of credit to Pat.

"He had a wonderful wife, don't forget," Kiefer said. "She had a lot to do with that. Better than most people. She's still running camp, isn't she? She's a smart gal."

As per her request, Tex held on until the end of the summer.

Though he was bed-ridden, he didn't stop influencing the programs he had created – even the ones outside of Camp Longhorn.

"His passion for swimming was the same when I first got here as it was the year before he passed away," DeLoss Dodds said. "He kept it burning the whole time, which is really wonderful."

He loved to stop by Longhorn swim practices during his life, but even when he couldn't physically be there he stayed in near constant contact with the coaches. Kubik continued to receive phone calls from Tex right up to the end:

> Tex was the king of keeping in touch. He'd call me probably once every two weeks and just say something wacky. "Hey Kris, this is Tex. I saw a raccoon and it made me think about you and the reason I was thinking about you is I was wondering, how are you guys looking in the 800 free relay this year?" I'd be like, "Ok." Or he'd send you a little pick-you-up letter halfway through the season. How'd he know how we were doing in meets? I got something at age ninety-eight from him. It was a picture or something and he'd say, "Give my love to your wife, April. I still remember how you two met." How could that guy keep attached to me when he's attached to 25,000 other people? Imagine sending out 25,000 other letters. How can he do all these things and still run a successful business? I found out that for Tex there was about thirty-six hours in every day.

He paid attention to swimming, even in his final days. Just before his death, Tex met with his Masters coaches to talk about the direction of his sport. Keith Bell said:

> We went to visit him about three days before he died and he was very, very weak. He was telling us that his heart had just about had it, but he was still so sharp and funny. And concerned and interested in swimming in the world. He was still interested in camp and running that business, but still interested in the swimming community. It meant a lot to us that one of the last things he told us was how proud he

was of us for what we'd done with the American Swimming Association. That meant a tremendous amount to us coming from him. He was a man of great stature. Loved and honored and tremendously respected by thousands and thousands of campers and other people we came across, and we had tremendous respect for him and admiration for him, and he was our friend.

Kubik also came by to meet one last time with the old coach, who had become a mentor to him.

I was really fortunate. In Tex's later years I got to spend more time with him because the family would allow my wife and I to go by and visit. I would talk to him about the past and swimming and had lots of what I'd consider special conversations. But one in particular, I asked him one time why he got out of coaching. I said, "Tex, you obviously had a gift for coaching, why did you get out of coaching?" and he paused for a little bit and he said, "You know what? I wanted to be around more kids." He certainly did. He went from around twenty-five or thirty guys a year to now thousands, and it's amazing to me what he did and his legacy continues to do for kids throughout the state of Texas and around the country.

He stayed involved and he stayed connected. But at the end of the summer, he was done.

"I'm ready to go to Church Mountain," he told Pat.

The following Monday, August 27, 2007, Tex Robertson died. The family buried him at the top of Church Mountain. There was a private ceremony with his children and grandchildren. The following weekend Camp Longhorn hosted a public ceremony. More than a thousand people attended.

He died exactly as he lived: on his own terms. He was done. Like the beginning of his coaching career and his camp, it happened when and how he said it would.

He was as ready as any person can be for death. Shortly before he died, he wrote a poem, which in part reads: "Being in wonderful overtime of life, I was ready for this, with goals complete and family bliss. Put a dent atop my grave for the rain to fall in through; intermediate freestyle, but backstroke will do. Our five (kids) and theirs made this a wonderful life, but I owe it all to a wonderful wife."

TEX'S LIFE is the story of what a single person can bring into existence by sheer force of will.

"He just looked at the world and thought, 'That's the way it ought to be.' It was his way," Robby said.

"He had three ambitions in life," Bill Johnson said. "That was to be a great swimmer, to be a successful swimming coach, and to run a successful camp to teach kids how to swim. How many people do you know have three definite ambitions and have accomplished them all?"

But for all he created, an even greater impact is felt by what others created because of him. He was a coach to so many, and even a surrogate father to some.

"He's an inspiration to everybody that knew him, including me," Adolph Kiefer said. "I'm successful. I would say that I should thank him for ninety percent of it. Not eighty percent, ninety."

It's why Tex was so loved by so many. He was the great promoter, often described as swimming's "carnival barker," but he was truly loved because he was able to impact a tremendous number of individuals.

"I worry a little bit about the fact that they say artists are better after they die. Tex was appreciated when he was here," Reese said. "It just seems like he was always in my life, one way or the other. He was obnoxiously positive. He was perfect."

It's why so many legends about him sprouted forth from Camp Longhorn. Many originated from Tex's proclivity for grand exaggerations. But as the story of his life has revealed, a surprising number of those legends are true. The grand plans and exaggerations of reality that existed in his head became true. They became true because of "sure you can," because of "attawaytogo," because he refused to accept that the world had to exist as presented.

"He didn't give up on something because someone told him he couldn't do it," his son, John, said. "Darned if it didn't get done."

Afterword
by
Nan Robertson Manning

In the fall of 1962, Dad and Mom bought 385 acres from long time friends, the Duncan family. This rough and rugged ranch, located on Hoover's Valley Road (early history states that it was Fort Mason Road) is about a twenty minute drive time from Camp Longhorn Inks Lake, but as Dad would always say, only four miles as the crow flies.

As a child, I have the fondest memories of going to the ranch for picnics with family and friends along the creek. The ranch was stunning with beautiful, old oak trees among its hills, and crystal clear water in its creeks. Exploring the ranch on horseback was my favorite thing to do during the winter months, because the horses spent their "vacation" there. I would often get lost among the vast cedar, and as it would get dark I would lay my reins down on the horse's neck and then he would always find the way home. The landscape of the ranch is so unique; the creek widens and the banks turn into cliffs as you venture down the creek. We would hike the cliffs of the gorge (Dad always said they were called that because they're so "gorgeous"). One of the tallest cliffs was called Devil's Hollow; named for the loud sound of rushing water flowing over its edge after a big rain. Legend has it this gorge was the location of the Indian Maiden leaping to her death after her love was killed, leaving behind her devastated father, the crying Chief whose face is etched in the stone of the cliff. His tears flow rain or shine. This was one of Dad's favorite stories, and campers still hear this legend when they go on their cookout and hike down into the creek to see the gorge and its spectacular views.

Soon after the purchase of the ranch, a darn (we don't cuss at camp) was built and the artesian springs that filled it made for a beautiful lake. Dad would bring the fourth-year campers from Inks to hike the gorge and end up at the lake to swim and have breakfast. A trolley (zip line) with a seat had been built to travel from the cabin above the creek down to the water. More often than not, the trolley would get stuck stranding campers above the rocks. It became a ritual that before they could get back on the bus they had to each pick up ten rocks to clear the area around the cabin. It was always an adventure leaving the ranch. He would drive the bus up the airstrip and pretend the brakes did not work. The poor Indian Guide (counselor) would scream and jump off the bus as it was gaining speed to make the whole adventure more exciting. The bus would run right into the fence to make it stop to the relief of all the campers. Never a dull moment with Dad. The fence was repaired for another day and the Indian Guide went to the Pit Stop. Dad took the fourth-year trip and hiked those cliffs with the campers well into his late eighties.

As he explored the ranch he found an abandoned shack by the creek and learned it was a Pony Express stop manned by Eli Peters, who the creek is named after. Dad loved the history of the land, especially the Indian stories he had heard from ranchers in the area.

He had a few of his own, as well. There was a story he'd tell for why he called the ranch "Indian Springs." He said that during a hike he sensed someone was watching him. Quickly he turned to spot a man in the distance. As the man turned and ran Dad followed him down into Devil's Hollow where he saw him crawl into a cave. Dad approached him in the cave and could see this person was in distress and holding his leg. As he got closer he was shocked to see the outline of this person's face; he was an Indian and about the same age as Dad. The leg looked bad; he had been bitten by a snake. Doing everything he had ever learned Dad tried his best to treat him. After a few days, the Indian began to regain his strength and spoke in broken English to say his name was Peta and that he was chief of a small tribe of Comanches hiding in the canyon. He was thankful to be alive and promised Dad his tribe would always be an ally. In return, Dad promised his tribe would remain a secret.

The legend of Peta and other legends of the land are told on horseback trail rides and during cookouts. To this day when campers are out on the trail and they see someone in the distance they raise their right hand as a sign of peace.

I think all along the wheels were turning and Dad had a vision for a second camp. The character, ruggedness, and especially the beautiful and abundant water of the ranch suited him perfectly. In 1974, Dad asked to meet Sally and me at the Ranch. He told us we were going to have camp here next summer – he loved to call it the "sister" camp. We looked at him for a long time in disbelief, and then at each other. "But Dad..." we pleaded, "Let's wait another year." But of course he had already had "Ranch Branch" fliers printed. And Camp Longhorn Ranch Branch was started! With a lot of dedicated builders, an office, cabins, and chow hall (original cabin by the creek) were built.

Soon Sally and I, along with Mary Patt and Frank Everest, and some very brave and coerced counselors, escorted in the happy and excited first term campers of 1975. There were twenty-five boys and twenty-nine girls. The boys (the Rattlesnakes, Apaches, and Comanches cabins), lived above the chow hall and would rise and shine to the smell of LT's bacon. The gals had three cabins; the Seahorses above the office, and a two-story cabin right next door housing the Pintos and Palominos. A floating bridge led the way to campfire over the lake which usually ended up with us going back to the cabin to change into dry clothes. The bridge also made for a great hiding spot for counselors trying to scare each other at night. The first uniforms had to be solid blue or orange, no white, because the St. Augustine hadn't had time to fill in so it seemed like we were always in the dirt. We took those first campers to the Inks Camp for the Merit Store, special events, and extra activities. When we took our first trip there, we were worried our campers would not want to go back to Ranch once they saw the Inks Lake camp. When it was time to leave, we were totally astonished when they ran for the bus saying "Let's go home!" A few years later, the only bus rides were for an afternoon of water skiing. The rest of that summer camp was full, and in 1976 four more cabins were added.

One afternoon in 1977, I was taking campers on a trail ride to the Indian burial ground on the west side of the ranch and a camper was swinging his lanyard merit pin. Up into a big tree it went and hung on a limb. A counselor climbed up into the tree and yelled, "You have to see this!" From the tree we could see Lake Buchanan, Inks Lake, and the Inks camp's Church Mountain. I instantly called Dad and when he climbed up that tree he proudly proclaimed, "We found our Church Mountain." Church Mountain was always Dad's favorite place where he felt most at peace, besides in the water. He was immensely spiritual. He felt it was the perfect place to talk about his favorite rule, the Golden Rule, and emphasize camp's slogan that "everybody is somebody." Looking at the clouds from Church Mountain he never failed to take time to spot animal shapes in the sky with the campers. We didn't know it at the time, but that day when he climbed in that big tree, he had another vision, a friendship flash between the two camps. The sun was long gone, the torches were the only light, and every camper held their flashlight tight and just before

Taps one of the camps would point those flashlights toward the other camp. The Reverend (staff counselor in charge) counted "one, two, three on...one, two, three off" and then silence...as we would wait for an answer. As soon as the other camp's friendship flash illuminated the sky, you could hear a unified gasp from our campers, and after nearly forty years, the reaction is still always the same.

In September of 1978, Dad walked me down the aisle to marry the love of my life and best friend, Bobby Manning. Thank goodness he was a great camp man too. We both joined camp full time the next year. With Bobby as the Boys Camp Director and me in the Girls Camp, we learned a lot from Dad. We were working for the ultimate coach; he was demanding and relentless in his mission to create and mold us into the best we could be. He had such a confidence and will to work hard even when the odds were stacked against him. He pushed on and pushed all of us too. He would stand on the chow hall balcony and instruct the counselors teaching swimming below, and then turn around and praise and pat them on the back which meant the world to them. Every detail of camp was important, and Dad would always say, "It's all the little things done right that make camp great." He was meticulous about everything: the libraries (bathrooms) had to be spotless, activities needed to be fun and safe, KP (kitchen patrol) needed be executed correctly, no one could be in the sun after lunch, merit questions and inspection were a daily treasured ritual, yes ma'ams, yes sirs, and the merit system were at the heart of what made camp run, but above all, the passing down and continuing of camp traditions was most important to him. Counselor meetings were an adventure with Dad, always some kind of critter or snake with a nature lesson. He would let them go right in the middle of the room and everyone would wonder if there was still a snake or two in the living room after he left. He never minded missing a quiet time to speak at our counselor meetings. He knew the counselors were the key to a successful camp, making camp life great for the campers. When he and Mom would come to the first Monday night campfire they would be introduced to a roar of applause and standing ovation. The duty counselor knew to never introduce them as "visitors" as he would tell them you can call me anything, but don't call me a visitor. Brand new campers would get a merit from Mom, and then Dad would take the stage to talk about earning their Early Bird, the greatest reward, an invitation back to camp.

Camp Longhorn Indian Springs grew every year. Another lake was built and by 1994, more space was needed, and a hundred more acres were bought for expansion. Dad would always brag that we were a "five-star... oops... five-Blob camp" and we were.

Dad would always say "we don't want a camper for a year, we want them for a lifetime." Generations of families carrying on that loyalty and love for camp. And then there is the extremely dedicated and talented staff, which most have been a part of camp for thirty, forty, and fifty-plus years. This combination of truly wonderful people carry on Dad's vision for Camp Longhorn to be that "heaven on earth."

Dad never ceased to try new things, dabble in new hobbies, and challenge himself; he was a tried and true renaissance man. Dad wanted to grow tomatoes near the front gate. He tried growing them in old tires and left-over cans from the chow hall with little success. Bobby asked him if he wanted to plow an area by the front gate – one of the only places with some dirt – and plant some tomatoes. As always, the challenge was on to make it work. The garden soon flourished and became another one of his favorite places with abundant fresh vegetables and fruit changing with the seasons. Its famous tomatoes are used in the chow hall and sold to parents on V-Day. Every summer hundreds of campers run through its orchards, picking peaches, apples, and blackberries. In 2002, we were all so excited to hear that Hoover Valley Road was going to be improved as a Farm to Market road. That is until we heard its new path was going to run right through the garden. Bobby and I met with the County Commissioner and other officials without much luck to change the road's path. One day Dad showed up with that very same County Commissioner, stood by Old Hangman's Tree, and told him the tree's history. They immediately called the surveyors and changed the course of the road to stay outside the garden to not disturb the ground around the hangman's tree.

Now, thirty-eight years later with forty-two cabins of happy and enthusiastic campers, his vision of Indian Springs is a reality...and he was durn proud of it. There were times he would talk about building camp and get emotional and teary-eyed. Even in his nineties he would make the trip to see the campers and counselors. As we would travel around camp in the golf cart before campfire the campers would run out to greet him with cameras and paper for autographs. He would talk to each and every camper. He was the most famous person on earth in their eyes, the creator of something truly magical. Alumni who return and walk through camp and every child who has ran barefoot on its grass can feel his presence. His spirit lives on through visual reminders such as the sycamore trees he dug out of the creek and planted to shade the tennis court, or the spiritual ones left through traditions and songs. He left his mark on all of us: love of life, appreciation for nature, positive attitude, humor, fortitude, inventiveness, compassion, and a never ending love for camp and what it does for these kiddos.

Teacher of the Golden Rule. Builder of Dreams. Teammate. Friend. Mentor. Immensely spiritual husband of sixty-seven years to the love of his life. Always to live in the hearts of all of us.

Every time a camper smiles, that is Tex smiling back.

NOTES

These notes document the primary sources of information utilized for each chapter. Given my relationship with Tex and growing up on the property of Camp Longhorn, much of the book was also informed by experience.

Prologue
The primary source for the Prologue is a recording of Tex Robertson's induction into the International Swimming Hall of Fame, as well as interviews with Adolph Kiefer, George Lillard, Sally Lucksinger, Nan Manning, Bill Robertson, John Robertson, and Robby Robertson.

Chapter 1
My sources on Tex's childhood in Sweetwater were interviews with Bill Robertson, John Robertson, Pat Robertson, Robby Robertson, Sally Lucksinger, and Nan Manning; a series of letters written by Tex's father to his stepsister and stepbrother; *Tex Robertson: Attaway-to-go!*, by Dr. Samuel J. Ayers; Ayers' notes from his interview with Tex; and Tex's self-written eulogy. Information on Robertson family history comes from birth records found in the Julian "Tex" Robertson Papers at the Briscoe Center for American History in Austin, Texas, and from Alline Angier Wallce's information on Henry C. Robertson in the Walker County History Book. General information about Sweetwater was provided by the Sweetwater Chamber of Commerce, The Handbook of Texas Online, and AllAcrossTexas.com. Texas history and railroad expansion data comes from *The Rise and Fall of Great Powers*, by Paul Kennedy; *Encyclopedia of the Industrial Revolution in America*, by James S. Olson; and *By the Way - A condensed guide of points of interest along the Santa Fe lines to California.*

Chapter 2
My sources on Sweetwater were an interview with Bill Robertson, *Tex Robertson: Attaway-to-go!*, Ayers' notes, The Handbook of Texas Online, and Tex's eulogy. Information on Nancy Emerson Robertson's death comes from her front-page obituary in the *Sweetwater Reporter* and a

Robertson family photo album compiled by Frank and Nancy. My sources on the "Free State of Galveston" were "Grande Dame of the Gulf," by Paul Burka of *Texas Monthly*; "Sam Maceo is the Kindly King of Texas Gambling Realm," by Hal Boyle of *The Free-Lance Star*; "Beaches Bring Out Island's Diversity," by Peter Davis of *The Galveston Daily News*; and "Museum to Honor Galveston Lifeguard," by Kelly Hawes of *The Galveston Daily News*. Along with the interview with Bill Robertson and Tex's eulogy, miscellaneous information on his life in California comes from the California Department Fish and Game's entry on abalone; the history of the Studebaker Corporation found in the Lehman Brothers Collection at the Harvard Business School; and information from the International Swimming Hall of Fame on Buster Crabbe, Duke Kahanamoku, Johnny Weissmuller, and Fred Cady. My sources on swimming and the 1932 Olympics were "Johnny Weissmuller Made Olympian Efforts To Conceal His Birthplace," by Arlene Mueller of *Sports Illustrated*; Keio University; and George A. Hodak's interview with Tex's water polo teammate – "An Olympian's Oral History: F. Calvert Strong."

Chapter 3

My sources on Tex's years as a swimmer at Michigan were interviews with Adolph Kiefer and Bill Robertson; *Michigan: Champions of the West*, by Bruce Madej; *Tex Robertson: Attaway-to-go!*; Ayers' notes; *Swimming Fundamentals*, by Matt Mann and Charles C. Fries; "Adolph Meet Adolph," by Amy Dyson of *The Alcalde*; "Adolph and Tex," by Kari Jones of *USMS Swimmer*; information from the International Swimming Hall of Fame on Tex, Forbes Carlile, and Matt Mann; "Taylor Drysdale, 83, Swam in '36 Olympics," by Mike Oliver of the *Orlando Sentinel*; and articles on Tex's swimming accomplishments in the *Sweetwater Reporter, Austin American*, several 1935 Michigan newspaper clippings of unknown origin, and Tex's 1981 speech to the College Swim Coaches of America.

Chapter 4

My main sources on Tex's early years as the head coach at Texas were interviews with Denton Cooley, Johnny Crawford, Eddie Gilbert, Bill Johnson, Becky Crouch Patterson, and Bill Robertson; *Hondo My Father*, by Becky Crouch Patterson; *Longhorn Football: An Illustrated History*, by Bobby Hawthorne; "Colleges Have Seen Money Woes Before," by

Ivan Maisel of ESPN.com; "The Swimming Legend You Never Heard Of," by Frank Deford of NPR; "Adolph Meet Adolph"; "Adolph and Tex"; "Tex's Longhorn Swimming: Julian 'Tex' Robertson and University of Texas Swimming 1936-1950," by Trip Hedrick, and articles in the *Austin American*, *The Daily Texan*, and the *San Antonio Light*.

Chapter 5

My primary sources on Tex's time in the U.S. Navy were interviews with Adolph Kiefer, Pat Robertson, and John Robertson; *The Frogmen of World War II: An Oral History of the U.S. Navy's Underwater Demolition Teams*, by Chet Cunningham; *The Naked Warriors: The Elite Fighting Force That Became The Navy Seals*, by Francis D. Fane; and *The Histories* by Herodotus of Halicarnassus.

Chapter 6

My sources on Tex's style of coaching were interviews with Johnny Crawford, Eddie Gilbert, Bill Johnson, and Mary Johnson; *My Memories of Camp Longhorn* by Bill Johnson; and "Tex's Longhorn Swimming: Julian 'Tex' Robertson and University of Texas Swimming 1936-1950." My sources on Tex's later years as coach and the end of his career were "Adolph and Tex"; "Jane Dillard, The Natural," by Steve Emanuel of *Swim Texas Magazine*; articles in the *Austin American* and *The Daily Texan*; information from The International Swimming Hall of Fame on Tex and Skippy Browning; and the UT Athletic Council's record of minutes on April 25, 1946, and March 24, 1948.

Chapter 7

All dialogue at the beginning of the chapter comes from Pat Robertson. My main sources on the founding of Camp Longhorn were interviews with Johnny Crawford, Eddie Gilbert, Jeff Heller, Bill Johnson, Mary Johnson, Sally Lucksinger, and Pat Robertson; VHS tapes of raw interviews for the Camp Longhorn 60th anniversary video with Tex Robertson, Pat Robertson, Cactus Pryor, Wally Pryor, Bill Johnson, Mary Johnson, and Frank 'Zark' Withers; *My Memories of Camp Longhorn*; "No Telephone? Try Carrier Pigeons," by Regenia Shepperd of the *Houston Chronicle Magazine*; a letter from Tex to LCRA General Manager Joe Beal regarding the LCRA's history with Camp Longhorn; a paper written by Tex titled "Starting Camp Longhorn," and a recording of Tex's public memorial service.

Chapter 8
My main sources on the expansion of Camp Longhorn were interviews with Johnny Crawford, Eddie Gilbert, Jeff Heller, Bill Johnson, and Mary Johnson; interview tapes with Tex Robertson, Pat Robertson, Emory Bellard, Wilson Cozby, Bill Johnson, Mary Johnson, and Frank Withers; *My Memories of Camp Longhorn*; and "Longhorn Murray-Go-Round," by Tom Murray of *The Alcalde*. My main sources on the founding of girls camp were interviews with Margret Butler, Bill Johnson, Mary Johnson, and Becky Crouch Patterson; a letter from Butler to Pat Robertson; and *Hondo My Father*.

Chapter 9
My main sources on the history of Camp Longhorn were interviews with Johnny Crawford, Eddie Gilbert, Jeff Heller, Bill Johnson, Mary Johnson, and Gardner Parker; recorded interview tapes with Tex Robertson, Pat Robertson, Barney Baker, Bill Johnson, and Mary Johnson; *My Memories of Camp Longhorn*; *The Complete Book of Frisbee: The History of the Sport & the First Official Price Guide* by Victor A. Malafronte; "Tex Robertson, a Texas Swimming Legend (and Masters Great) Is Honored," by John Maher of the *Austin American-Statesman*; and a letter from Tex's father to his stepsister written at Camp Longhorn.

Chapter 10
My sources were interviews with Nan Manning, Gardner Parker, John Robertson, Robby Robertson, and Sally Lucksinger; recorded interviews with George W. Bush and Cactus Pryor; *My Memories of Camp Longhorn*; and letters received by Tex Robertson from President George W. Bush, President George H.W. Bush, President Gerald Ford, Senator Kay Bailey Hutchison, Senator Phil Gramm, Representative Robert Turner, Representative Harvey Hilderbran, Representative Lamar Smith, and Texas Attorney General John Cornyn. My sources on "East Germany" were a summation of the feud written by Tex; Tex's letter to Beal; "Judge Joe R. Greenhill Memorial Story" from the Texas Supreme Court Historical Society; Greenhill's obituary in the *Houston Chronicle*; and

information on Charles Ferguson Herring in records of the Texas State Cemetery. My sources on Tex's opposition to federal regulation of camps were "Mitch Kurman Loses His Son and Turns Into an Angry Crusader," by Ross Drake of *People*; profiles of Kurman by the *Associated Press* and the *Washington Post*; several articles by Tex in *CAMP News*; and a transcript of the hearings before the Select Subcommittee on Labor of the Committee on Education and Labor regarding H.R. 1486.

Chapter 11

My main sources were interviews with Margret Butler, Bill Johnson, Mary Johnson, Kris Kubik, Nan Manning, Eddie Reese, Bill Robertson, Robby Robertson, and Dotson Smith; *My Memories of Camp Longhorn*; Ayers' notes; and information provided by the Texas Swimming and Diving Hall of Fame.

Chapter 12

My sources on Tex's work with UT swimming were interviews with Denton Cooley, DeLoss Dodds, Jeff Heller, Kris Kubik, Becky Crouch Patterson, Eddie Reese, Jim Robertson, Jill Sterkel, and Jim Willerson; *Hondo My Father*; Ayers' notes; "Aqua Carnival Makes a Splash" from *The Alcalde*; "The politics of campus planning: How UT architecture restricts activism," by Mark Macek of *The Polemicist*; a letter from Tex to the University of Texas Athletic Department recommending Pat Patterson for the Longhorn Hall of Honor; a speech written by Tex in 1975 on the founding of the Frank Erwin Award; UT's data on the Lee & Joe Jamail Texas Swimming Center; the LA84 Foundation's official report on the 1972 Summer Olympics; information from Hawai'i Athletics on diving coach Michael Brown; information from the International Swimming Hall of Fame on Paul Bergen, Robert Clotworthy, and Richard Quick; "Olympic Coach Quick Dies" from the *Associated Press*; and a feature on Jim Robertson by TexasSports.tv.

Chapter 13

My sources on the founding of Indian Springs were interviews with Clem Love, Sally Lucksinger, Nan Manning, and Gardner Parker; recorded interviews with Frank Everest and Tex Robertson; *My Memories of Camp Longhorn*; Tex's written "Ghost Town" story; and a profile of Guitch

Koock by John Hallowell of *Hill Country Magazine*. My sources on the structure of Camp Longhorn were interviews with Sally Lucksinger, Nan Manning, Gardner Parker, Bill Robertson, John Robertson, and Robby Robertson.

Chapter 14
My sources on Tex's Masters swimming career were interviews with Keith Bell, Sandy Neilson-Bell, Kris Kubik, and Eddie Reese; articles in the *Austin American-Statesman*, *Burnet Bulletin*, and *Citizens Gazette*; information from the International Swimming Hall of Fame on Tex and Neilson-Bell; information from FINA's database of Masters swimming records; information from U.S. Masters Swimming; and a profile of Tex by Pam LeBlanc of the American Swimming Association.

Chapter 15
My primary sources were interviews with Keith Bell, Sandy Neilson-Bell, DeLoss Dodds, Bill Johnson, Adolph Kiefer, Kris Kubik, George Lillard, Clem Love, Sally Lucksinger, Nan Manning, Gardner Parker, Becky Crouch Patterson, Eddie Reese, Bill Robertson, John Robertson, Pat Robertson, and Robby Robertson.

BIBLIOGRAPHY

Books

Ayers, Samuel J. *Tex Robertson: Attaway-to-go!* San Angelo, Texas: Lubbock Christian University, 2002.

Cunningham, Chet. *The Frogmen of World War II: An Oral History of the U.S. Navy's Underwater Demolition Teams.* New York: Pocket Star, 2004.

Fane, Francis D. *The Naked Warriors: The Elite Fighting Force That Became the Navy SEALS.* New York: St. Martin's Paperbacks, 1996.

Hawthorne, Bobby. *Longhorn Football: An Illustrated History.* Austin, Texas: University of Texas Press, 2007.

Herodotus of Halicarnassus. *The Histories.* Ancient Greece. 484-430 BCE.

Johnson, Bill. *My Memories of Camp Longhorn.* Wimberley, Texas: Sabino Enterprises, 2000.

Kennedy, Paul. *The Rise and Fall of Great Powers.* New York: Vintage Books, 1989.

Madej, Bruce. *Michigan: Champions of the West.* Urbana, Illinois: Sagamore Publishing, 1997.

Malafronte, Victor A. *The Complete Book of Frisbee: The History of the Sport & the First Official Price Guide.* Oceanside, Calif.: American Trends, 1998.

Mann, Matt and Charles C. Fries. *Swimming Fundamentals.* New York: Prentice Hall, Inc., 1940.

Olson, James S. *Encyclopedia of the Industrial Revolution in America.* Westport, Connecticut: Greenwood Press, 2002.

Patterson, Becky Crouch. *Hondo My Father.* Austin, Texas: Shoal Creek Publishers, Inc., 1979.

Santa Fe Railroad. *By the Way - A condensed guide of points of interest along the Santa Fe lines to California.* Chicago, Illinois: Rand McNally and Company, 1922.

Periodicals/Online Publications

AllAcrossTexas.com. "Explore: Sweetwater, Texas."

"Aqua Carnival Makes a Splash." *The Alcalde*. March, 1973.

Burka, Paul. "Grande Dame of the Gulf". *Texas Monthly*. December, 1983.

Burns, Chester R. Texas State Historical Association. "Epidemic Diseases." The Handbook of Texas Online.

Burns, Chester R. Texas State Historical Association. "Sweetwater." The Handbook of Texas Online.

Deford, Frank. "The Swimming Legend You Never Heard Of." NPR. August 13, 2008.

Drake, Ross. "Mitch Kurman Loses His Son and Turns Into an Angry Crusader." *People*. June 16, 1975.

Dyson, Amy. "Adolph Meet Adolph." *The Alcalde*. July, 2008.

Emanuel, Steve. "Jane Dillard, The Natural." *Swim Texas Magazine*. April 14, 1996.

Hallowell, John. "Guich Koock." *Hill Country Magazine*. Fall, 2009.

"In Memoriam: Tex Robertson." *The Alcalde*. November, 2007.

Jones, Cindy. Texas State Historical Association. "Privett, Samuel Thomas, Jr. [Booger Red]" The Handbook of Texas Online.

Jones, Kari. "Adolph and Tex." *USMS Swimmer*. January-February, 2009.

Lerner, Mitchell. Texas State Historical Association. "Erwin, Frank Craig, Jr." The Handbook of Texas Online.

Macek, Mark. "The politics of campus planning: How UT architecture restricts activism." *The Polemicist*. Austin, Texas. May 1990.

Maisel, Ivan. "Colleges Have Seen Money Woes Before." ESPN.com. July 13, 2009.

Market Watch. "F. Gardner Parker, CPA." *The Wall Street Journal*.

Mueller, Arlene. "Johnny Weissmuller Made Olympian Efforts to Conceal His

Birthplace." *Sports Illustrated*. August 6, 1984.

Murray, Tom. "Longhorn Murray-Go-Round." *The Alcalde*. May, 1961.

Stanford Athletics. "Richard Quick."

The Handbook of Texas Online. "Santa Fe Lake."

Shepperd, Regenia. "No Telephone? Try Carrier Pigeons." *The Houston Chronicle Magazine*. September 12, 1948.

TexasSports.com. "University of Texas Facilities: Lee & Joe Jamail Texas Swimming Center."

Newspapers

"All-American Honors Likely For Local Lad." *Sweetwater Reporter*. Sweetwater, Texas. 1935.

Boyle, Hal. "Sam Maceo Is the Kindly King of Texas Gambling Realm." *The Free-Lance Star*. Fredericksburg, Virginia. April 24, 1947.

Davis, Jeff. "Around the Plaza." *San Antonio Light*. San Antonio. March 11, 1938.

Davis, Peter. "Beaches Bring Out Island's Diversity." *Galveston Daily News*. Galveston, Texas. May 2, 2008.

"Former Sweetwater Youth, Champion Swimmer, Here Today." *Sweetwater Reporter*. Sweetwater, Texas. 1935

Hawes, Kelly. "Museum to Honor Galveston Lifeguard." *Galveston Daily News*. Galveston, Texas. May 2, 2005.

"Highland Lakes Challenge Re-Named for Tex Robertson." *Burnet Bulletin*. Burnet, Texas. June 17, 2009.

Lee, Bill. "Tex Robertson Resigns as Texas Swim Coach." *The Austin American*. Austin, Texas. May 16, 1950.

Maher, John. "Tex Robertson, a Texas Swimming Legend (and Masters Great) Is Honored." *Austin American-Statesman*. Austin, Texas. January 15, 2003.

"Mitch Kurman, Camp Safety Advocate, Dies at 86." *Associated Press*. October 8, 2007.

Oliver, Mike. "Taylor Drysdale, 83, Swam in '36 Olympics." *Orlando Sentinel.* Orlando, California. February 11, 1997.

"Olympic Coach Quick Dies." *Associated Press.* June, 11 2009.

"Pastor Praises Mrs. Robertson." *Sweetwater Reporter.* Sweetwater, Texas. July 30, 1924.

"Pre-Olympic Swimming Carnival to Be Staged Thursday Night." *The Daily Texan.* Austin, Texas. January 7, 1936.

"Robertson Becomes Victim of Conference Eligibility Ruling." 1935 Michigan newspaper clipping of unknown origin.

"Robertson Succeeds First Year as Coach." *The Daily Texan.* Austin, Texas. June, 1936.

"Robertson Takes Three Gold Medals." *Citizens Gazette.* Burnet, Texas. June 7, 1995.

Robertson, Tex. "Camping Wins Freedom, No Federal Control Yet." *CAMP News.* Burnet, Texas. June, 1972.

Robertson, Tex. "Texas Has Own Safety Law." *CAMP News.* Burnet, Texas. June, 1973.

Sullivan, Patricia. "Mitch Kurman; Lobbied for Camp Safety." *Washington Post.* Washington, D.C. October 10, 2007.

"Tex Robertson's Resignation Brings Student Objections." *The Daily Texan.* Austin, Texas. May 17, 1950.

"Texas High Court Justice Greenhill Dies at 96." *Houston Chronicle.* Houston. February 11, 2011.

Thomas, John. "Tex Robertson Now One of Mann's Best." 1935 Michigan newspaper clipping of unknown origin.

Vincent, Curt. "Tex Swims to Gold in Tokyo." *Burnet Bulletin.* Burnet, Texas. 1986.

Manuscripts

Burleson, James E. "Tex Robertson's Impact." Essay. 2008.

Hedrick, Trip. "Tex's Longhorn Swimming: Julian 'Tex' Robertson and University of Texas Swimming 1936-1950." Kinesiology Thesis, University of Texas at Austin, 1987.

Hodak, George A. "An Olympian's Oral History: F. Calvert Strong." 1988.

LA84 Foundation. "1972 Summer Olympics Official Report."

Parker, Gardner. "East Germany." Essay published in the Second Edition of *My Memories of Camp Longhorn* by Bill Johnson. 2000.

Robertson, Tex. "Ghost Town." Date Unknown.

Robertson, Tex. Self-written Eulogy. 1997.

Robertson, Tex. "Starting Camp Longhorn." 1997.

Robertson, Tex. "The Frank Erwin Award." 1975.

Robertson, Tex. "The Story of the East Germany Purchase." 1999.

Wallace, Alline Angier. "Henry C. Robertson." Published in the Walker County History Book, 1987.

Papers, Letters, Collections

Ayers, Samuel J. Notes from his interview with Tex for *Tex Robertson: Attaway-to-go!*

"Charles Ferguson Herring." Texas State Cemetery records.

Harvard Business School. Lehman Brothers Collection – Twentieth-Century Business Archive. "The Studebaker Corporation."

International Swimming Hall of Fame. "Clarence 'Buster' Crabbe."

International Swimming Hall of Fame. "David 'Skippy' Browning."

International Swimming Hall of Fame. "Duke Kahanamoku."

International Swimming Hall of Fame. "Forbes Carlile."

International Swimming Hall of Fame. "Fred Cady."

International Swimming Hall of Fame. "Johnny Weissmuller."

International Swimming Hall of Fame. "Matt Mann II."

International Swimming Hall of Fame. "Paul Bergen."

International Swimming Hall of Fame. "Richard Quick."

International Swimming Hall of Fame. "Robert Clotworthy."

International Swimming Hall of Fame. "Sandra Neilson."

International Swimming Hall of Fame. "Tex Robertson."

"Judge Joe R. Greenhill Memorial Story." Texas Supreme Court Historical Society.

The Julian "Tex" Robertson Papers. Briscoe Center for American History. Austin, Texas.

LeBlanc, Pam. American Swimming Association. "Tex Robertson."

Robertson family birth records. Walker County, Texas.

Robertson, Tex. Letter to LCRA General Manager Joe Beal regarding the LCRA's history with Camp Longhorn. June 1, 2005.

Robertson, Tex. Letter to Representative Sam Johnson regarding H.R. 1194. January 17, 1996.

Robertson, Tex. Letters to Representative Lamar Smith, Senator Phil Gramm, and Texas Attorney General John Cornyn regarding water rights and EPA regulations. June 15, 2000.

Robertson, Tex. Letter to the University of Texas Athletic Department recommending Pat Patterson for the Longhorn Hall of Honor. (Date unknown.)

Letters received by Tex Robertson from President George W. Bush, President George H.W. Bush, President Gerald Ford, Senator Kay Bailey Hutchison, Representative Robert Turner, Representative Harvey Hilderbran.

Multimedia

DVD. Recording of Tex Robertson's induction into the International Swimming Hall of Fame, May 9, 2003.

DVD. Recording of Tex Robertson's Memorial Service, September 1, 2007.

VHS. Camp Longhorn 60th Anniversary Video, September 15, 1999.

VHS. Raw interview tapes for the Camp Longhorn 60th Anniversary video: Barney Baker, Emory Bellard, George W. Bush, Wilson Cozby, Frank Everest, Bill Johnson, Mary Francis Johnson, Cactus Pryor, Wally Pryor, Pat Robertson, Tex Robertson, Frank Withers.

TexasSports.tv. "Jim Robertson Preserving Family's UT Swimming Legacy."

In-Person Interviews

Dr. Keith Bell, Margaret Butler, Dr. Denton Cooley, Johnny Crawford, DeLoss Dodds, Eddie Gilbert, Jeff Heller, Bill Johnson, Mary Francis Johnson, Adolph Kiefer, Kris Kubik, George Lillard, Clem Love, Sally Lucksinger, Nan Manning, Sandy Neilson-Bell, Gardner Parker, Becky Crouch Patterson, Eddie Reese, Bill Robertson, Jim Robertson, John Robertson, Pat Robertson, Robby Robertson, Dotson Smith, Jill Sterkel, Dr. Jim Willerson

Miscellaneous

California Department Fish and Game. "Abalone."

Encyclopædia Britannica. "Olympic Village."

FINA. Masters Swimming World Records.

H.R. 1194, the "Recreational Camp Safety Act," March 9, 1995.

Hawai'i Athletics. "Diving Head Coach Michael Brown."

"The Hero." Speech to the International Academy of Trail Lawyers by Broadus Spivey.

Keio University. "Keio In Depth."

Robertson, Tex. Speech to the College Swim Coaches of America. 1981.

Robertson family photo album.

S. 258, the "Children and Youth Safety Act," January 14, 1977.

Sweetwater Chamber of Commerce. "The Rich History of Sweetwater."

Transcript, Hearings before the Select Subcommittee on Labor of the Committee on Education and Labor, House of Representatives, Ninety-Third Congress, Second Session on H.R. 1486 and Related Bills, Bills to provide for the development and implementation of programs for youth camp safety. Hearings held in Washington, D.C., May 15, 16, 1974; June 12, and 13, 1974; and Bear Mountain, N.Y., June 7, 1974.

U.S. Masters Swimming. Records. "USMS Top Ten Swims by Tex Robertson."

UT Athletic Council. Record of Minutes. April 25, 1946, and March 24, 1948.

AUTHOR'S NOTE

Being a grandson of Tex obviously framed much of my research for this book. There were many notable advantages. As a member of the family, people told me many details of his life they would not have otherwise revealed and I was given access to a host of documents others would not have seen. In fact, I wrote much of this book sitting at Tex's desk in his office at Camp Longhorn Inks Lake. Many hours were spent combing through his "files," which were stacks of cardboard beer flats containing documents arranged in his nonsensical, incongruous filing system.

This relation brought many challenges as well. I grew up on the property of Camp Longhorn Indian Springs and my subject was a relative I respect. This no doubt armed me with a significant number of preconceived assumptions heading into the project. But I attempted to write as accurately as possible about who he really was and cut through the myths and legends to the truth of the man, which proved far more interesting than the exaggerated tales.

It would be disingenuous to say I have no bias. I love Tex, and I love the world he built for my family. But I wanted to tell his true story. In this effort, I found myself inspired most by Nicholas Thompson, author of *The Hawk and the Dove*, a dual biography of Paul Nitze and George Kennan, two of the most influential figures in American foreign policy during the Cold War. Nitze was Thompson's grandfather, yet the book is written with honesty and fairness.

As Thompson wrote in the final pages: "It's also true, of course, that writing about someone you knew and admired means that there's always a faint sense that he is looking over your shoulder. Fortunately, I'm certain that my grandfather would chiefly have wished that the book be as rigorous and accurate as possible...If I have cut Paul Nitze slack, I have done so unconsciously."

ACKNOWLEDGMENTS

As there are thousands who were affected by Tex and what he created, there are more people who played a role in the story than can be named in these pages, but I can list those who were directly involved in bringing this book into existence.

As Tex was my grandfather, the family provided a great deal of support and information. Foremost, I thank my brother Jon for his superb editing work. Having a professional editor for a brother is a tremendous resource for a writer to have – doubly so when he has no qualms with being honest about parts of the book that needed significant improvement. This advantage was doubled again by having an English professor for a sister and another brother who is deeply involved in the day-to-day operations of Camp Longhorn. Thank you so much to Jon, Annette, and Daniel for your constant support.

The whole family played a role, but the book is chiefly dedicated to Pat, who was by Tex's side for sixty-eight years and knew him like no one else. I would also like to give a special thank you to my uncle, Bill Robertson. As president of the Texas Swimming and Diving Hall of Fame, he was a wonderful help locating sources, information, and interviews.

As the book's interior and cover designer, Will Gallagher played an important role in bringing this story to life. Thank you to Will for your hard work and all your help down the stretch as the book neared publication.

Senator Kay Bailey Hutchison provided the wonderful foreword to the story, and her staff, especially Dean Pagani, Jeff Nelligan, and Melinda Poucher, deserve thanks for their assistance. In addition, David Sherzer from President George W. Bush's office and Ashley MacKenna each provided help coordinating the effort.

I did a great deal of traveling for the book, including visiting the International Swimming Hall of Fame in Ft. Lauderdale, Florida, but the farthest I traveled for a specific interview was to Chicago to meet with Adolph Kiefer. Thank you to Adolph and to his wife Joyce for being so welcoming and thank you to Chip Rives for providing additional information about Kiefer.

Thank you to Eddie Reese, Kris Kubik, Travis Feldhaus, and everyone over at the University of Texas swim program. Among those who provided additional documentation for the book were James Patton, who assembled the Julian "Tex" Robertson Papers, Trip Hedrick, who interviewed Tex in 1987, and Sam Ayers, who interviewed Tex in 2002.

Each person who added their memories to the story by giving their time for interviews deserves thanks: Dr. Keith Bell, Margaret Butler, Dr. Denton Cooley, Johnny Crawford, DeLoss Dodds, Eddie Gilbert, Jeff Heller, Bill Johnson, Mary Francis Johnson, Adolph Kiefer, Kris Kubik, George Lillard, Clem Love, Sally Lucksinger, Nan Manning, Sandy Neilson-Bell, Gardner Parker, Becky Crouch Patterson, Eddie Reese, Bill Robertson, Jim Robertson, John Robertson, Pat Robertson, Robby Robertson, Dotson Smith, Jill Sterkel, and Dr. Jim Willerson.

Because the book covers a man's lifetime of experiences, those who played prominent roles in the story covered a wide span of ages. There are eight people who are a part of that story who died in the past few years. This book is also dedicated to the memory of Emory Bellard, Joe Greenhill, Tom Haynie, Clem Love, Jane Kneip Patterson, Cactus Pryor, Richard Quick, and Frank "Zark" Withers.

164, 168, 171
Curtis, Lawrence, 115

149, 198

Yale University, 30-32, 35, 64, 83, 147, 158
year-round school, xv, 158
YMCA
    Austin, 10, 19
    Central Los Angeles, 19-22, 24-25, 28, 54
    Lawson (Chicago), 41
    Maine, 153
YMCA National Championships, 24
Yoyogi Olympic Pool (Tokyo), 191

Zark, *see Withers, Frank*
Zihuatanejo, Guerrero, 165

ABOUT THE AUTHOR

Ross Lucksinger has written articles for ESPN.com and FoxSports.com, been a correspondent and producer for ESPN Radio, and served as the editor of *Inside Texas*, a magazine and website that covers University of Texas sports. He is a grandson of Tex Robertson and lives in Austin, Texas.

Day is done
Gone the sun
  from the lake
  from the hills
  from the sky
All is well
Safely rest
God is nigh